# Why I Do VFX

## The Untold Truths About Working in Visual Effects

### VICKI LAU

First published by Vicki Lau, 2021
Copyright © 2021 by Vicki Lau

All rights reserved.

*First edition*

ISBN: 979-8-743-64979-2 (paperback)
ISBN: 979-8-201-11252-3 (ebook)

# CONTENTS

# FOREWORD

## by Leif Einarsson

VFX veteran and Visual Effects Society (VES)
Award nominee for *"The Kite Runner"*

(VFX on *"Stuart Little," "X-Men: Days of Future Past,"
"Spider-Man: Homecoming"*)

When my friend, Vicki Lau, invited me to write this foreword I was humbled. Throughout the book, she refers to industry veterans who have been doing their jobs for twenty or more years; I am actually one of those old fogies that she is referring to. I got into digital media at the age of twenty-four, straight out of college. Nowadays, twenty-four is kind of old to be getting into visual effects (VFX) and games, but back in the mid-nineties that was early. I spent over five years at the University of California, San Diego (UCSD) pursuing a degree in Structural Engineering with a minor in Surfing. I ended up failing at both.

With degree in hand, I approached one of my professors and asked him, "what am I going to do with my life?" He was a loving and eccentric character who spent more time in class talking about Madonna and screenplays than applied physics. He told me to get into something called 'Virtual Reality'. He had seen a lot of his friends die of AIDS and found that a common deathbed wish was to just be able to stroll once more on a beach. At one point, my professor threw me a book on 'C++' and told me to "get to work." After a week of me reading this book on the beach, I realized I was also not a programmer. I returned to my professor, told him that I had failed yet again, and that was when he advised me to check out an after-hours business school pitch. It was there that I saw a presentation by a local game company with their final slide stating that they were "Looking for Interns." Several pencil drawings and an interview later, I was working for free at Presto Studios.

The world of digital graphics opened up to me like magic in the form of CD-ROM games. Remember those? I didn't think so. Now google "Macintosh Quadra." It would be many years of making games, and even more of making movies, before I ventured back into that space called virtual reality. As of today, I have developed and shipped almost a dozen virtual reality products with my fellow coworkers. It's funny how things come full circle.

Dreams can come true, but it takes hard work. And once you achieve those dreams, you come out on the other side with a reality check and (hopefully) a better understanding of who you are than the younger you that was a dreamer. I'll tell you a story:

While still in San Diego, before spending a decade in La La Land, we used to go to Comic-Con. Back then you actually went for the comics; now it's a spectacle where a pricey ticket gets you access to see Angelina Jolie for a split second. Well, at some point, during its years of growth, I found myself in the audience listening to Sam Raimi and Tobey Maguire talk about the upcoming *"Spider-Man 2"* film they were making. Pretty cool for me as I am an *"Army of Darkness"* fanboy. Fast forward a year and I'm hanging at my buddy's loft in downtown Los Angeles when I get a call that they are filming *"Spider-Man 2"* nearby. So, we dress up as construction workers – doesn't everyone have a construction worker costume on hand – and find our way to the underground mall tunnels that were closed off. We pop up on the other side only to witness a car drive by, shooting guns at a Spider-Man stuntman. You can only imagine our elation. Raimi yelled cut as it was time to take a break, and we get rounded up with the extras for the next shot. We were wearing fluorescent vests mind you, which is a terrible thing for VFX compositing and post-production color grading. So even though we stood out from the crowd, we did our best to act the way an extra might. After a few takes, it was time to break for dinner – who am I to say no to free food? After our meals, the crew was preparing to set up for the next shot, but this time I was near the director's monitor tent. How lucky I felt to be standing next to Raimi, shadowing him as he directed this big action sequence.

Fast forward years later and I get a call from a friend asking me to be interviewed as a previsualization artist for *"Spider-Man 3."* Raimi himself interviewed me and even singled out things in my reel that he knew were directly inspired by him. I get the job. In no time I was working in Sam Raimi's office, helping brainstorm and design key action sequences for him. It's a dream come true, but again, dreams take hard work.

Through laser-focused dedication, I pulled more all-nighters on that job than ever before. Sleeping under the desk was not uncommon. Being the only person on the entire Sony Pictures studio lot was not uncommon either. Raimi was intent on creating some of the greatest action sequences ever (some were thirty minutes long). A thirty-minute action sequence was not very realistic in a less than two-hour movie, mind you. You learned how every frame counts and you learned not to get attached creatively. An idea that was great on Friday could be axed on Monday and then brought back on Wednesday. But this was my dream and I'm happy to have experienced it, even if my physical body was not.

There's one thing anyone should know about working in glamorous industries is that they do instill fear. In fact, the closer you are to the top, the more fear amongst the workers that is ever pervasive. I've been on a job where I was told not to have certain books on my desk for fear that David Fincher might see them. While directors might be a pleasure to work with, you will find individuals two tiers below them enveloped by paranoia and fear. Fear that they might screw up or look foolish; but most importantly, fear that they might lose their status. It contrasts heavily with the sincere desire to serve.

After a year or so on the film, an individual who was in power for a weekend singled me out as the one person who would not give in to his bullying. It became a 'me or him' scenario and I was forced to leave because this individual had more connections to Raimi outside of the workplace. Regardless, the producer on the film was a great guy and apologized profusely for what had happened. It seems like the old adage of 'connections are everything' is very true.

I was free from the all-nighters but sad to leave. Even sadder when the film received poor reviews on release. They never told us Tobey would have an emo dance sequence! All this made me reflect. Having pulled back the curtain I was so curious to see behind, the experience inspired me to pivot my career and life to other arenas. I storyboarded a film. I became a character animator. I moved out of Los Angeles. I had a kid. Lots of wonderful things.

Even to this day, I continue to pivot. Because why not? We are all artists. We are malleable. We can redefine ourselves at every moment of our lives. You can be a scientist, a cowboy, or both. Every job I've had has been a unique experience: all those impressions weaved together make for a very complex me and it will be the same for you.

This Spider-Man story is a microcosm of my whole career. No, not "With great power comes great responsibility." What I mean is that when you get to the core and humanize your idols, it truly makes you wonder "What do I really want? What is best for me? And am I in pursuit of that?"

I couldn't have predicted these experiences happening. I worked hard at each and every job to be the right person for when the right opportunity came (unexpectedly). Plans just don't play out as envisioned. Instead, you often get exactly what you need, but not necessarily what you want. However, when you know what you want, luck often finds you.

I wish you all good luck on your journeys. Enjoy your read of *"Why I Do VFX"* and learn a thing or two about yourself as you go along.

# 1

# WHAT IS THIS ABOUT?

When I was young, I always imagined what life would be like if I had the ability to play God. The ability to control the outcomes in one's life, eliminate those who bullied you when you were just a helpless child, and perhaps even create events or elements that could only exist on cinema screens. That would have been ideal.

Of course, the real world does not function that way – at least, not directly.

You see, when I was only six years of age, I was singled out by the girls at my primary school (and consequently secondary school) to be the target of bullying. At the time, I honestly did not know what was happening and was never properly taught by any of the adults in my life what differentiated bullying from child's play; in hindsight, having my birthday party invitations stolen and being forced to eat the shavings from a pencil sharpener were definitely predatory behavior from these girls, but I digress.

The point is, through this period of ostracization and isolation, I was conveniently given a camcorder for fun – sort of a hand-me-down device. Being stingy Asian (more specifically, Singaporean) people, rather than selling or discarding old, unwanted devices, parents would often hand them down to their offspring for use. It is through this camcorder that an attachment was formed – an attachment to a potential outlet for self-expression.

Being the shy, quiet, and bullied girl that I was, I eventually found my voice through video-editing my recorded clips; consequently, this passion for video-editing developed into a passion for post-production visual effects. After all, who wouldn't enjoy immersing oneself in an imaginary environment made entirely by fake backdrops or, even better, having the ability to "shoot" the bad guys (or girls) with digital additions of blood spurts and gunshot wounds, all in the name of storytelling?

Writing this now, having utilized visual effects as a channel of self-expression since I first discovered video editing at the age of fourteen, and with close to nine years of cumulative visual effects industry experience (working on transmedia projects, independent features, blockbuster movies, television shows, commercials, shorts, and student projects), I am exhilarated to be sharing my experiences, knowledge, and insights about the inner workings of the visual effects (VFX) industry that not many books in this field, thus far, have dared to expose. Then again, who could really blame them? A quick Google search on VFX literature will result in an overwhelming majority of books focused on methods of the trade rather than the psychology involved or the economy of the trade itself.

I do have to disclose that I am most definitely not a native of the United States (in other words, consider me a foreigner/immigrant), thus, this perspective will be slightly more detached from the state of the American economy and its national affairs. I am also not going to pretend to be an economics expert, nor will I be filling this book with lots of graphs, statistics, and data, which would be outdated by the time this book is released. Instead, treat this treatise as a collection of astute observations about the inner (and outer) workings of the life of a VFX artist (mine and others observed and analyzed), corporate and industry psychology, and the larger elements at play on a global scale. We know that trends and technology can change almost rapidly, but human behaviors fundamentally persist for a longer period of time – and are definitely much, *much* harder to change overnight.

As such, I am speaking to the ordinary person, the reader who simply wants to forgo the data deep-dives, analysis-paralysis, and endlessly droning texts about the history of visual effects and how the Hollywood film industry developed over the decades. While all that is indeed important to a certain extent, it doesn't tell you what *really* goes on inside the people and the systems that make visual effects work for the machine that is Hollywood.

I am not here to give you a step-by-step guide on how to get into visual effects or Hollywood, for I believe it to be presumptuous of me and on the part of the reader to believe that anyone would actually give you a detailed guideline for the cost of a book whilst ignoring the myriad of internal and external factors that will be at play regardless. In addition, I am presuming you as a reader are intelligent enough to know that there will always be different ways to achieve the same result. What I *will* give you in this book are my truest thoughts, conclusions, and observations on the inner workings of the industry and, ultimately, how I think (and perhaps even *how* to think).

So, if you are in the interesting position of deciding if you should or should not dedicate your entire existence to visual effects, or are currently in the industry looking to comprehend the unspoken human elements at play in your field, you are invited to explore everything I have to say about why I do VFX and, more importantly, the untold truths about working in VFX.

# 2

# "I LOVE TO WATCH MOVIES"

Sometimes, at work, I get to listen in on the conversations that float around me. It's hard not to when you are packed rather tightly in an office space. This doesn't surprise me as VFX studios are also businesses and maximizing office space is most likely something many business owners would be thinking of. "Hmm ... how many bodies can I fit into this corner of the room?" they might ponder. Out of the over twenty studios I've been to and worked with, only two of them actually had enough room for you that you could have a twin-size bed running parallel to your desk with that entire space being yours. For the most part, us VFX artists would be packed quite closely next to one another, perhaps an arm or so apart from the person sitting next to you in the same department. Either way, unintentional eavesdropping is quite easy with this kind of setup, and oftentimes you'll hear things you wished you hadn't – corny jokes, banal small talk that has absolutely zero substance, and random tidbits about the current state of affairs that you frankly couldn't care less. On a few rare occasions, I would hear a mainstay artist ask a newbie or a freelancer what got them into VFX. The answer is almost always the same – "Oh, well, when I was a kid, I used to watch [insert favorite movie here] and was inspired by the VFX, so that's why I am doing it," or "When I was young, my dad/mom would always bring me to the local theater and I just loved watching movies. I just knew that I had to get into entertainment."

## A stupid reason to get into VFX

Firstly, if you are new and thinking of entering the visual effects industry just know that "I love to watch movies" has got to be the *stupidest* reason for you to decide to pursue a career in visual effects. Here's why:

If you are a successful artist, which I suppose is what any sane artist in any endeavor should aspire to become, you'll soon find that your time is short and any time that you do have will not be committed to watching movies. In fact, some of the most successful or experienced veterans I know who are still in visual effects today would always tell me that they eventually got to a point where they simply didn't have the time to even watch their own work in the films and shows they had worked on. This, of course, makes absolute sense. As your success as a VFX artist grows, so does the demand for your services – which includes the increasing demand for exclusivity of your time.

Another reason that "I love to watch movies" is such a stupid motivator is that watching movies isn't exactly the same as creating them. As someone with experience as both a movie-goer and movie-creator, I can confirm that the latter definitely requires much more work, time, and effort on the part of the individual. Contrast that with kicking back – stale popcorn and an oversized jug of sugary drink in hand – and enjoying a two-hour movie about superheroes. As I spend more time listening in on such conversations that involve divulging one's motivations for being a VFX artist and tracking certain fellow colleagues on their VFX journey (not consciously or with deliberation, just through casual flicks on LinkedIn whenever they make a random post or job announcement), I notice a trend: a large majority of these individuals who prop up "I love to watch movies" as a motivation for being in VFX eventually, years or even months later, leave VFX to pursue other fields such as game development, television sports, or technology.

This should not be surprising since a passion for watching and enjoying movies does not necessarily equate to an equal amount of passion for creating them – let alone spending forty-to-fifty-hour weeks sitting in front of a computer screen with ten small bags of Doritos, clicking away in After Effects or Nuke (and yes, I have been in that lucky position to overconsume Doritos, free of charge). Many who do get into VFX for this reason soon find themselves either not enjoying the amount of work it entails – and the kind of work it involves – or simply wanting to do something else that they weren't allowed to (more on that later). Ultimately, only a few of the "I love to watch movies" types learn to adapt to VFX and learn to enjoy the craft for its own sake, independently of whether their shots come from a fantastic production or a really low-budget one.

## Another stupid reason to get into VFX

On that note, while this reason is not as stupid as the first, if you're thinking that you get to eventually make your *own* movies by working in visual effects then I hate to burst your bubble, but this simply does not happen often, if ever. In my experience, I have found that the VFX artists (whether they'd be compositors, supervisors, 3D animators, or the like) who eventually *do* end up directing and making their own movies are the ones who had, in some capacity, left the visual effects industry some years ago. A few of them did something else for a while, but for the most part, they never actually returned to work in visual effects as an artist or supervisor (or even as a manager, for that matter). Now, this isn't to say that it would be impossible to eventually create your own movies or bring your own stories to life as a VFX artist, it's just that the industry and to a larger extent Hollywood itself has a way of ensnaring you into certain roles where, twenty to thirty years later, you will find yourself wondering why you never got a chance to actualize your own feature film script. Believe me, I actually *know* a few of these said VFX artists who – twenty to thirty years later – still have not turned their film scripts into productions.

Of course, "I want to make movies" is definitely a recognizable step-up from "I love to watch movies" as a form of motivation to get into the field of VFX, but this reason still falls short depending on the type of person you are. Here is a simple example to enlighten you:

Let's say you had a camcorder ever since you were eight. You filmed everything – your meals, your family members, your pet(s), the bird carcass on the side of the road, even the random bus driver who yells at you about their right to not be filmed (perhaps threatening to sue you to oblivion). Fair enough. Now, you get into VFX about fifteen years later expecting to be able to get the same level of creative control over storytelling. "Hey, I get to *actually* create movies that matter now!" Unfortunately, if you are the kind of person who wants to have your own story told, VFX may not be the right niche to get into.

However, through my conversations with many artists as well as conversations overheard at the various studios I've worked at, I have found that many chose to stay put. They stay and they stay there ... until they have lost their focus or purpose in life, which was "I want to make movies" or more likely "I want to make my *own* movies." Now, this isn't to paint a grim and dismal picture of the world of VFX – again, it depends on the type of person you are. Some people who do "want to make movies" are completely happy playing second fiddle and being part of the creative process without actually *owning* anything of their own. Sure, your VFX techniques may be your own (somewhat), you may have your own ways of executing and delivering top-notch VFX shots and assets to your team and supervisor(s) but technically, you can never really call it *your* production. This also extends to the people doing post-production sound and, to a certain extent, special effects on-set as well as production design. Sure, you did work on that production, but it isn't really *your* production.

Once again, this really depends on who you are. Yes, being a part of VFX does allow you to make movies. They will never be *your* movies, but you did *help* make them happen. If you are satisfied with that, then go ahead and proudly exclaim "I want to make movies!"

## How veteran VFX artists last for 20+ years

With my attempt at dry wit and some kind of snarky humor aside, all in all, your 'why' has got to be a lot stronger than "I love to watch movies when I was a kid" or "the VFX in *Star Wars* was so inspiring;" you will soon find that VFX requires a lot of patience, technical dedication, and will also drain you of your most precious resource – time. The artists who make it to twenty or thirty years, I find, have usually found some kind of solace or peace with the craft of visual effects (whatever their specialty may be) and actually derive some kind of enjoyment and pleasure from sitting in front of a computer screen and solving problems, because that is what VFX ultimately is all about – problem-solving. Sure, while some of these veterans may never get to actualize their own film projects or ideas due to the sheer lack of time and resources required to accomplish such feats, through my conversations with them, I could tell that it's a fair trade-off in order for them to experience that bliss one gets from solving a complex visual problem with the tools given to you.

It is rather fascinating to see their eyes light up whenever they discuss their next project, upcoming works, or even a film shoot they had just supervised over the weekend; from those bursts of conversations alone, I can already tell that they are most likely going to die as hardcore VFX artists (am putting this in as positive a light as I can, I know anything involving death might be too taboo a subject; forgive me, dear reader, if you were oddly [though understandably] offended by the mere mention of the word 'die').

Of course, after twenty or thirty years, there are always going to be those who do shift to different sectors or areas of the entertainment world and that is also natural, given human nature and our craving for variety in certain aspects of our life. It really depends on who you are, your perspective on your craft, and what you are comfortable living with for the rest of your life.

In my line of work – including the extension into teaching VFX online since 2016 – I have had the pleasure of interviewing and speaking with many veterans in their fields (VFX-related or otherwise). The common patterns from our conversations – of the veterans who lasted for twenty over years doing the same thing over and over again – tended to be that they simply integrated their lives with their craft. In other words, it extended beyond passion to a positive relationship and bond with their work. Because let's be real for a moment – passion can only get you so far in life. You need to have that intense desire, that overwhelming lust, that insatiable appetite for your craft – something that the mere underling 'passion' can only hope to comprehend. So, don't be fooled. "You need to find your passion," is what they will always tell you because it's easier to understand it that way; anything else would probably require a long exposition on the determinants of passion, how it works and does not work, basically, all that extra information that doesn't sound as good of a sound bite as "you need to find your passion." Of course, everything involves a lot more moving parts than your initial comprehension, but this book is not about that so I will just sum it up as-is:

Generally, these mainstay artists made it this far, for the most part, because of the successful integration of their lives with their respective crafts. All their goals and ambitions may not necessarily have been fulfilled by their craft (to be realistic), but you can bet that their most important needs and wants as individuals have most certainly been met.

## My abstract-sounding 'Why'

As for me, with about nine cumulative years in this industry, I still get that gratifying surge of dopamine whenever I'm presented with a challenging shot or a tight turnaround, like that one time I rapidly churned out over twenty shots in an hour or was given a really complicated (but interesting and exciting) keying shot. I can remember the excitement and zeal I would experience. In fact, I was so pumped that I was almost passionately – or aggressively and excitedly – demanding for more shots from my direct supervisor at the time. It was fun. Of course, all this 'fun' – including the type of shots you get to tackle – is entirely subject to your relationship with your peers and supervisors, which I will cover in a later chapter.

Earlier, I did express why and how I got into visual effects and my reason for being in this industry – self-expression. Frankly, it is a very abstract reason – perhaps one might even say stupid as well; after all, you could literally pursue any channel or path for self-expression, so really, why visual effects? Well, perhaps it could be that visual effects happened to be the outlet I discovered first – or rather, the outlet that first discovered me. I would like to believe that it was simply a matter of coincidence that I happened to be given a camcorder at a really young age and that I also happened to enjoy the power it gave me in terms of a voice to a once voiceless being. To be honest, I could have pursued any outlet for self-expression, but it just so happened that I was exposed to this world first.

# 3

# ARTISTIC DEVELOPMENT

When it comes to any endeavor – whether it be the arts or sciences – it is a no-brainer that one has to put in the work to develop one's skills. As cliché as it sounds, this truly applies to a field like visual effects – though not in the way you are thinking. You see, visual effects post-production (or even on-set production supervision) is really all about problem-solving; so, yes, while you will be developing your technical and artistic skills through repeated exposure to a variety of shot types, shot issues, and projects in general, what you are in essence doing is practicing and enhancing your ability to solve (mostly) visual problems. Your development comes in the form of becoming a better problem-solver rather than solely becoming a better technical artist. Of course, I understand that some of you reading this may be coming into the field (or deliberating on coming into the field) with perhaps a blatant lack of critical thinking and problem-solving skills. Not to offend you, but I have met those people and they do exist. There *are* people who work in the field who *really* need to be told what to do and exactly how to do it or they will be completely lost; unsurprisingly, these individuals don't last very long in technical visual effects roles and usually end up taking a more administrative or clerical position at studios or randomly becoming photographers (not that there is anything negative about being in such positions).

## Everyone started somewhere

If the last statement – which I acknowledge is a rather long statement on its own – somewhat applies to you, reader, fear not, for I will preface by reminding you that everyone has to start somewhere. For me, my very first attempt at visual effects was with After Effects. I believe I was about sixteen years of age at the time. I recruited a schoolmate and did a very quick music video for a cover of a song, planning everything with storyboards, scripting, and editing with Premiere Pro. In 2007, YouTube was just starting off as a little startup (before I even knew what a startup was) so you would not be able to find anything close to what amounts to libraries upon libraries of After Effects tutorials online today (and not just on YouTube, mind you); plus, to be completely upfront, the idea of looking up tutorials just did not cross my mind as a youngling of sixteen.

With nothing but my curiosity and passion for the craft, I dove right in, grabbing the pen tool in After Effects and doodling away at what would be, in hindsight, my first ever rotoscope mask (for those who are not familiar with the term, feel free to look up 'rotoscoping' on Google). Leaning back in my hard, wooden chair, I felt proud of what I had done. Of course, it looked terrible, but hey, I was so new to the craft that I did not even know what terrible was – and honestly, if you are truly new to the field, it would most likely take some time for you (and your creative eye) to get acquainted with what differentiates terrible from perfect rotoscoping, but I digress.

The point is – everyone has to start somewhere. You bet that I did. Your friend that you happened to know who recently got into visual effects did, and so did that random, nerdy, talking-head guy with the glasses on your favorite VFX YouTube channel. We all did. We just don't really talk about it because, I suppose, nobody asked us to, or it isn't really a part of our past worth mentioning in any context today (unless you happen to be interviewed or choose to write about it in a book). Do I look back at my first-ever VFX piece and sulk? No. Do I know what to do to it today in order to make it better? Yes, though I am not going to because I honestly like the way the music video turned out – it was raw, authentic, made with the best of intentions, and, most importantly, made out of sheer curiosity using software I had no idea how to use at the time, even with the weird VFX set extension attempts at turning urban Singapore into a mystical forest with some still images of trees (matte painting at its finest).

Reader, I hope you know by now that it does not matter where you are at in terms of your skill level or even knowledge of VFX.

If you want to get into the field, just get into the field. Be aware that there are many ways to do so, and I will highlight two of these ways below.

## Enrolling in an art school

Yes, schools do serve a purpose, much to the chagrin of the hardcore advocates of not going to school and learning from the metaphorical 'School of Life'. As a disclaimer, I did complete my schooling years in Singapore and in the United States – and even sought out additional enrollment at other institutes for other subjects – so I am a fan of enrolling and going to school as a personal preference. Here's why:

Schools provide you with a safe environment to experiment, make mistakes, and – here's the catch – incur no *reputational damage* to yourself while at it. In other words, you can make all the mistakes and execute all the failed experiments in the world and your reputation in the field is protected (until you graduate). I can imagine some of you shaking your head right now, thinking, "Well, technically ... I could do the same thing out there in the *real* world and also get *real* feedback!" Sure, you can. I am objective and I can see that working just as well; you could most certainly apply yourself out there as a beginner and make those same mistakes as you would whilst in school. Of course, depending on the mistake, who you are, who you are working with, which studio you are at, or perhaps what you did, you *may* experience some form of damage to your reputation as a professional or artist; this could have been avoided if performed in a school but again, I can completely see all sides here. For me, personally, I would prefer to start off on the right foot since I know that life is not fair and frankly some mistakes, once made, can never be undone. Likewise, some people, when crossed, will always have something against you for the rest of their lives. In a small industry like VFX especially, word really does get around. You'd be surprised how one single mistake – even as a beginner – when done at the wrong studio, wrong time, or to the wrong person, can haunt you for the rest of your career.

Scaring you aside, enrolling in art schools is merely one of the ways to develop your artistic and technical skills in VFX. If I haven't stressed it enough, not only do these art schools provide you with a safe space to explore and experiment to your heart's content, but they also expose you to a variety of people. You get to meet people from different countries, with different experience levels and on different artistic paths. That alone should be a huge upside for the case of enrolling in an art school – the exposure to people, which gives you the opportunity to not just network but also train your people skills. If you want to be really creative with it, you could even experiment with your people skills at school. Don't try to ask me what that means, I'm just that eccentric.

Do note, however, that once you get out of school and enter into your respective field – in this case, VFX – the people you meet are most likely going to be similar types of people. This should not be surprising since an industry is simply a collection of specific types of people, specific types of actions, and specific types of outcomes or products; certain types of people are drawn to certain industries based on their personality, goals, and desires, so expect that you will most likely be working with a homogenous group of colleagues who are really not markedly different from you. Some of you might even wish for those good ol' art school days with the variety of colorful and spicy people.

Another case for enrolling in an art school as a path to artistic development is having the option and accessibility to have your hands in many pots of VFX. If you happen to be one of those students who does not want to do or learn anything unless forced to by an institution, well, an art school would work just fine for you. You see, sometimes it is hard to get around a curriculum that is forced into your selected art major; so, even if you loathe 3D rigging, you will have to suck it up and complete that class if you would like to graduate. Another perspective on this is that being forced to have your hands in all the pies would give you the insight and option of understanding what you do like and what you don't like. If you happen to enjoy doing all aspects of VFX, congratulations – though be prepared to never be able to use all those skills at work again (with the exception of a few specific positions).

On the other hand, should have entered the industry without having attempted all elements of VFX, you will most likely have a very narrow and skewed view of what the life and tasks of a VFX professional entails. Perhaps you got into an entry-level rotoscoping role and that is all you have ever known about VFX; imagine not even being aware of all facets of VFX artistry, and thus, not knowing if you really, truly *do* want to do rotoscoping as a VFX artist for the rest of your VFX days. Hence, art school provides the much-needed exposure for those who are clueless as to where and how to start and want some structured learning to be placed by an educational institution or by someone else (this comes with its pros and cons).

Now, this all sounds fine and dandy but let's not forget the big, powerful elephant in the room when it comes to art schools – student tuition fees. This treatise is not about how to go about dealing with tuition fees, but I thought I'd bring this up as this may not be as viable an option, depending on your individual situation, for those who do not have the personal or familial funds or have access to any educational funding. My scenario was a bit unique in the sense that I did not have to pay any tuition at all and had the entirety of my education covered and funded by a Singapore government organization's scholarship along with two other additional artistic and merit-based scholarships I had nabbed from my United States' art school (Savannah College of Art & Design – SCAD) as well. It is strongly advised, however, that you look at your very unique and very specific personal situation before determining if you could or could not bear the costs (and subsequent debt) of attending an art school.

What about online art schools you might ask? Well, I have had a bit of experience with those as an educator, instructor, and student myself. My objective viewpoint is that whilst they most likely do equip you with the tools, knowledge, and skills you could have gained from an on-location, physical art school, most of these online schools lack the true support you would actually need to develop artistically as an individual. It is undeniable that you would have access to like-minded peers, some form of the instructor's knowledge, and perhaps even get some kind of mentoring; however, let's be realistic, these schools are honestly not as invested in their students as an actual, on-location art school would be. You might be fine if you are more of an independent sort and know how to figure things out on your own; on the other hand, those who are much more clueless and lost would most likely complete these online schools only slightly less clueless and lost than before. In addition, these online art schools simply do not have the brand and name power that physical art schools command. Exclaiming and updating your LinkedIn profile to reflect that you have a certificate from "So-and-So Online Art School" simply isn't as appealing as someone who can proclaim their allegiance from "ArtCenter College of Design" or "Ringling College of Art & Design," for example.

## The fashionable trend of dropping out of school

Alright, with art schools aside, let's discuss the oh-so-fashionable trend of dropping out of said schools – or any school for that matter. Personally, I have not done such a deed, but I am sure you are aware of all those famous entrepreneurs and business tycoons who did – and then went on to make a big killing in their markets. This is where the buck stops. Reader, I hope you are aware that the media only highlights success stories of dropouts and that just because someone chooses to drop out of school, doesn't immediately make them the next big thing since sliced bread. In fact, what lurks underneath the surface of all those success stories you hear of dropouts are piles of bodies, bones, and corpses – to elucidate, I am referring to the tens of thousands of *failed* entrepreneurs and business owners who *also* dropped out of their respective schools. No one ever talks about those, and why would they? Those stories don't make people feel good and do not guarantee that people may ever return to that news or media outlet to read about other people's failures and bankruptcies. Besides, everyone loves a good story about the hero who defied all odds and came out victorious in the end.

Objectively, there is really nothing wrong with dropping out of your school to then pursue the arts or learn the craft of VFX on your own – whether through experimentation or online resources. It really depends on who you are, what works best for you, and of course, your tolerance for footing expensive tuition bills on your own accord. Needless to say, there will always be pros and cons to any decision you make, and dropping out of school is no different than enrolling in one. A major pro that comes with being a drop-out is most definitely the time you have now freed up for yourself to focus on your own personal growth and artistic development at your own pace. Instead of attending courses and classes that have zero appeal to you, you can now concentrate your efforts on those few areas that do matter. Instead of being forced to learn art history or 3D sculpting with recycled materials, you can now work on improving your VFX 3D modeling and texturing skills. The opportunities to develop your artistry are boundless with that extra time. And yes, not having to pay (expensively) to learn from an accredited institution could also be a major benefit if you are taking out loans to foot the tuition or are living on the fringes of destitution (or both). That being said, the cons are also present with the decision to drop out of school. For one, it may reflect poorly on your ability to finish things, which could affect how you are perceived by studios or employers. Yes, I understand it is completely biased and you may be wondering, "How could they judge me this way!? Me dropping out of school just goes to show that I know what I want and don't take no crap from others!" Well, yes and no. You see, VFX studios – and to a certain extent, Hollywood – are not part of the startup or tech community where people brag about dropping out of Stanford or Harvard like it's a legitimate degree from those institutions. VFX and Hollywood are more on the artistic and creative side of things, and their reverence is for people who can finish and deliver results (pertaining to film and TV). They may not care where you get your skills from (or whether you dropped out of school or not, frankly), but if you choose to make being a dropout a bragging factor, then you won't really be sure how the studios or producers will perceive you as a person to work with. They might see you as someone who doesn't finish what they start. On this point, it is far better to err on the side of caution. Also, let's not forget that if you were in art school and took out a loan for it, you are now without a degree *and* stuck with mandatory debt that you *have* to pay off – a lose-lose situation, in my opinion.

Throughout my own journey and forays in the VFX world, I have encountered artists from all walks of life – those who actually completed a Master's in VFX and went on to do exceptionally well as a particle FX senior artist, for one; and those who dropped out of high school or art school and went on to do exceptionally well in whatever their VFX specialties were. Unlike mathematics where one plus one is always two (without being creative with the equation), there is no singular path to developing yourself as an artist in the VFX world – or in any artistic realm for that matter. It all depends on what suits your style and your learning preferences.

Don't let anyone convince you that schools are a waste of time and money if that is the route you really want to pursue, and don't let anyone tell you that dropping out is for quitters if you truly believe that the uncharted path would serve you better as an artist. Just be smart about it and know yourself well. Resist the urge to blindly follow others just because that's what Steve Jobs did or that's the school that Bob Iger graduated from. Not everything is about one side versus the other.

## Developing as an entry-level artist

Assuming you have selected your learning path of choice – what's done is done, you cannot undo the past. Now what? Dear reader, if you are just starting out fresh as a wide-eyed entry-level artist, you need to be aware that being a sponge will be your most important asset when it comes to working with and at various VFX studios. Yes, your skills are and will be important – that's how you got your entry-level job after all; however, these studios aren't just hiring you for your skills. They are primarily hiring you for your age, youth, vitality, and all other qualities affiliated with being young and naive as an entry-level person in the field. They know you most likely don't have other offers as a fresh graduate or newcomer and most likely won't be married with children. How, then, can you prove your mettle and develop yourself further as an entry-level artistic sponge in VFX?

When I first started out, I was definitely that sponge. A skinny, foreigner sponge, but a sponge nonetheless. I devoured everything in that studio – its VFX shot submission protocols, artist management systems, even the free snacks and crafties (film lingo for on-set munchies). That's how I developed over time as an entry-level artist. And soon you'll learn things that they don't teach you in school about VFX but happen to be important to that particular VFX studio or the VFX community at large. This is where that phrase of "what you learned in school doesn't apply at work" comes about; many, typically from other industries, would extol themselves for being that one man or woman in the office smart enough to realize how the knowledge they had gained from school was not relevant to their current professional careers. This is only true to a certain extent as you still needed that base knowledge to get into those offices or studios to begin with – so, I would not be too quick to dismiss your degree or online foundations just yet.

Ultimately, at this phase of your career, one of the best things you can do is to be a sponge and soak up as much applicable knowledge related to and about VFX as possible – especially at your new job. Remember though that each studio has its own personality so be sure to store all that knowledge you have soaked up from one studio in a bucket at home before entering another studio as a fresh, dry sponge ready for another soaking.

## Developing mid-career

Weird analogy aside, you will eventually ascend in your career in VFX to what one would call the 'mid-level artist', also known as a 'mid' or 'mid artist'. Typically, you will know when you have entered mid territory as you will start to notice that tasks and shots that get assigned your way will have an extra layer of complexity to them – that, or you will experience an increase in the volume of shots where previously you had a whole day just to tackle one. As an experienced mid artist myself, I would say that this could be where the lull starts to set in. You are comfortable, you know you get around in the industry, and depending on the lifestyle you are looking for, you could either remain an employee or try becoming a freelancer. It is still important, however, to continue developing yourself as an artist at the mid-level, and here are a few suggestions how.

Understand that right now, your best assets are not just your skills or your youth (or your ability to work overtime without question), your best asset at this stage is your ability to execute quickly and almost flawlessly. Of course, everyone makes mistakes and sometimes clients don't know what they want; your ability to grow and develop as a mid artist is hence, to be able to quickly iterate and problem-solve with as high an accuracy as humanly possible. This becomes easy when the studio you are at is already assigning you lots of shots or a few really complex shots as you'll get a chance to practice speeding up your problem-solving skills whilst customizing your solutions to the task at hand.

What if you are a freelancer though? Well, you could still develop artistically by taking on a variety of tasks or VFX projects. VFX shots and tasks are as varied as they come, and sometimes you get a greater variety (and option) of shots to practice performing your problem-solving skills as a freelancer, compared to a mainstay employee. Again, don't just take my word for it – try it out and see how the experience is like for yourself. As a mid, it is presumed that some of your life priorities may have shifted since you first began your journey into VFX, so take that into account if you are deciding to be an avid freelancer or remain as a stable employee.

## Developing as a veteran (speculative)

This section would be entirely speculative for I do not consider myself to be a veteran in VFX by any means – at least not yet, at the time of the writing of this treatise. However, upon gathering intel and insights from various colleagues and acquaintances of mine in the VFX world, for the most part, I have determined a few specific patterns and trends in how these individuals operate and develop their craft – even when they have over twenty years of experience in their industry.

To them, it is all about relevancy. They have already proven to be sponges, they had youth and vitality on their side when they began their journey, and they also proved to be the studio's weapon of choice when it comes to delivering shots and completing VFX tasks at record speed and accuracy; now, in order for these veterans to develop further as artists, it is crucial that they invest into keeping up with the latest tools, methods, and means of performing certain tasks differently (usually more efficiently).

In fact, I have an acquaintance who is a very experienced VFX producer who had recently been accepted into a program to learn virtual production using game engines. To be upfront, virtual production has already existed for a while but with virtual reality (VR) being at the forefront of certain integrations with tools that were once mainly used for game development, it's quite interesting to see someone whom I know to be a veteran up his game by being willing to enter a program meant for complete beginners.

Regardless of where you are at, reader, I hope you are aware that being and staying relevant is not just something you do once you hit the coveted (or not, depending on your perspective) veteran status in VFX. In fact, in order to stay in the industry, being relevant is usually a must at all stages of one's VFX career. I am only bringing this up here since it is the topmost recurring trend that I could detect in those veterans I have spoken to or have come to know personally. That being said, just because one is a veteran does not give them the latitude to forgo being that skinny, dried-up sponge they once were when they were a young – and let's face it, probably thinner and healthier-looking – artist, nor does it give them the permission to stop completing tasks quickly and with high accuracy. If anything, older veterans are sometimes stuck in a pickle where they know they have the track record and portfolio to back them up as viable and skilled artists yet still have to prove their mettle in terms of being able to perform at the speed and accuracy that artists younger than themselves (like the mids) tend to excel at. While it is slightly ageist, it is not as bad as one thinks. I still know plenty of veterans who remain relevant and get around in VFX just fine.

## Shifting into VFX

Alright, alright, this all sounds fine and dandy if you already had your eyes set on becoming a VFX artist when you were younger, but let's say you are a little on the older side of this journey. Perhaps you got a degree in engineering from a top Indian university, worked at one of the 'Big Techs' for about ten years or so, and then, at the age of thirty-five, decided that enough is enough. "That's it! I've had it with these politics, bro culture, and toxic environment. I want to do something fun and solitary like work on Hollywood VFX!" you exclaimed with a unique blend of rage and excitement. Even though the above path could still work out for you where you either go to a school, enroll in an online academy or just learn things on your own, your situation is actually a lot harder to work with, realistically. Here's why: remember the one true asset that studios value most in entry-level positions? Your youth and naivety, of course. Now, I am going to presuppose that as a thirty-five-year-old engineer in tech, you have a family of sorts or are at least thinking of planning some kind of a stable home life for yourself and/or your significant other(s). Fair enough. I am also going to presuppose that at this stage in your life – not your career, your life as a living person – you are looking for more fulfillment and a healthier work-life balance (or the term I would prefer – work-life integration). Not surprising. In fact, it is fairly commonplace for the healthy-minded thirty-somethings to already be in some sort of a serious committed relationship and, having experienced a form of work life in whatever industry they were in, seek for a greater synergy of work and time off.

Unfortunately, those two desires alone could work against you should you be starting out from scratch as an entry-level artist at the age of thirty-five. Unless you are exceptionally talented, and highly convincing and appealing as an artist to these studios, transitioning into VFX from another industry after ten years or so in this other industry will be a challenge. In this case, your chances are best placed in investing and enrolling into an art school that will likely supply you with all the foundations of VFX in a nutshell. You could pursue a master's degree in VFX or animation, depending on your interests, as the school's brand would lend you some credibility and visibility when restarting your career path to enter VFX. That being said, you could of course pursue the online school route or learn from random VFX courses online – I'm just suggesting the options that would give you, as a career-switcher, the *best* and *highest* possible chance of being considered as an entry-level artist whilst competing against all the other younger fledgling artists out there today.

That being said, it is not impossible for career-switchers or jumpers into VFX to make their marks having already spent their prime in another field. A quick Google search and you can easily find a couple of artists who managed to successfully shift into VFX – a few of whom were also foreigners like me, which made the switch for them appear even more impressive. It might require much more effort and luck on your side, but with the right strategy and mindset, you can get into VFX even if you are forty. Just be realistic with your market position and skills coming in – know that studios generally prefer someone younger with the exact same VFX skills as you, with all else being equal.

## Sum of Averages

"You are the average of the five people you spend the most time with," is a quote popularized by Jim Rohn. While I could happily write a ten-page essay debating why this is not necessarily the case nor does it apply to every single human being in existence, the quote most likely does apply to you, dear reader. I am presuming that you, reader, at least have family members or next of kin you genuinely care for or love; perhaps a close friend or two, or three, or five whom you occasionally hang with. Even for someone like me who sometimes claims to have no friends and no kin I genuinely care for – other than my dog, who has passed – the sum of averages still applies. We do tend to soak up the personalities, habits, intensities, and attributes of our environment

– it's human nature. Like real estate, we as individuals would prefer not to stick out like a sore thumb, and by silently assimilating the traits of those in close proximity to ourselves, this ensures and fulfills our subconscious need for acceptance and communion amongst our own kind (as in mankind).

This sum of averages also applies in VFX and how you develop and grow as an artist in this industry. And I don't mean go out and hang out only with your colleagues from your VFX studio, nor am I specifying that you should live, breathe, and sleep VFX and only hang out with the VFX community or "artistic" people. You see, while I can confidently state that I do not have friends, I can also proudly state that I do have a *lot* of acquaintances – and not just in VFX. As a matter of fact, not only do I never date someone in my industry of VFX, but I also don't only hang out with VFX professionals just because I work in VFX. It gets boring. Frankly, a lot of VFX people are also dreadfully boring as individuals. At work, most of the conversations encompass movies, the latest technologies (but not discussed in-depth because, frankly, no one sitting at that desk would be an expert in those technologies), episodes or shows from Netflix, or random "how did you get into VFX" questions. Sometimes, you'll get the occasional sexist (or sexist *and* racist) conversation but thus far, I've only encountered that once – and the perpetrator was a woman who worked in production who had a thing against Asian women taking away Caucasian men. Anyway, I digress.

The point is, do not go out of your way to only surround yourself with VFX peers and professionals all the time. Get out of your field and out of yourself for a while. It was easy for me since, being hypercompetitive, I didn't exactly enjoy hanging out with my "competition" (with competition defined as peers of my age range, who specialize in the same area of VFX as I do) outside of work, so I hung out with people outside of VFX the majority of the time, without judgment. Oh, reader, please do not misconstrue this message (or myself) as being a non-collaborative team player though. Let's not forget the nuances of human behavior. One can still be an awesome team player at work whilst showing absolute disinterest in forging closer relationships with your work peers *outside* of work due to personal conflicts of interest. Not everything is black-and-white. Life is usually a shade of grey – and the biggest matters that tend to be black or white tend to involve the giving of life or taking of it anyway.

In short, do not fret if you do not like hanging around your colleagues outside of work or feel obligated to be present at every single VFX-related event or meeting. Whilst those are useful in your artistic development to a certain extent, you'll find that your mind and your world opens up a lot more when you choose to explore outside VFX and meet people from all walks of life – again, the kind of experience usually provided for at schools, albeit that experience is more of a sampler than the main course. If anything, let's not make your entire life as a VFX artist all about VFX – life's way too short to be that narrow.

# 4

# THE LIFE OF A VFX ARTIST

Ah yes, it's time to divulge the life of a VFX artist. Firstly, it is important to establish that regardless of your exact specialty in post-production VFX, your typical day-to-day activities will most likely follow the same pattern. The only differences in the day-to-day activities when it comes to positions in the VFX industry are when we compare post-production artists to on-set VFX supervisors and more administrative positions such as VFX producers and coordinators. For this treatise, we will be focusing more on a day in the life of a typical post-production VFX artist – an endeavor I have had plenty more years of experience in, in comparison to being a VFX supervisor or producer. Do take note, however, that the following is merely an outline and of course, expect that there will always be variances from person-to-person and studio-to-studio. Your level of seniority at a studio will also determine a few adjustments in your daily routine as a post-production VFX professional.

## Day in the life of

Here I will be laying out what typically happens during my day as a VFX compositor (employee or freelancer, it doesn't really differ in routine) at most studios:

**8 AM**: Wake up and get ready to commute

(I do not drive, so I tend to get up early in order to catch the buses and trains in Los Angeles – yes, they are not as bad as the people [who actually never tried them] make it out to be)

**9.50 AM**: Enter studio premises

(depending on how large the studio is, this can take some time and generally requires getting through security or having a key pass, et cetera)

**9.55 AM**: Get my milk, tea, bagel, or whatever breakfast was laid out bare

(breakfast availability depends on the studio and their budget – don't expect it all the time; this is also the time where I may perhaps hoard a packet of snacks or two for later)

**10 AM**: Get settled and check your shots using the studio's artist/shot management software

(the majority of studios use the Shotgun Software, some may use ftrack and others; and no, there is no real need to learn this before you get a job)

Check studio email inbox and reply if necessary (optional)

**10.10 AM:**     Start work on your shot(s)

(depending on the priority of the shots, you may either address shots with notes or work on a newly-assigned shot – the former is more likely; also cue the task of sitting for prolonged hours [which can cause health issues in the future, but I digress])

**2 PM:**     Get lunch by yourself or with co-workers

(sometimes lunch is a set time, or it could be any time you want, as long as it only lasts an hour; you would either log this in your timesheet or stop the timer, depending on which system the studio uses for artists)

**3 PM:**     Back to working on those shot(s)

(and back to sitting and getting fat with snacks – kidding; sometimes you may get fresh notes from the client or supervisor after lunch, depending on how dailies are scheduled at the studio [look up 'dailies' on Google if you are unsure what the term means])

**7 PM:**     Time to clock out!

(yay, time to leave the office; you will update your time card/timesheet or stop the timer and turn in whatever shots you had completed before you leave for the day – again, turning in shots happens throughout the day and will depend on studio protocol)

**7.15 PM**:         Commute back home

(common sense, unless you want to sleep at the office – which I did see people do at one particular major studio I had worked at long ago)

**9 PM**:         Get settled back home

(consider this as your spare time as a working VFX artist; if you go for an 8-hour sleep then you really only have three hours to yourself [don't forget to include the time you need to get dinner and shower])

**8 AM (next day)**: RINSE AND REPEAT

If you are thinking – after looking at the above routine very carefully – that this sounds like a typical, regular ol' desk job – it is. Don't get me wrong though. VFX can still be fun and exciting depending on your perspective but I kid you not, the above is exactly how a typical day in the life of a VFX artist goes. Perhaps things may change in the future as more advanced technology disrupts more industries but for now, take this as your reality as a VFX artist.

I do want to enlighten you, however, on the possible variations that can occur during one's daily routine as a VFX artist. The following distractions and interruptions that occasionally do occur at various studios could perhaps spice up your life a bit as a VFX artist:

- Sequence or scene screenings of your current top-secret project.
- Mini-group pow-wow stand-up meeting: to discuss next steps, updates from clients, shot priorities, and expectations from the team.
- Short 30-minute or an hour talk on topics unrelated to VFX.
- Short 30-minute or less game time: soccer, ping-pong, other minor games.
- Short group trips to Starbucks or the local food place for snacks: sometimes all-expenses-paid but don't rely on it.
- Birthday or anniversary celebrations of certain co-workers or people you don't know who work at the studio: happy birthday, whatshisface from the IT department?
- Free pizza and drinks to celebrate working on certain holidays – sometimes they are just randomly served for dinner for artists staying overtime.
- Setting up or confirming artist schedule with the producer or human resources (HR) personnel.

The above is not an exclusive list and there can certainly be other random events that occur during the day that could detract from the typical doldrums of your VFX desk job. As you can see, quite the colorful variety, especially now that free dinners and food are mentioned. Speaking of free food, yes, there are usually free snacks available at most studios. In fact, the only studios I have been to with no free snacks provided are those that happened to be downsizing or impacted by a sudden reduction in their project revenue; there was a studio I had worked at that had a majority reliance on Disney for their incoming work – I was told that when Disney took all the creative work in-house, that severely impacted that studio so much that the owner had to lay off almost ninety percent of their staff. It was even quite difficult to find their office at first since they shared a little cubicle with another company.

Of course, not all is that dismal and dull in the VFX world when it comes to the day-to-day grind (did I mention that overtime work is likely a possibility with your job as well?). As mentioned previously, your routine would be vastly different as a VFX supervisor or VFX producer. With some experience as an independent VFX supervisor on set, I would say that their day-to-day activities allow for more variety and flexibility – plus, it gets you out of the office more. Their duties generally involve quick, on-the-go problem-solving on set and guiding of VFX teams both on set and during post-production (depending on the production's budget, in general). However, our focus here is on FX jobs in post-production, so I will leave it at that when it comes to what VFX supervisors do in a day.

Honestly, regardless of how you slice it – yes, our daily routine is exactly like a typical desk job. You are most likely paid by the hour as well, irrespective of your status as an employee or a freelancer, when it comes to working at studios. Whilst those minor intrusions and celebratory moments at the office are nice, the irony of it all is that you still end up being a slave to your employer and enslaved to your desk and daily routine as a VFX artist. It is part of the game and comes with the territory, unfortunately. But hey, a few of these studios have actually invested in standing desks, so maybe instead of sitting yourself to death, you could afford to stretch your legs a bit?

## So-called spare time

Ah, spare time. Don't we all wish we had more? Well, clearly, if I can write this book right now without hiring a co-author or a ghostwriter then I have loads of spare time – and that's because, in some way, I am not currently on a studio project (due to geographical reasons, for the most part). Unfortunately, if you are seeking to become or currently are a VFX professional in the industry, spare time may only come by sparingly. You will have much more flexibility in a managerial, non-technical position but for the most part, your spare time sometimes gets occupied by the dreaded (or exciting, depending on your view) overtime work. As someone who freelanced a lot, this overtime rule also applies to you. I would say I have done overtime at almost seventy-five percent of the total studios I have worked at. Expect that the odds of you doing overtime as an entry-level artist will be somewhat similar. In fact, I have observed that the higher in seniority you get at any given studio, the more hours you will have to work – including that overtime. That's because when it comes to the grind – or 'crunch time', as it's known in the industry – senior artists with more experience will be asked or required to stay behind to pick up the slack on any missing or overdue shots, sometimes tackling shots that were not able to be completed by the mid or entry-level artists in time. So then, if you happen to be one of the "lucky ones" to not get called for overtime work, how much spare time could you expect to have, realistically?

Assuming you drive to and from work (rather than taking public transportation on a dollar, like myself), you could muster up to about four to five hours of so-called spare time per weekday, and of course, the full days on the weekends (assuming you aren't required to work on the weekends). Tell me, what can you do for five hours? Your shift ends at about 7 PM or 7.30 PM, usually; with driving, you would be home by around 8 PM, let's say. Some VFX artists go home and get straight back to sitting in front of a computer screen, whereas some head to the gym and train (probably poorly because let's be real, I have yet to meet a VFX artist who *actually* trains hardcore – most just don't have that coveted gym knowledge). If you date – most people I know in VFX are already in relationships and not really newly dating (and if they are, they surely don't make mention of it) – you may spend your spare time doing that on a Friday night. Or perhaps you may spend your time getting intimate or playing with the kids; whatever it is, you really only have about four to five hours per weekday to get them all in. Sad, but true.

Hence, weekends were brought up for a reason as they're really the only days off you have from your job as a VFX artist – unless, of course, you have to work on weekends too. That actually happened to me once at this major studio that enforced almost an eighty-hour work week from Monday to Sunday, including all overtime hours. Sure, you do make a hefty sum from the time-and-a-half artist rate from all overtime hours (mandated by law), but you can kiss your weekends and any weekend plans goodbye. Truthfully and thankfully, however, such cases where the studio demands your full weekends for a long period of time are rare. That eighty-hour workweek stint lasted for about a month and a half if recollection serves me well. In fact, it was becoming so tedious and difficult to commute to and from work by public transport that I had to temporarily put up at a random co-worker's place in the living room. Notably, they were all obese or morbidly obese men with beards, with one really random stick-thin newcomer into the industry; fantastic people and wonderful roommates who offered me their place when in need, though you can tell by now what tends to happen to those who stay in VFX for too long (especially at desk jobs).

The bottom line is this: treasure your precious spare time as a VFX artist. You will never know when studios may take your free time away with planned or unplanned overtime. Sometimes, I do get the occasional text, call, or email on a Saturday to come in on a Sunday for a VFX emergency. Also, treat your weekends like gold and try not to sit for too long even on the weekends. Get out of the house, do some sports, get in shape, and stay healthy – or just rest, there is always that option to just do nothing on the weekends, if you prefer. We all know our eyes definitely deserve a break from staring at computer screens all day, for a minimum of forty hours per week.

## "Work-life balance"

With that comes the point of establishing a healthy work-life balance as a VFX artist. I prefer the term 'work-life integration' as it seems rather silly to think that work and life are to be treated as if they were separate entities. If one were to get philosophical for a moment, work is technically a subset of life; so, to have a concept developed based on balancing or attempting to balance work and life appears to be wanting in logic – that the two are not truly mutually exclusive elements at play to begin with. Thus, let's talk about work-life integration for a moment.

There is a general consensus that exists out there that we as a society develop our intellectual consciousness and awareness of things as we breed new generations of people. Intrinsically, it is fair to state that the generation that comes after yours is probably better equipped with the fundamentals of certain concepts that would most likely have taken a longer time for your generation or the generations of your parents or grandparents to grasp. An example would be the use of the Google search engine and intelligent devices such as smartphones. It is a safe bet to assume that Generation Z has had earlier access to these tools and technologies at a younger age compared to Gen Y (Millennials), who would have had even earlier access to these tools than Generation X and consequently the Baby Boomers. With that foundation, we can start to understand how the concept of a 'work-life balance' will start to be overruled by the newer generations' ideal of work-life integration. Through my observations and experiences with people of all ages, I can see this happening online and in-person, where it is most notably the younger generation (sometimes even the youngest generation) that has started to show companies and corporations how to successfully integrate work and life harmoniously. I believe as studios tend to prioritize and hire younger and younger talents – usually in hopes of grooming them to become mainstays at the studio if they are particularly talented – we can start to see the VFX industry slowly attempt to tilt towards balancing work and life as one. How that will happen remains to be seen, though I have a pretty good prediction and vision of what that would look like that I'll keep to myself.

For now, however, at least at the time of publishing this book, I do want to state that regardless of where you are in the VFX pipeline when it comes to your position as an artist, technician, or producer, it is always best to approach your outlook on work as a form of integration with your life and lifestyle, rather than as an object that needs to be balanced against it. Of course, as described in this chapter thus far, that does present a challenge in and of itself with the way your daily routine is scheduled and with the limited amount of spare time available to you. Unfortunately, it is just the way the industry is, and it is presently a fact that has to be accepted by all coming into the industry as an artist or practitioner – you have to be willing to eat into your leisure time in order to work in VFX at studios. Presented with this reality, rather than shunning or trying to bypass it, we as VFX artists should learn to accept it and adapt our schedules accordingly – hence, the work-life integration.

The problem then arises as your life and lifestyle changes over the years – I know mine did, and it wasn't for any major reason such as wanting to have kids, start a family, or all that human jazz; I'll get to that part later in the book. For the majority of you readers out there, I am sure you all have your own goals, dreams, and aspirations outside of just working on VFX work and cool projects for the rest of your life. Now, perhaps you're one of those who went, "Nope, I pretty much want to spend my next fifty years doing VFX at any studio until the day I die." Good for you, you're pretty much set working on other people's projects – and I am saying this positively; it is completely fine to just want something stable and to not be at the helm of any film projects. As for the rest of you, understand this: it is absolutely normal to want to do something else or achieve your other dreams and goals; whether that is to start a family, have more vacation time, or just travel the world, you are only human to have such aspirations throughout your lifetime. Unfortunately, I do want to be upfront in saying this, unless you transition into a different type of position within VFX that allows you a bit more flexibility (but not necessarily a reduction in any more responsibility), as a VFX artist over the years, your daily demands and hourly requirements at work will *not* change to suit your lifestyle changes. Sacrifices *must* be made on account of your other dreams and ambitions should you wish to continue being a seasoned VFX artist at any studio over the years. Also, no, your spare time availability will not change to accommodate your changing life goals either, unfortunately.

## Perks of being a VFX artist

Alright reader, admit it, you have been getting a lot of negative vibes from me thus far when it comes to my outlook on VFX and being a VFX artist. Now, here comes the part where I actually shatter some of that negativity that I have been building into your soul and highlight some of the perks of being a VFX artist. As with almost anything else in life, they all come with their perks and downsides. It is up to you as an individual to determine how much of the downsides you are willing to take in order to experience said or perceived perks. There is no right or wrong answer – only good or bad when it comes to the experience being worthy of your time and beneficial towards your personal goals.

1.  **The VFX industry is predominantly filled with smart, talented people**

While there is a case to be made that every industry has smart, talented people, this is even more so in highly technical and process-oriented industries such as VFX, animation, and game development. Having worked with a vast number of artists, technicians, supervisors, producers, and production personnel, I would say that the VFX industry is predominantly a place where people with higher intelligence flock to. Not to make this about IQ, EQ, or whatever (look them up on Google if you are confused by these acronyms), but it does not and would not surprise me if the VFX crowd, in general, has an above-average intelligence compared to, let's say, the trucking or farming industries. This isn't to say they are geniuses – and after meeting enough people in the industry, I can attest to the fact that not everyone in VFX is really at genius level (not even close) – but they are more intelligent than your average Joe walking down the street. Hence, as a VFX artist, know that you will not only be surrounded by smart and talented people most of the time – who can only help further your own development as an artist – but being in the industry for an extended period of time does show that you *do* indeed have the talent, smarts, and VFX chops to make it for the long haul.

## 2. Being a VFX artist helps sharpen your mind (if you are in the right role)

Being in VFX also brings the added bonus of daily mental training if you are in the right VFX role. To clarify, there are roles in VFX that are certainly mind-numbing and unstimulating such as most entry-level positions like rotoscoping and prep artists. However, if you are in a more mentally stimulating position such as 3D animation, compositing, or scripting, then being a VFX artist will certainly aid in sharpening your mind for old age. In fact, as a compositor, one of the industry's most competitive and hottest positions to be in these days, I would get a mix of shots with interesting and unique problems or challenges. Something as simple as a clean-up could even take some mental effort to conjure up a solution if, for example, production provided zero clean plates or footage from set to work with for that particular shot. Thinking of slicing a zombie's head off? That comes with its own host of unique challenges and problems to solve if you don't have a background plate provided to you from the set. Again, the combination of problems is endless – and that's a good thing. That is *exactly* what you want (although costly and not ideal for the producers of the production) as a VFX artist – to solve challenging, unique, and interesting problems every day, under a tight deadline (if you work on television projects).

**3. You get to work on amazing projects spearheaded by creative (sometimes well-funded) people**

Throughout my career as a VFX artist, I have worked on films and television shows I never could have imagined that I would have worked on. I had worked on *"The Walking Dead"* before I even knew what all the fuss was about with that show – and now, I'm a fan. Then there were *"Guardians of the Galaxy," "Alice Through the Looking Glass," "War for the Planet of the Apes," "Aquaman," "Grey's Anatomy," "Parks & Recreation,"* and so on and so forth. I could name-drop all I want in this book, but that's beside the point. The experience of working on what would turn out to be incredibly inspirational and amazing titles, and alongside equally amazing and talented people in VFX, cannot be replaced nor priced. The coolest part of my working experience was when I get to meet or work collaboratively with the directors of some of these projects as well. Again, depending on your role in VFX, some positions in VFX allow you access (or visitation rights, ha) to the director of the production. And to be bold, these directors look as creative and well-funded as they come. Since I promised to make this section about its perks, I am going to sidestep how production funding is funneled through all cast but mostly crew members on a project (and how the VFX people are factored into this equation). In general, yes: amazing projects, talented people, and well-funded directors.

### 4. It is fulfilling to complete a VFX shot and see it on the big screen

Yes, yes, I am sure a few of you budding artists are looking forward to this one and I must admit, it really *is* fulfilling to complete a VFX shot and see it on the big screen (and have it be seen by millions and millions of mostly VFX-oblivious viewers worldwide). Just as it was tantalizing to see a VFX shot through to completion, it is just as exciting to see your completed and finished work be appreciated and admired by the masses. To be honest, it is highly unlikely for an audience to go "Wow!" on great VFX shots as their focus is primarily on the storytelling and narrative unfolding before them, but even if you don't hear the "oohs" and the "ahhs," at least you were part of the process that helped tell and sell the story. Despite VFX being a supportive industry and niche in the macrosphere that is the filmmaking and entertainment business, the film most likely would not be as convincing and as successful had it not been for all the behind-the-scenes, supporting industry players at work – from VFX to post-production sound, editing, and creative color grading. So, kudos to all of us VFX artists for completing those VFX shots under a time crunch and helping make Hollywood magic possible.

## 5. It is rewarding to see your name in the credits

Yet another perk that most coming into the industry seem to go after – having your name in the credit roll of a film or television series. We will discuss the specifics of what and who gets the credits and why but for now, let's just say that it is indeed rewarding to see your name in the spotlight, on the silver and small screens. Of course, you will most likely be sharing that spotlight with thousands and thousands of other names; in fact, VFX is easy to spot in the credits typically by being the section with the longest list of names most people in the audience would never actually bother to read (most of them would probably have left by that point). Regardless, it's a nice pat on the back – even if it's a name that only you would actually care to spot or actively look for amongst the sea of back-to-back names in VFX.

## 6. You get a good variety of problems to solve in your work (it's never dull, depending on your role)

Depending on your exact specialization and position in VFX, there is never really a dull moment at work. Sure, your daily routine may be repetitive, but your mental acuity will surely be enhanced after a few years in this industry – at least when it comes to visual problem-solving. As a VFX compositor mostly for independent and television projects, I have come to love the fast-paced critical thinking and versatility that compositing for television requires. At any typical job, I would get shots that involved compositing for driving scenes (also known as driving comps), greenscreen keying, removing blemishes or marks on an actor's face (also known as beauty work), enhancing lighting in an existing shot, and removing crew equipment visible in the shot at odd places. So many different problems, so many ways to solve them. I really do get a dopamine kick out of all that problem-solving – even just thinking about it!

## 7. If you freelance, you get to choose the projects/contracts you want to work on

This mainly applies to freelancers who hop around and work at different studios throughout their career – frankly, everyone is sort of a freelancer in this industry, but there are some who would be your traditional freelancers more often than most, in the sense that they deliberately do not stay for more than three months or so (a term greater than that would then typically be viewed as an 'employee' status instead). If you are in demand, then the coolest part of being a freelancer is that you get to actually choose the projects and contracts you want to do. In fact, there was one time in the summer, many moons ago – around 2014 or 2015 is my guess – when I had the opportunity and pleasure of selecting one or multiple contract offers from a pool of fourteen. Yes, I had fourteen work offers during the summer with most of them happening simultaneously. Then, depending on your individual stamina and appetite, you may take up as many or as few offers as you would like. Again, this is not something you should expect all the time, but it is something that can happen if you are in the right position for it to happen.

**8. Senior artists are always willing to help and mentor junior artists (to a certain extent)**

From speaking with dozens of others outside the VFX industry – such as in finance, investment banking (think Wall Street), technology, software development, and civil service – I can attest to the VFX industry's willingness to genuinely mentor and guide junior and fledgling artists who are just starting out in the industry. I have observed this in action as a mid artist seeing newer artists get mentored by the mainstay seniors at studios and have also been on the receiving end of such mentorship when I first started out with my first break on AMC's *"The Walking Dead."* This is personally one of my favorite perks of being a VFX artist –that you get direct access to these smart and talented artists who are always willing to help you get acquainted with the software, proprietary tools, or other new techniques up their sleeves. Of course, don't expect them to be your career counselor or life coach or anything like that – you're asking way too much. These senior artists, however, will gladly mentor you through a shot or help out by providing some pointers and tips – especially if you are just coming in at entry-level.

## The lies you uncover for yourself

All in all, perks and lack of spare time aside, my observations of the lives of VFX artists – more specifically, my own life as a VFX artist – have been quite insightful. You see, I am sure you, dear reader, have had some sort of preconceived notion about what the life of a blockbuster-movie VFX artist would be like. Sullied by images and expectations placed by film biographies or dramas about filmmakers and artisans on set (forgetting the fact that these films are usually about a producer or director and *not* a VFX artist – because really, nobody cares about watching a movie about a VFX artist, it's boring), thinking that that is probably going to be your life as well. Well, I hope that after reading this chapter, you've abandoned those rose-colored lenses. Welcome to the real world of being a VFX artist.

Glamour and talented people aside, the more time you spend in VFX, the more you will start to uncover the lies you have been told about working in movies or animation/VFX. The reality isn't as glamorous as it seems – and you wouldn't want it to be (or you'll have lots of competition in the field). The biggest lie studios try to sell you on is the false narrative of a "work-life balance." To be honest, we cannot really blame them. It is just how the industry is. Frankly, if you want to get into the trenches working on some of the best and toughest VFX shots and tasks, you can forget about having any semblance of a proper life outside of work. There is, of course, nothing wrong with that if you are a true workaholic. You've just got to accept that you will have to be that workaholic in order to serve a studio or production that you ultimately will have zero personal stake in and that you do not own, for an end product that you will ultimately not be lauded for – at least when compared to the cast, director, and producers of the production. And no, VFX will not make you famous, nor will it make you rich (unless you stay in the industry for a *really* long time and try not to incur any bad debts along the way), if that's what you're expecting.

Yes, it is rewarding to *help* bring a production to life. It just depends on whether you are comfortable being in the backseat or actually driving the car of your dreams. You will have to accept the good and the bad and understand that much like everything else in life, there is no perfect job, perfect industry, or perfect place to call home. There is not even a perfect country – trust me, I've tried to find it. The United States and Singapore each have their own annoying flaws and fantastic benefits. And don't even bet on New Zealand either just because they have sheep. Ultimately, each industry and niche will be entirely subjective, unique, and flawed with a life and personality of its own. It is up to you to choose the life of a VFX artist or decide if it isn't for you, based on how well you know yourself. So, know yourself. Know yourself *well*.

# 5

# HOW THE VFX INDUSTRY WORKS

If you have made it this far and have decided that you can afford to live the life of a VFX artist, then congratulations on making that decision. The next few chapters are where I will unleash a whole lot of truths, insights, and information about how the VFX industry, Hollywood, and global markets work. So, do bear with me if this is not your forte nor interest – I understand some artists are not all that concerned with discussing such phenomena. Regardless, reader, if you want to know all about the external factors at play that could possibly grind your career to a halt (or expedite it rapidly), these next few chapters are not to be taken lightly. No, I will not be boring you with the history or development of VFX over the years as frankly, those have zero impact on your career trajectory (or mine) whatsoever. I will in fact be elucidating on the various types of market players, job-related tenets, and systemic aspects of the VFX industry that you ought to know regardless of whether you plan to stay or leave VFX anytime soon. I guarantee you will be way ahead of the curve by simply understanding how the VFX industry functions to keep itself alive, and ultimately keeping you employed in the long run.

## A segregated world

I have read enough market statistics and analyses from various firms to know that the VFX industry is indeed a segregated world (and my firsthand experience in the industry only serves to prove these firms' analyses). Meaning, its industry players are segmented into different categories, most of whom attempt to compete for the same types of productions or projects. Understandably, stronger brand names such as Industrial Light & Magic (ILM) and Digital Domain will command the majority of major blockbuster film and television projects, leaving other independent or less-funded productions as scraps for the other studios. Not all hope is lost for those studios, however, as manpower is always limited even at places such as ILM and Digital Domain, which is why you will always find a long list of different VFX studios on the credit roll of any well-funded, studio-backed film. In addition to the evident hierarchy of powerhouse studios within the VFX world, you also have studios divided by their specializations and focus. For example, we have studios that focus solely on creature FX or particle effects using the software Houdini; we also have studios that only do title or motion graphic sequences for films, shows, commercials, and so on and so forth.

I would name them, but the thing is, these studios usually realize that specialization and focus aren't enough to sustain their businesses. Hence, they eventually generalize to become like every other studio on the Hollywood block. This shift should already prove how studio changes and shifts in focus are also to be expected across all studios in the VFX world – no matter how big their brand names are.

Another form of segmentation in the market of VFX is the types of projects that each studio would prefer or generally accept. There are in fact studios, some of which I have worked for, that only focus on delivering VFX for television shows or pilots, for example. There are also those that deliver VFX only for commercials and even fewer who solely concentrate on games. The point being, there are multiple forms of segmentation amongst industry players in this field that would make it hard to group certain VFX studios together under multiple categories, since each of them differs from the other in some way – whether that be their studio manpower, VFX specialization, or types of projects accepted. It is highly unlikely that the segregated nature of the VFX industry will change over the next decade since there will always be new studio entrants into the industry and studios change in specialization and brand notoriety over the years. We can only expect to see further market segmentation in VFX as a greater variety of projects require post-production VFX editing, and VFX starts to make a more pronounced presence with on-set manipulation and real-time post-production VFX.

As a VFX artist entering this segmented world, consider it a privilege to be able to experience the myriad of projects, studio environments, and specializations of different studios, big or small. While prospects as a VFX studio owner are rather dim – and rightly so, given how much the majority of well-funded projects are instantaneously funneled into big-branded VFX studios by default – the opportunities are practically boundless if you are playing the industry as an ordinary VFX artist (regardless of your specialization). The segregation mainly works in your favor should you decide to freelance, as studios most heavily rely on people that have had experience with their unique workflows and systems. Essentially, if you have worked with one studio that had its own proprietary software, know that it is unlikely that there will be much competition for return projects at that particular studio, since no other studios will have that tool that you had to learn in order to get the job.

## Mainstream VFX studios

Speaking of studios and the many aspects of segregation, let's discuss those big-name VFX studios which are, broadly speaking, the studios that would make up your mainstream VFX studios in this industry. Just as any other industry has its incumbents, the VFX industry is no different. I don't have to list all their names in order for you, reader, to get acquainted with these mainstream VFX studios as most of them have most likely been exposed to you through your basic interest in VFX. The ILMs, Digital Domains, and Framestores of the VFX world are literally the only ones that could say that they are the ILMs, Digital Domains, and Framestores of the VFX world. In other words, there is *no other* ILM out there that could be the ILM of VFX – only ILM. Likewise, there is *no other* Digital Domain out there that could be the Digital Domain of VFX – there is only Digital Domain. You get the picture. These industry titans, some of whom have lasted for more than three decades, make up your mainstream VFX studios that production companies typically turn to for reliable VFX work and that you, reader, most likely aspire to work for at some point in your VFX career.

Whilst I was close to getting to work at Framestore (and also Method Studios, but let's focus on Framestore for this particular case) – but couldn't due to the dreaded scheduling conflicts – on several occasions, I had one or two interviews there and was able to quickly assess how the insides of one of these titan VFX studios looked like. I also had the opportunity to tour ILM through an inside connection who had worked there at the time. I will say that these mainstream VFX studios do give off that aura of excellence and superiority (and I mean this in a positive sense) and from the brief glimpses of work I was able to see from these artists' screens – after signing a bunch of non-disclosure agreements – these studios do in fact live up to their renown and reputation for being the best of the best in the business.

With that being said, while they do have access to a larger pool of manpower in terms of numbers, their recruitment standards are definitely very specific and refined. The cool trick is that once you get into one, you generally have access to all the rest as long as you did actually perform and do the work right. In other words, had I gotten into Framestore at the time when they were hiring for some commercial work, the chances of me gaining another contract or job at Digital Domain, ILM, or Pixomondo would have increased. Again, this is *not* a guarantee, but it sure seems that way, based on the other artists and technicians I have met. Basically, once you get into one major VFX studio, the doors to the other major VFX studios have cracked opened for you. You still need to show them your chops, but they will essentially have warmed up to you from the get-go compared to someone who had done a lot of work at random smaller VFX studios (or studios specializing in a different project type). Do I regret not sacrificing my schedule or whatever contract I had at the time to get into Framestore all those years back? Not at all. What I was doing at the time proved to be more beneficial for me in the long run, as proven by the results I am seeing today, with regard to that particular thing I was doing at the time.

## Smaller/boutique VFX studios

Moving on to the smaller and/or boutique VFX studios, firstly, I'd like to clarify what a boutique VFX studio is. A boutique VFX studio is a small (though this may not necessarily be the case) company that focuses specifically on a very niche area of VFX. They could either focus on this niche by serving a very specific set of clients (for example, features, television shows, commercial projects, et cetera), performing and providing a very specific set of results for the VFX industry as a whole (such as previsualization or stereoscopic conversion), or a combination of both. Technically, some of these boutique VFX studios also qualify as mainstream VFX studios due to the power of their brand names – many of whom I have worked with and for during my career as a VFX professional. These studios are generally easier to get into, but they also do have very specific processes and systems that you should follow; sometimes, they don't necessarily translate into other competing VFX studios as well, if at all. For example, a few of these boutique VFX studios may use After Effects – some even use Fusion or Shake, even though those are rare nowadays.

Of course, I am not forgetting the studios that also fall under this category that are both small and boutique in nature; and when I say small, I mean they could be running on a skeleton crew of only three to seven people – including yourself. Their office space is usually also limited to a few cubicles and, most likely, they are only renting those rooms rather than having the entire building dedicated to their facility. I have even seen big corporations, such as Intel, rent rooms at production facilities when I was part of their small team of VFX artists consisting of only three people (myself included) at the time, for this one special production. While it may not appear to be glamorous, most small and boutique studios do this out of convenience, to be closer to their source of production (or funding), or because it's cost-effective. Yes, there were a few rare instances where a small studio did that because they were downsizing but those are uncommon.

Alright, reader, maybe you are reading this as an owner of a mid-sized VFX company – hang tight, I am going to get to your studio as well, just so that we have all our bases covered. So, we have the boutique (but not necessarily small) VFX studios and the small-and-boutique VFX studios, now let's touch base on the mid-sized companies. Interestingly, what I have encountered and experienced with mid-sized VFX studios is that the vast majority of them actually do have star power; meaning, they are quite well-known. These studios might not necessarily have the brand recognition of ILM or Framestore, but they most certainly have had their fair share of amazing projects come their way – the majority of them from television and commercials. Perhaps what makes these mid-sized studios even more unique is their ability to work on a huge number of projects at once while maintaining their mid-sized company status. This is usually accomplished through a string of seasonal freelancers but even then, the amount of work churned out by these studios is just as high in quality as those delivered by ILM or Pixomondo (with these mid-sized studios probably delivering at an even faster rate).

A few notable studios that I would consider mid-sized (and boutique in nature) would be studios that focus on previsualization and post-visualization (also known as previs/postvis) – two of which I have worked for multiple times in the past. Again, their focus is strictly on delivering half-completed shots at a rapid-fire rate in order for the director of the film (yes, the *actual* director of the film) to review and approve, before passing these "half-completed shots" to the actual VFX studios that will spend days and weeks finishing and polishing those few shots. In this example, the core purpose of the mid-sized previs/postvis studio is simply to sketch out and translate the director's vision onto the computer screen, in preliminary form. While these shots will never be seen by the audiences in cinemas (because that is not the purpose of previs/postvis), they are important in the sense that they lay out the foundation as to how the VFX in these shots are to appear and be designed, with direct approval from the director. Ultimately, these types of boutique VFX studios form an integral part of the VFX industry as a whole. After all, you don't just go from a blank canvas to a finished masterpiece without a few preliminary sketch lines laid out on the canvas first.

## VFX studios owned & operated by a few individuals no one has ever heard of

With the small exception of a few individuals who were able to pull this off based on their cults of personality, the majority of the VFX businesses or studios that fall under this category are usually not faring too well – from a logical business sense. Either set up as sole proprietorships or partnerships (sometimes as corporations or LLCs), these VFX studios that are owned and operated by one or two people you've probably never heard of are most likely just independent freelancers who thought it would be a good idea to register a business or have attempted to start their own VFX studios (and failed on that front). Not to be a downer on these folks, I have seen some of them try, but honestly, most of these people simply do not understand how business works, as well as the other important aspects that come with "starting your own company." There are a lot of factors that go into it and your own name alone isn't going to be sufficient – unless, as mentioned, you have a strong cult of personality (or cult following) to back you up.

As of the writing of this book, I cannot tell you how many times I have accidentally stumbled across one of these nameless entities. Their only team members are themselves and maybe one or two other people and when you reach out via their contact page, they never get back to you. That's because they probably aren't hiring (and never were hiring) and they have probably moved on from that "company" by now. Again, there are many of these entities out there that make up the further segmentation of the VFX market. For now, most of them simply exist just to exist, or are technically independent freelancers who have created a company thinking that it was necessary for tax purposes (for your information, it isn't).

Other than the above, there really isn't much else to say about these studios other than that they exist, and you may occasionally stumble across them. Take my word for it though: they are not and most likely are never hiring. These companies exist mainly to serve the owner's own needs or for perceived tax benefits.

## Freelancers, *returnlancers*, and employees

With the understanding of the different types of companies you will encounter on your journey to becoming a professional, industry-approved VFX artist, it is important to now understand the various employment positions you may ultimately find yourself in, in the VFX world – though I would imagine that any other artistic or creative industry would also function similarly. Of course, interns are a given in almost any industry, so I am not going to be addressing those – I am presuming you, reader, understand how internships work and how that position generally goes. Not exactly a glamorous type of position but you do learn a lot as an intern if you know how to use your internship wisely irrespective of the industry you are in.

Let's jump straight into freelancers and freelancing in VFX. Here's the thing: VFX and Hollywood are gig-based micro-economies. You would be going against the grain in trying hard to stay put as an employee at any one studio unless your position serves a very specific kind of business-related function. Then again, I have encountered employees throughout my time as a VFX freelancer so I will address those groups of people later. For now, let's just say that you will most likely find yourself freelancing at some point as a VFX artist, simply because there isn't enough work to go around to keep extra manpower at these studios sometimes. As an aspiring or current VFX artist, you will have to get used to jumping from studio to studio and, sometimes, the occasional employment gap, if you are keen (or unlucky). Personally, I know a few VFX colleagues who were mainstay employees but later converted into freelancers and have been enjoying the experience ever since.

Remember the time when job-hopping on a résumé was deemed to be undesirable in an employer's eyes? Well, one of the benefits of working in the VFX world as a freelancer is that studios generally expect to see a lot of job switches on your résumé. This is absolutely normal in the world of VFX and Hollywood. Likewise, it is also absolutely normal to see an applicant with only one to three VFX studios in their ten-year career – it just depends on what each studio is looking for and how strong the applicant's VFX portfolio is, in the end. In other words, studios don't care if you have worked with over twenty studios in two years or two in ten years, they only care that you can perform (and have a strong portfolio). One of the notable benefits of freelancing as a VFX artist, thus, is the opportunity to test the waters working at and for multiple different studios. Not only will you get to see how they conduct their studios, get a feel for what their systems and processes are like, and gain the experience of working on various types of projects; you will also get to see how you fit in with their culture and how you feel about working with their current in-house teams. Don't like the nasty attitudes of some of the co-workers? You will never have to see them again if you don't want to. Like how the company offers a lot of other incentives aside from just cool projects? You can choose to continue working with them for a longer term if they are also in agreement. You get the idea.

This brings me to the next type of position you may experience – something I would like to call *returnlancers*. Last I checked, this word does not exist yet so I am staking my claim here and coining this word as my own (please credit me should you ever use it, ha). A *returnlancer*, according to my definition, is someone who is technically a freelancer that has finished a contract at their previous studio and has gone off to another studio or two, before returning to the former studio for a second, third, or subsequent contracted work. You are not a full-time employee, and neither are you a permalancer (a freelancer who is treated as a full-time employee, minus the employee benefits – in other words, an employer taking advantage of your freelance status to not provide you with said benefits); you are simply a freelancer that returns to the same studio, after performing work elsewhere, at different points of the year. It can be described as being similar to the concept of serial killers, where they kill once, experience an interval of a few weeks or even months, then kill again. A morbid example, I know, reader, but it does illustrate the point ... I suppose.

*Returnlancers* (or serial freelancers, though it doesn't quite capture the essence and nature of the work) are essentially a step-up from freelancers since they now have an established rapport with the studio they have worked at, and they are seen as a viable option to keep for returning projects and contracts. I have had this type of relationship with some of my studios and I will say that if you get the right studios (the ones that allow you to work on great projects and meet your needs as a VFX artist), you are basically in VFX heaven. Not only did taking the time off and away from my favorite studios allow me to cultivate my skills even further before returning, the projects as a *returnlancer* also got better with each return. Studios, moreover, continue to gradually build their trust in you as you return and work with them on different projects.

I will discuss the concept of *returnlancers* and how they impact studio dynamics later; for now, let's take this conversation a step further.

Employees. I don't know about you, but back when I started as a wide-eyed and happy artist (alright, maybe not necessarily happy, I have always been rather stoic), my idea of a great VFX life was to get a mainstay, *permanent* job at my favorite studio and then stay there forever until I die. Reader, don't laugh, for I am almost certain you had a similar ideal back when you just started – perhaps you were eyeing Disney, Pixar, or DreamWorks instead. If that were the case, I would invite you to review the second paragraph of this sub-chapter on how VFX and Hollywood are a freelancer's world. There is no getting around that fact. Of course, hope is not lost if your dream is to become an employee at your favorite VFX studio someday; just understand that that is most likely not going to happen in the way that you are expecting.

Long-term employees do exist in VFX and whilst you may be eyeing the insurance and week-off benefits, every position has its pros and cons. Being an employee does absolutely provide you with *better* stability (though stability in VFX is entirely relative) in your career compared to freelancing or interning but bear in mind that your upward mobility and growth as an artist generally get stunted or limited to that one studio alone. There are certain positions such as VFX supervisors, coordinators, and producers that are transferable to other similar or better positions at other studios, but even as you ascend the so-called corporate ladder in Studio A to become a 3D supervisor, for example, that may not necessarily translate over into a similar position at Studio B (who may already have their own 3D supervisors in-house). You may, rather, get a position as a 3D lead or senior 3D artist at Studio B instead (a downgrade from your initial supervisory position at Studio A, if you see it that way). Again, there will always be exceptions to this phenomenon, but it is better to cautiously assume your position to be the norm rather than expect yourself to be that special, exceptional snowflake right off the bat. We will dive deeper into the employee versus freelancer (or *returnlancer*) in VFX later, but for now, the stated insights into these positions should be sufficient at this point in the book.

## Understanding your contract and privileges

Whether you are currently an intern, entry-level artist, mid, or senior, understanding your contract as a VFX artist (or as any kind of artist, really) is key to knowing what you can and cannot do while employed by the studio. Your contract, of course, would also include the relevant privileges that come with your position. Bypassing the obvious technical differences between contracts based on your VFX role – in other words, whether you are a texture artist, compositor, technical director, or production assistant – we will mainly discuss the generalities of the types of contracts you will encounter and what to expect out of each. To be deadly serious (if only you could see my screen right now), I have all my contracts opened up and placed right next to me whilst typing this section. Having worked with so many filmmakers and studios throughout my career as a VFX professional, here are some of the contracts or types of paperwork I have encountered and signed (in no particular order):

- Independent Contractor Agreement
- Non-Disclosure Agreement(s)
- Independent Contractor Confidential Information & Inventions Agreement
- Proprietary Information Agreement
- Standards of Conduct & Employee Performance
- Freelance Data Sheet – yes, it's what it was called by this studio
- Project Employment Agreement
- Screen Credit Form
- Deal Memo(s)
- Employment Agreement
- Terms & Conditions of Employment
- Request for Taxpayer Identification Number & Certification
- Disclosure Regarding Background Investigation
- Emails containing details of employment but with no paperwork signed digitally – yes, they exist
- Other tax-related forms and tax information pertaining to the country you are working in
- Other background information checks, drug-testing checks, et cetera – yes, some studios may *actually* want to test you for drugs (not sure why, but I digress)

Of course, there may be others but the above generally are the types of contracts you will encounter in this field. Some documents I received were as short as one page (or two sentences in an email), others were as long as seventeen pages – it varies.

What you will notice in the above list is that there will be contracts that are fairly similar to one another whilst others may stand out from your usual obligatory paperwork. Either way, we will dissect what each type of contract generally entails. If this part is way too boring for you, feel free to skip ahead.

### 1. Employment Contracts

These contracts include independent contractor agreements, project employment contracts, and your usual employment agreements. The key here is that they define the terms of your employment in great detail. Information includes your role in VFX, your expected VFX responsibilities, location of work, payment terms and schedule, termination clauses, contract extensions (typically known as 'dates on hold' in order to allow studios to book you for a longer term in the event that they still need your help on a project), and other typical legalese (like attorney fees, arbitration, and whatnot). Some employment contracts include a confidentiality clause, but it really depends on how the contract was drafted by the studio's legal counsel. In general, this document alone tells you where you need to be for work, how much and when you are getting paid for your VFX work, what project you are assigned to (sometimes studios use code names for confidentiality purposes), and the length of your at-will contract. If you are getting an employment agreement (as a position of an employee), then your contract will also include a few clauses on employee benefits. Sometimes these are listed in an addendum or on a separate sheet provided by the studio altogether, but in general, you will know what you are entitled to as an employee at that studio.

## 2.   Confidentiality and Non-Disclosures

You will most likely sign this document even before you step inside a studio for an interview. I know I did, and I had signed a bunch of non-disclosure agreements (NDA) even for something as simple as taking an insider-led tour at one of the bigger studios. More commonly known as NDAs than confidentiality agreements, these documents generally restrict the kind of information you can share with the public – mostly pertaining to the project you are working on, namely, the shots that only you and a few others get to see. Spoiler alert: as a VFX artist, you will be one of the few people in the world who gets to know who dies at the end (in a movie or television show). With such important information about the plot at your fingertips, NDAs are strictly enforced, and you *will not* get away with any kind of information leak whatsoever. In fact, I was told a story of how this one particular foreign artist (I believe he was from India) was working on the movie *"Garfield"* at the time. It was his first project, and he was pretty excited; so excited that he actually took a screenshot of his computer screen and shared it with his family back home in India. Of course, supportive Asian parents being supportive Asian parents, I was told that one of them (the mother) actually went on to share that screenshot with her friends and, as you know how gossip goes, the rest is history (and so was that VFX artist). Since he broke his NDA, his work visa was revoked, and I believe he was forced to return (or was deported back) to his home country by the studio. It was a shame since that was one of the well-known studios that had hired him and sponsored his visa. So, word to the wise, don't send a screenshot of *"Garfield"* (or your top-secret studio project) to your mother.

### 3. Film Industry-Specific Documents

Then we have the industry-specific documents. In this case, as a VFX artist, you may encounter deal memos, screen credit forms, and the occasional call sheet (if you are an on-set VFX supervisor or production assistant). These documents are usually one-pagers with the screen credit form requiring you to input the name you would like to be reflected in the credits of the project you are assigned to (if you meet the other credit requirements) and the deal memos essentially being simplified versions of employment contracts. For example, I have signed deal memos for project-based hires at startups and also signed deal memos as a VFX supervisor on-set. They differ in the technical terms and wording used but provide you with the same information as any typical employment contract would, minus the detailed legalese. In general, expect to see your planned start date (anticipated or otherwise), end date, employment status (whether you are a freelancer, employee, or other), supervisor name, hours per week, compensation, overtime, any benefits, and privileges from this typically-one-page deal memo. Again, there is a myriad of other industry-specific documents out there that you will encounter based on your exact position in the VFX industry. I presume you don't need me to go into all of that right now. After all, that is what Google is for – if you *really* need some handholding.

### 4. Standard Employment Processes

In case you had forgotten, a VFX job is still a job and that studio that employs you is still a corporation. Thus, standard employment processes still need to occur, even if anyone believes that the creative industries are above all that "corporate stuff" – hint: they are not. So, it is highly likely (in fact, probably one-hundred-percent guaranteed) that you will be required to go through their typical employment checks and standard proceedings, which includes filling out any requests for tax identification or information, background, and criminal checks (the latter is not common but does happen) and conceding to any mandatory reference phone calls and checks that the studio's human resource personnel might require. If you have been a good person (or at least, what society defines as a "good" person) in general, you needn't fret endlessly about this portion of the onboarding process. It is just standard procedure that *any* corporation in the world has the right or obligation to perform. And yes, they will conduct "informal" checks on you and your online presence as well, which I will discuss at greater length in a later chapter of this book.

### 5. Email-Based Agreements

Finally, we have the all-too-ambiguous email-based agreements. Think of these as your typical handshake deals that you would make after a hearty brunch at a local café or your scribbled agreements on table napkins at Mel's Drive-in (except in email form). Personally, I've worked with both new and old studio clients through this format, not of my own volition, but because it seemed that the person whom I was speaking to via email at the time preferred to confirm the agreement only via email. Perhaps the producer is busy, they are a new studio in the market, or they simply don't have the time to bother to draft up a contract, an email agreement is as solid as all parties involved make it out to be. I take my agreements *very* seriously (and so do these studios) regardless of their form, so expect that should you experience and *agree* to an email contract (where the only information provided in the email is merely a confirmation of your payment amount, location of the studio and start date/time), it is happening, and it is real. Hence, be sure to make good on your word and actually show up. At times, I would receive paper contracts to sign on my first day of showing up, but if that does not happen, know that someone at the studio (depending on how organized or disorganized the studio management is) will eventually request for your tax information – which is how you will know that they are serious and not stringing you along without paying you. Whilst an email-based agreement is not ideal, I have yet to encounter an issue stemming from this type of arrangement; you may chalk that up to luck or my ability to discern the good eggs from the bad. Either way, what is neat about email-based agreements is that you can clarify your employment privileges, benefits, et cetera (if you choose to do so) in email directly with the producer or supervisor (who is usually the person you will be communicating with in this type of arrangement) and you will get a response in writing directly from the producer/supervisor of that studio.

## Pricing and rates

Moving on from the dull topic of contracts, it's time for the juicy bits of your job – your pay and rates as a VFX artist. Firstly, I'd like to premise this by saying again that I hope you are getting into VFX for the *right* reasons. Although it is tempting to use one of those "there is no right or wrong" quotes, in the case of working in an industry as intensive as VFX, there actually *is* a right or wrong – namely, a right or wrong reason to be in VFX and to create as a VFX artist. Of course, I am not here to judge you, dear reader, for I know nothing about you, who you are, or what led you to be reading this book in the first place. I do know for a fact, however, that you will *not* get (insanely) rich as a VFX artist – *ever*. At least, not in the traditional way and not if you only do VFX in specific positions for the rest of your life. Do I know rich old men who did VFX and are still doing it today who are people I would classify as "rich" people? Sure. Though for every one of those rich VFX veteran artists, I also know an equally-old VFX veteran artist who lives out of his dilapidated van and looks like he actually doesn't even have a proper roof over his head – not even a rental unit. I would say, as a mid artist myself, I have fared quite well, but that's because I knew and would consider myself quite well-versed in the internal and external factors that impact rates, which I will touch on much later in the book.

For now, let's bring our focus squarely back on pricing and setting your rates as a VFX artist (irrespective of the technical specialty). Chiefly, I'd like to state that you should *not* rely on Glassdoor for all your answers. Heck, I was interviewed by a magazine once and they tried to force a number onto my salary. I told them that you cannot simply steal a number from Glassdoor and say that that's what I make because it's simply too relative. Besides, depending on whether you are an animator, compositor, or pipeline technical director, your pay rates *will* differ from your peers in other positions (or even in the exact same position). On that note, I am not going to pretend to know the rates for all positions, nor will I list them here as if they are set in stone, for they are not and never will be. However, what would then be set in stone, as far as rates go, is how much studios are willing to offer (or have offered) to someone in your position as well as how much *perceived and utilized value* you will be bringing to the studio table. Let me explain. You see, studios are just like your typical corporations. In fact, they *are* corporations. When it comes to choosing employees or contractors, know that, just like any other corporation out there, they will want someone useful, that can do the job and ideally can do the work at a fast pace for the lowest possible price (typical, I know). Depending on the studio's level of experience in the industry, you may have some who have already set out a budget for people in specific positions; this is normal. However, if you can clearly show (usually in your portfolio) that you offer and provide other skills *relevant* to the job that they could *use* you for, then you may have a chance at negotiating for a better rate. Again, there is always going to be a risk in doing so but if you can prove your point, it will not cost you the job compared to someone trying to negotiate for a schedule change – I've tried the latter, it doesn't work.

The key here is that you have to have skills that the studio *actually cares about*. Basically, if you are applying as an animator, saying that you know how to do film-editing with Premiere is as useless of a mention as telling your math teacher that you are a star basketball player on the school team. Likewise, if I am being hired strictly to work in the capacity of a studio's 2D department as a compositor, mentioning myself being a whiz at Houdini particle effects is redundant and unnecessary. Now, do those additional skills help make you a more well-rounded VFX artist? Heck, yes. But do the studios *actually* care about that when hiring you as a compositor, for example? Nope. Again, if we are referring strictly to being hired by the living and breathing VFX studios in Hollywood, your additional skills that don't apply to the job don't matter – unless they say that they do in the job listing. Hence, in order to increase your *perceived and utilized value* in order to aim for a higher pay rate, you would actually have to show that your skills *directly* apply to the position you are interviewing for. There is a fine line between showing you've got the *bonus* chops that make you a useful artist in that position versus showing that you've got all the best chops in the world for the sake of showing that you've got all the best chops in the world. Studios just don't care about the latter if they cannot *use* you in the way that they want.

I went from an entry-level rate of about $15 USD to as high as a beginning senior artist rate whilst still being only about two or so years into my VFX career in Hollywood (and technically, having only graduated from SCAD about one year and some months ago before hitting that rate). Let me tell you that that wasn't by accident. Of course, reader, please do not use me as a benchmark in terms of setting a timeline for yourself, and neither should you take everything I say in this section as gospel. The industry changes all the time – even if you do not experience or feel the change occurring – and that also applies to pricing and artist rates. At times, getting to a higher pay rate does not necessarily increase your quality of life (or shots) as a VFX artist. It is entirely relative to the studio and your work history, among several other external, unseen factors (such as the studio's budget and other available applicants) that are usually out of your reach. The best way to set a rate for yourself as a VFX artist is to know what other studios have once offered you, know your worth (also known as your résumé and portfolio), and know the studio with which you are dealing with. If you are a newcomer to VFX, then you may have to take what your first studio offers, just to have that pay rate history established for yourself as a reference to compare your future self to. And once and for all, don't just rely on Glassdoor for your rates. To be honest, I never even *looked* at Glassdoor (let alone loaded up that site) when I got my jobs at those studios or with those filmmakers. I am not even embarrassed to say that for the majority of my career, I didn't even know that Glassdoor existed. Heh, I guess in that case, ignorance was bliss (to my rates).

## Studio hierarchy and the order of things

With an understanding of what you will do, how you will do them, and how much you will be paid for it, it is important to understand the hierarchy at your studio. Now, I am not saying that things get political – politics are the byproduct whenever groups of different personalities congregate for a purpose or cause – but you do have to be aware of the studio hierarchy in terms of who is in charge (and more importantly, who you should or should not be speaking to). Thus, as a VFX artist, regardless of your technical specialty, you will definitely be coming into a studio hierarchy that has already been established since the studio's existence. If you happened to be working at a VFX startup studio, however, things may be a bit different, though in general, you should expect there to be a hierarchy of sorts (even if they tell you they don't have one).

Naturally, the founder of the company will be at the top of the food chain. This position also includes executive producers and studio general managers. We are deliberately bypassing the unseen top power players here – namely, the investors and company shareholders – since those are people you would *rarely*, if ever, encounter on studio grounds (as someone in your position). Anyway, back to founders and executives, as a VFX artist, you won't be communicating much (if at all) with these busy executives, though you will occasionally see them in general company meetings that you may be invited to attend (just to get the lay of the land). Next down the line, you'll have your VFX producers and supervisors. These individuals are the ones who are in the position to execute technically and lead teams. Whereas executive producers, general managers, and founders may only need to lead (without technical execution), the VFX producers and supervisors have to deliver tangible VFX results *and* lead. Regardless of which VFX studio I was working at in Hollywood, I have observed that almost every – if not all – VFX supervisors in-house were also working on VFX shots just like you; perhaps their shots are much more complex, fancy, or reel-worthy than yours, but at least you know that they aren't just big shots with their feet on their desks, doing nothing but barking orders all day. You'd be hard-pressed to find a VFX supervisor or producer whose sole purpose is to only lead without being an example. There are, of course, different types of VFX supervisors, but we're not here to delve into those details right now.

Going down the food chain, you have your team leads – otherwise also known as leads, for each respective department; depending on how the studio organizes their hierarchy, your leads may also be known as seniors. As a VFX artist, these are the individuals you will be reporting to most of the time. Basically, your team leads are only a few steps away from potentially being supervisors of their department or are employees who have been there for a long enough time (years, maybe) who have earned their positions as leads based on how familiar they are with the studio's workflow and systems. If you are comfortable staying put at one studio for decades, then you would most likely ascend to senior-level status (within the company), though you will still have to compete against others who have also sacrificed years at that one studio for the sole position of lead. Whether it is worth it or not, you will have to weigh it out on your own.

Ultimately, all this is relative to your current position as a VFX artist at that one particular studio. In general, you will not have a lot of corporate power nor say as a common VFX fellow; and if you are totally fine with having zero corporate authority and are happy just to have the autonomy to execute shots and solve creative problems, good for you. All in all, this hierarchy has been in play for many decades (perhaps even a century) in both the VFX and Hollywood spheres, so resistance is futile – and frankly, a waste of your energy. As a VFX artist, you are expected to accept and respect the chain of command at your studio, as the established hierarchy is what keeps film productions and the working pipelines going and flowing effortlessly. If you have a bit of a rebellious streak in you, allow me to enlighten you on why this studio hierarchy is in fact necessary for productive VFX and film production.

You see, we humans like order and having structure (if you don't like that word, then replace 'structure' with 'a sense of direction'). Regardless of how "free and spontaneous" one claims to be, in general, people are people and people like having some kind of sense and structure in their lives. This is where the structure of a film or VFX studio's hierarchy comes in. Let's imagine this scenario for a moment: you have the writer-producer who generally hires or finds the director (more commonly, you will find people coming in as a producer-director or some similar kind of combo). This director is then solely responsible for the creative vision and outlook of the project. An entire ensemble of cast and crew in all departments and related niches are then gathered together solely to realize this one person's creative vision and film production. The film is then distributed to millions, who will then be exposed to one unanimous visual splendor and creative direction of the film. Now imagine a different scenario: you have the director-producer who believes in giving an equal say to all members of the cast and crew when it comes to the creative direction of the film. In essence, everyone and their mother on this lateral hierarchical creative structure have equal say in the film's creative results. Knowing how each individual has different preferences and tastes, conflicts (and conflicts of interests) will arise throughout the entire process from pre-production to post (if this type of team is even lucky to have made it to post-production). The film is then (finally) distributed to millions, who are then exposed to a hodgepodge of random creative directions and a chaotic mess of a film. You get the picture.

Now, this isn't to say that heeding input from your creative team as a director or writer is box office suicide. It's just that you need to be aware of your position in a project and how much of a say you are technically allowed to have, with regard to the bigger picture of staying loyal to the director's macro-vision.

Realistically, the more lateral the hierarchy, the more time required to get things done. Hollywood – and to a certain extent, VFX – is not exactly a patient industry to be involved in. Hence, having that traditional, vertical hierarchy actually facilitates production efficiency to its fullest. As a VFX artist, you have got to respect that hierarchy at the studio you are with. Don't overstep your bounds or else – and most unfortunately – you will most likely be told to "just do your job."

## Other things you bring to the table

Remember when I discussed the other skills you may possess that may or may not be utilized at the VFX studio you're currently at? Well, it is time to unload on those other things you could bring to the table as a VFX artist at any stage – whether it be technical and creative skills or certain aspects of your personality and beliefs. As someone who has been around the VFX block for many years, I can attest to the fact that one of the biggest positives of being in the VFX niche of Hollywood is that the people in VFX generally do not care about your religious or political beliefs (thankfully). As long as it doesn't interfere with your job or the task at hand, the VFX industry generally does not give two hoots about where you lie on the political spectrum, who you pray to (if anyone), and what your views are on law and order. Unless you choose to disclose them through casual conversation with your colleagues, no one really cares. It's an industry that I would describe as being the most professional in that regard if you ignore the occasional crass and crude innuendo and jokes along those lines. As with anything else in life, so long as you aren't unnecessarily extreme (in the negative sense), the VFX world will accept you.

As mentioned earlier in the book, what the industry will prize you for is your vitality, technical skills required for the role, speed, and your overtime (ha, yes). Hence, expect those to be the default when showing up for any role in VFX. Studios don't generally care what you look like, but they do expect you to bring your professionalism and punctuality if we are to go into expected character traits for a VFX role. As for the other skills you may have and how much those will be utilized, again, it depends on the size of the company as well as the company culture in general. From my experience, I have yet to witness an artist at any company I have been with getting paid to successfully utilize *all* their VFX skills – unless it was already part of the job requirement. The consensus in VFX is that your skills outside of what your current role requires are generally irrelevant – especially if you are coming in at entry-level – so whether or not you have any additional VFX skills to bring to the table is not as important as what that VFX studio is presently looking for.

All in all, as a VFX artist, you don't need to be the perfect pinnacle of a VFX generalist if the specialized role you are applying to does not even care about those extra chops. My recommendation on the extra things you could bring to the table is your professional neutral stance on most broader issues (or just don't share the extremities of your beliefs, if you have any), your punctuality, and of course, your ability to execute and do the job right. Everything else – from whether you know CPR to the countless models you 3D-printed last weekend – is irrelevant and secondary (maybe even tertiary). The VFX world just doesn't care about those things.

# 6

# HOW HOLLYWOOD WORKS

Carrying on from our previous chapter, let's broaden our perspective and zero in on the world of Hollywood itself. Now, I do not presume to know every single detail or involved mechanism that makes Hollywood but, given the myriad of exposures beyond my desk job as a VFX artist, and having been a producer, assistant director, and VFX supervisor myself, I would say that the following information will be insightful enough for any and all young minds looking to grasp what working in Hollywood is *really* like. As evidently described, the VFX world is merely a subset of Hollywood – it keeps Hollywood running but it is not necessarily the most crucial niche of the entertainment industry as a whole. Think of it this way: you can have access to all the best gadgets, hardware, technology, and even post-production talent, but without the story, the script, or the proper organization of its production, all that will not matter. Think of VFX as the components in your Ferrari, whereas the script or narrative makes up the entire Ferrari itself – whether or not it sells depends on how appealing that Ferrari is to particular groups of people. Some people just prefer Teslas, others might prefer to get their hands dirty with a Harley, whatever floats their boat. VFX will always be the unseen components in your favorite vehicle – important, but not what truly entices the viewers to watch a movie. Car analogies aside (which is funny considering I don't care about cars), I will lay out how Hollywood works with respect to you being that VFX artist (and that unseen cog in the machine).

## Getting credit as an artist

Ah, credits. Everyone loves credit. After all, if we weren't getting paid for it, the majority of aspiring VFX artists would do it for the credit. While Hollywood is absolutely notorious for enforcing this and ensuring that the right people get credited – to the extent that you may even be credited under a pseudonym or nickname – the qualification for an on-screen credit is actually something else that we have to unpack. From what I have experienced directly, you are most likely guaranteed an on-screen credit if you work on set and have submitted the relevant paperwork to the production company or producers-in-charge. Meaning, if you are a production assistant (PA) or a set decorator, you will most likely get an on-screen credit if your name has been submitted by the supervisor or lead representing you or is handled by the producer you are directly working under in smaller productions.

The tricky part comes with most post-production departments as you now have an additional layer to filter through in order to get your paperwork (or your on-screen credit name form, for example) submitted to the producers of the film or show. This extra layer is the VFX, sound, or post-production facility that hired you. You see, getting an on-screen credit is actually not that difficult – it is all about submitting the right paperwork and having it be implemented in post-production before the final film is printed for distribution. The showstoppers come in the form of the additional requirements that the middleman (in the case of VFX, your VFX studio) may impose in order to have you *earn* that on-screen credit. Again, this is absolutely normal. Take me as an example. I had one person reach out to me with a comment saying that they were not able to find my name in the credits for *"Alice Through the Looking Glass,"* a film I had worked on as a postvis artist. Well, my simplest and most direct response to that comment is that I simply was not working at the studio for a long enough period of time to have qualified – based on their studio protocol – for that on-screen credit. I was not bothered by it as it was part of the nature of VFX freelancing: you either jump around to work on a myriad of projects or stay put at one studio until you rot and die. The latter is an exaggeration, but you get the idea. Basically, some post-production houses (VFX, sound, or editing-related studios) may impose a requirement that you have to work on a particular project for a set number of months before you get the benefit of that screen credit you've craved so much since you were a little kid. Why is it this way for post-production-related niches? That's the wrong question to ask. Frankly, the answer doesn't change anything and if you really want that on-screen credit for minimal time commitment, consider getting work in one of the on-set or production-related niches instead.

Scaling back to the bigger picture of Hollywood, it is most likely that unless you are working on a small or independent production, production-related roles would soon follow suit in terms of adopting a minimum threshold to qualify for an on-screen credit. In essence, if you are a freelance PA on set who is only there for a day, then I'm sorry to say, but it is possible that you may eventually not qualify for that on-screen credit unless you have been on that project for a set number of months (or even for the entirety of that production's timeline). On the other hand, since most production jobs tend to be short and contracted – and most people in production generally have a harder time finding consistent work – I don't think this would be an issue for the on-set production folks, should this minimum threshold requirement be imposed for that coveted on-screen credit.

Of course, there will also be a few occasions where, regardless of how long you have been involved with the project, only the studio or production company's name and their executive producers and supervisors get screen recognition. I have seen this with a lot of VFX, post-production enhancement, and post-production sound studios working on television projects – though it does occur in traditional film and movies as well. It really depends on the studio, the terms of your contract, and, to a certain extent, your employment status with that production or company. Again, whether you are in VFX or are a non-VFX person looking to understand VFX, most of the "restrictions" and "limits" when it comes to getting an on-screen credit fall into the category of post-production services and less so on pre-production or production-related roles. On the bright side, whilst you may be limited in getting an on-screen credit as a short-term freelancer, the Internet Movie Database (most commonly known as IMDb) – the number one source the vast majority of filmmakers and professionals in Hollywood reference in terms of ongoing projects and the résumés of their peers – is definitely a good place to update all those credits you have rightfully earned, regardless of how long you have been on a project. After going through their verification process, IMDb will soon approve your additions to your public IMDb profile, of which you will find that having a lengthy, prestigious filmography may be just as great as getting an on-screen credit on one production after a year.

In the end, there are many ways to get credited on a production just as there are pros and cons to working towards getting an on-screen credit on a film. The obvious pro to getting an on-screen credit being, well, you officially getting your name recognized on-screen, the con mainly being that you most likely are only able to work on very few projects in your career compared to the serious freelancer. The choice is yours – either way, you still get credited in other ways such as on IMDb, which is just as honorable a credit as an on-screen name, in my opinion.

## Your name among thousands

Whether your name is in the credit roll of a film or not, one thing is for sure: you (and anyone affiliated with you who has an interest) will most likely be the only person sitting in the audience actively looking out for your name in the screen credits. In VFX, this gets more complicated with the thousands of names listed – often side-by-side – usually halfway through the credits; by then, more than two-thirds of your audience has already left. Whilst the list of names is generally shorter for the production portion of the credit roll (in other words, you can only have so many PAs on set), the VFX department tends to take a significant chunk of the credit roll due to the numerous VFX studios involved in any one major feature production. Heck, even a major television series may sometimes have three or more VFX studios involved. As a VFX artist in Hollywood, you are going to end up in that chunky portion of the credit roll (if you qualify) where you will literally be a name in a thousand. I will say it again: the only person who will even be looking for your name will most likely be you and your friends and family who are aware that you worked on that film; outside of those few people, no one in the audience generally cares – nor do most of them even stay behind for the entire credit roll outside of the main cast (and some portion of the crew).

Again, depending on your studio and your exact position in VFX, your name may be shuffled around, with VFX producers and supervisors usually taking the top of the list in VFX right after the name of the studio, followed by team leads, et cetera (see the earlier section on studio hierarchy if you need a refresher). In general, expect that should you qualify for a screen credit, your name will not be immediately noticeable among the sea of names in the credits – unless you are specifically looking for it. You will have much better luck in having your name read by being in one of the other niches of Hollywood like production design, the camera department, or even in post-production editing or sound. After all, it is not like you will have a thousand editors for a film compared to VFX artists – the former would be way too expensive and unnecessary.

## No one actually cares about you people

Whilst it definitely calls for some kind of celebration to have your name in the credit roll of any film (if you are one of those people, which is absolutely normal), in the larger context of Hollywood, only a few key roles are actually "cared" about by the people and the movie-going audiences. These individuals are your (in no particular order):

- Lead actors & featured cast members
- Secondary cast members
- Directors
- Writers
- Producers
- Directors of Photography (though to a lesser extent)

Whilst an editor could arguably be on that list as well, I find that not many movie-goers watch a film because they enjoy the work of an editor (even if they are well-known). The same goes with big-name composers like Hans Zimmer and James Horner, for example. Whilst there will always be those avid fans who will recognize their work, most don't actually care about it *that much* to want to invest in watching an entire movie just for its music (there is always Spotify for that). So, while being awarded with an on-screen credit is a feat of accomplishment alone for any production member or qualifying VFX artist at a studio, the sad truth is that no one else outside your industry and your current production's producers (if they are good producers) care about you people the way followers or fans care about their favorite celebrity actors, directors, writers, and producers.

This attitude, unfortunately, also applies to some of the key movers and shakers in Hollywood itself – namely, your investors, executive producers, directors, and writers. Us VFX people – along with post-production sound – are ... let's just say ... low on the totem pole of priorities when it comes to most typical film productions. And yes, whilst not all film productions treat the post-production niches as expendable, with a cumulating number of projects and years of experience in the field, you will soon find that the majority of them – in some way, shape or form – do. These filmmakers do this by under-budgeting VFX or expecting expedited VFX work for little to no creative input and investment from the director. Again, there are many ways the key players of any film production can show their disregard for VFX and post-production sound – what I have mentioned are only a few.

As I have witnessed this trend in attitude change over time, it has noticeably gotten better over the years; however, there are still many who subscribe to the idea that VFX and sound can be addressed in hindsight, without much preparation at all. That being said, the good thing is that those who do prescribe to those beliefs soon learn things the hard way, which then prevents them from repeating the same costly mistake in the future – changing the trend by not perpetuating those beliefs in subsequent productions. Perhaps I was lucky or know how to carefully choose my projects, but of the many projects I have been involved with, VFX has always been planned and prioritized during pre-production. Interestingly, the priority placed on VFX was most prominent amongst student filmmakers and some indie filmmakers. Call it budgetary restrictions or the producer's educated understanding of how things really work (and cost) in post, you'd be surprised if I told you that the biggest culprits of putting post-production VFX in the rearview are actually some of the bigger clients and projects I've had working with major studios for television and film. I won't name names, but I suppose some of these production companies or producers take their larger budgets for granted; hence, they can afford to adopt that nonchalant attitude towards VFX being able to "fix it in post."

Whether you are aspiring to get into VFX or consider yourself to be a filmmaker looking to get a different perspective on your craft, know this: no one actually cares about certain roles involved in the making of a film – and that's okay. It only becomes a problem when the key players and creators don't care since that would inevitably lead to unfavorable working conditions for those crew members, and unnecessary stress and expenses incurred on behalf of the production. While it is true that VFX people are often overlooked, I do expect this to get better over time. It is all about being upfront with the issue and bringing these "forlorn" niches to the direct attention of the filmmakers.

## Specialization vs. generalization in VFX vs. film

On that note, let's segue into the notion of specialization versus generalization in the broader context of the Hollywood film industry. As I may have touched on in an earlier part of this book – and if I did not, I apologize, dear reader, you have no idea how tedious it is to write for an extended period of time – VFX is all for the specialization of skills (for the most part). This is especially true when working at VFX studios where they are seeking very specific roles; again, if they don't need a compositor to know or understand how to use Autodesk Maya and Houdini, they don't need to hire a compositor that knows Autodesk Maya and Houdini. As I have mentioned, it really depends on the studio, their manpower budget, and what they are specifically looking for in an artist position. If you are planning on being an active, independent VFX freelancer, however, I find that VFX generalization tends to work more in your favor; this is mainly the case due to the fact that indie films and filmmakers have less access to funding and will most likely only want one or two people to handle a variety of tasks in order to cut costs in the long run.

Either way, being a generalist or specialist in VFX has its target audience when it comes to serving the VFX community in general. In the filmmaking or production side of Hollywood however, their main preference when it comes to crew talent is in an individual who is a generalist; that jack-of-all-trades character, that guy or gal who is able to light a film set, handle some props, and assist with the camera operation. That person. The ability to generalize becomes even more crucial if one is intending to eventually become a director or producer of a film. After all, if anyone on set should know a little bit about everything that goes on during production and about the production it's those two roles. Hollywood generally has a strong preference for directors and producers who demonstrate that they not only know their craft but that they also have a good understanding of the general work involved in a typical film or television production. This is also true of other ancillary positions on set such as stunt work, special/physical effects, and production design – just to list a few. While a VFX person can get away with not knowing the nitty-gritty of set design or how explosives work on a film set, someone doing stunts would be better served knowing how that car will be flipped, what VFX will be done in post-production to complement their stunt work, and how important it is to ensure the stunt double is wearing the proper suit for continuity purposes. So, unless you are working in a highly technical position such as post-production sound, color-grading, or VFX, generalization is the way to go for most positions on the Hollywood filmmaking side of things.

Of course, this isn't to say that if you happen to be a costume designer who only knows about costume design then you're doomed to fail. Nah. Hollywood is actually quite open to whether you are a specialist or generalist in your field. As long you are highly proficient in what you know, and what you don't know doesn't impede the filmmaking speed and process, the world of filmmaking is generally very accepting of what you bring to the table; just know that being a generalist generally serves you better for preproduction or production work. In the end, a producer will hire based on your portfolio and relevant merits; if they happen to find a costume designer who knows a thing or two about makeup, physical effects, and stunt work versus one who does not, they will go for the generalist, if their rate difference (if any) is not too steep.

## Cheaper, better, faster

Speaking of money and rates, Daft Punk/Kanye West (pick your favorite) got it right with *"harder, better, faster, stronger."* When it comes to Hollywood and their hiring practices, you can bet that ninety percent of the time they're looking for a crew member who is cheaper, but better and faster. And let's be real – isn't this every corporation's ideal recruit? Someone who is cheap (or young) yet excels in their position and does things efficiently and quickly. Perhaps Daft Punk/Kanye West (pick your favorite) was actually right about more than just Hollywood when it comes to that phrase since it appears that almost any industry would want a hire like that (cheap, better than the rest, and fast). This isn't even an exception when it comes to choosing an attorney or doctor – heck, if you could find a "cheap" doctor who also happens to have a solid reputation in his field and performs his tasks at the speed of a god, wouldn't you want them too? Well, it depends. The same goes with Hollywood – it really depends on their budget and what the producers prioritize in what they're looking for in their roles. For the most part though, you can bet that the majority of hires tend to fit that bill of being the best yet the most cost-effective and expedient in their performances. The few occasional exceptions then go to the situations where producers don't have a choice – such as a hire mandated by the studio executives – or where the producers actually have close ties with the individuals or entities in question. Either way, don't fool yourself into thinking that this mantra of "cheaper, better, faster" only applies to the filmmaking side of Hollywood – it applies even more in post-production-related roles such as VFX. This is especially true since the pool of VFX artists is substantially larger (depending on the type of VFX role you are eyeing) and VFX studios *can* afford to replace you with someone else who is cheaper, better, and faster than you. Remember – your name is just one in a thousand; if there could possibly be more than a thousand other screen-credited artists in VFX, what makes you think that it is not easy to simply replace you with someone else? It is not like the VFX industry severely lacks talent domestically or internationally.

Now, regardless of what your role currently is in the world of Hollywood, if you're thinking of how unfair it is to be replaced by someone who is simply a cheaper (in a good way) version of you, don't be. This ambitious mindset perpetuated by Hollywood in its search for the ultimate recruit ("cheaper, better, faster") continues to persist and exist because there *are* in fact individuals who are like that. They are cheap (relatively speaking), they are good, and they are fast. Since these individuals do walk the Earth, this mindset naturally trickles down into all other sub-industries of Hollywood, including VFX. Besides, Hollywood is what keeps VFX and all the other niche industries employed – and you don't really want to bite the hand that feeds you. In the end, as a fellow VFX artist, if you can understand where the pressure to be fast and good is coming from (and how Hollywood producers and directors tend to apply the pressure on VFX studios that are not keeping up the pace), then you will most likely be better prepared to adapt to your studio's harsh demands (or overtime) or understand where their unrelenting sense of urgency comes from. Who knows, perhaps knowing this may even help you decide not to pursue VFX for your own mental sanity. Anything could happen once you become enlightened.

Allow me to illustrate this with an example: you have the big, mysterious studio executives at Fox who recently greenlit a film for funding and production. As the bosses of the bosses, these executives will have set an estimated deadline for when all of this production work will be completed to then be distributed for viewing in the cinemas. The pressure is then on the producers of that production to deliver in order to meet their bosses' demands (yes, producers have bosses too). Hence, this urgency (as well as deadlines) from the top flows all the way to the bottom of the totem pole, for missing that deadline could mean the difference between tapping into a period of the highest profit potential to missing that window of monetary opportunity completely and contending with a strong competing film entering the box office during that period of time. It really is emotional mathematics – very, very strong emotional mathematics – at this point. Of course, given that delays tend to happen on any sort of a massive project like a film production, some buffer time will have been built into the timeline expected by these major studios and their executives. Missing the window of prime and maximized box office grossing, however (even if all this predicted grossing is conjecture during the planning stage), could make or break a film and its return on investment. We are talking big stakes here when dealing with Hollywood major productions and deadlines.

Yes, Hollywood is a creative industry; yes, Hollywood's goal is to produce entertainment; yes, Hollywood allows for all sorts of fun and crazy people to be a part of its progress. Regardless of how you wish to see it though, Hollywood is still a *business*, and just like any business, money has to be made. In fact, if you could remove your rose-tinted glasses for a moment, I would even go as far as to say that Hollywood is one of the more ruthless businesses to be involved in if you bypass the flashy movie gimmicks and colorful characters and personalities projected by your favorite writers, directors, and producers for a moment. They (your writers, directors, and producers) are that way because it's part of their job to be that way, and studios certainly don't tolerate any ill being spoken about their products (films) if it has the potential to ruin the marketability and profitability of a film. I am sure you, reader, have stumbled across news of actors being removed from films or sequels due to their bad or unsupportive behavior towards their own films; so, don't think that just because an actor is on the A-list that he or she is necessarily safe from being sacked – even if they are meant to play the titular character of said film. In Hollywood, any (unplanned) bad publicity that could sink a film's box office potential has to be dealt with swiftly and aggressively, even if it is just for show. Hence, the mantra of "cheaper, faster, better" will always be the touted standard of this mega-industry, alongside the fact that nearly anyone is or becomes replaceable if they no longer serve to benefit the marketability of the film (thus, getting rid of the bad eggs *faster*, to make the film's profitability *better*).

Now, you might be thinking that the great products (or movies) you have seen in cinemas, the likes of *"Joker"* or any other high-caliber films of late, were probably exceptions to the "cheaper, faster, better" rule. That, just because they are such impressive, amazing, and incredible movies somehow excludes them from this dirty mantra of the seedy underbelly of the Hollywood world. Well, don't be too quick to judge and be deceived. Whilst there are certainly nuances working on different productions of different standards, from what I have observed having worked on set and behind the scenes (mainly behind the screens) is that great movies *can* be made cheaper, faster, and better, which is not necessarily a bad thing. Those movies that went down in history but were made cheaper, faster, and better certainly *do* exist, which is perhaps why many filmmakers today continue to live up to that mantra seeing that some very successful filmmakers have applied it and achieved massive results. In other words, you can have your cake and eat it too. It may be hard to believe but Hollywood can simply be *that* adept at maximizing profit whilst minimizing time and financial expenditure (and waste); though, to be clear, it's really only the top few filmmakers who have managed to successfully do that. Perhaps that explains why they continue to remain as the top filmmakers in the industry.

Ultimately, it's the name of the game – something you should be aware of as well if you really want to be part of the world of Hollywood. After all, let's be real: not everything is about "doing it for creativity's sake." If that were the case, you would most likely have severely delayed projects or get paid less than the amount you were getting due to budgetary constraints. It is highly likely that that project would also not see the light of day. Believe me, I've worked on many projects helmed by all types of filmmakers to know this as a fact, albeit a sad one. Most projects done in the name of "creativity" simply don't make it out of the render in one piece (or at all). Sorry (not sorry), Hollywood is still a business. We don't create movies just to create movies *and* lose money. Everyone has to get paid somehow and they'll get the job if they're cheaper, better, and faster for the betterment of maximized profits at the box office – that's what Hollywood is *really* about.

## If it costs, it hurts

Now, with all that being said, this section might seem a little redundant given all that I had divulged earlier when it comes to the way Hollywood thinks and the way Hollywood works, but I am really here to remind you again that Hollywood is simply a business (perhaps in glamorized form) like any other business. Heck, one could even say that Hollywood deals in the business of glamorized, long-form attention. Whilst it is true that cheaper, better, faster is always going to be the way to go when it comes to the plethora of productions organized by Hollywood, there is another saying that if something costs, it hurts – especially if said object to be obtained could either have been obtained for less or for absolutely nothing at all. Of course, as with most things in life, this is only true to a certain extent. For the most part, however, it is largely *true*.

Now, I wouldn't want to bore you with a regurgitation of how Hollywood is much like any other business but yes, it is just that – like any other business. And like any other business, behind the glitter, glam, and packaging, the focus is *always* going to be on the bottom line. Think about that. It is the same with any single thing you purchase – be it a service or, more commonly, a product – behind all the packaging, its functionality, and purpose in your life, it is all about the bottom line for that business (whilst, of course, still providing you with value that you would willingly hand over your cash in exchange for). In the case of Hollywood, whose value is to enlighten, educate, or entertain by sustaining your attention with glamorous images to help take you away from your current reality, if a cost can be avoided then why not? As long as the avoidance of that cost does not impede the production or its quality in any way, good producers usually err on the side of caution when it comes to unnecessary spending of a massive budget.

Most productions, however, are well known for either going over budget – hence, the necessity to cut out certain expensive scenes or shots in post-production – or hitting the budget directly on the nail. It is a rare instance to find a production going under budget. You should be aware though that most studio executives generally prefer budgets that have been assigned to be fully utilized – executives tend to not like it when producers go over or even under budget. The former is easily criticized as the producers lacking foresight or management skills to distribute the assigned budget properly, whereas even the latter could be frowned upon as the producers misquoting budget calculations – leading to excess funding that could have been spent on a different project, to be unfairly occupied by the particular production in question. Of course, if you are an independent producer or filmmaker, I find that being the one who (reasonably) under-spends a budget tends to be looked upon more favorably in the independent spheres.

Ok, so, all that sounds fairly straightforward. Let's get back to why this even matters to someone like you – the aspiring VFX artist or currently-active VFX person: how does the avoidance of unnecessary expenditure amongst filmmakers and producers in Hollywood hurt you and your options? After all, if Hollywood is in the business of only spending what it has to in order to maximize its output, does that mean that fewer VFX studios and houses would be employed for specific productions (and hence, trickling down to the number of artists involved in a production itself)? Well, that depends as every situation as well as every production is quite unique. Frankly, I have never found this to be a problem at any of the studios I have worked at or with that has been funded by a Hollywood feature production. Typically, what usually happens is that a budget for the VFX department has already been carved out by the producers, who will then carefully peruse the different VFX production houses, selecting the ones that both meet their needs and their financial constraints. If it costs (unnecessarily) or if negotiations on pricing fall flat between a producer and a VFX house – for example, if a VFX studio ended up being too greedy or pricing itself way up there on the totem pole – then, of course, it is unlikely that that VFX studio will win that project as it would hurt or hamper the producer's production budget unnecessarily. The good producers will and should only spend where they know will get them the best returns and, honestly, most of that cost will be going to enrolling A-list cast and top-of-the-line creatives.

As a VFX artist in Hollywood, you're mainly hired by the VFX studio itself who would, of course, have an assigned budget from production whilst simultaneously aiming to retain a surplus in profit for the VFX studio entity itself. This assigned budget thus determines how many people you will be working with, how much overtime is allowed (yes, allowed), and all the other factors involving your contract and time required as well as shot delivery turnarounds. With that perspective and insight in mind, all that should matter to you (in the position of a VFX practitioner) is how to use that awareness to gauge where you are in the broader spectrum of things. You as a VFX person, after all, are merely one minuscule cog in the large macrocosm that is Hollywood.

## International film markets

And on the subject of macrocosms, what a fantastic way to transition to this segment right here on international film markets. Just to clarify, I will only be covering this topic in the context of how Hollywood works. Understandably, international film markets could be classified and discussed at great length in an entirely separate book, and I reckoned that you, dear reader, understood that fact; so, I am not even going to pretend to be a film academic here. Back on point, however, it is important to point out that there are indeed pockets of film markets and industries internationally that have since risen or are presently rising to prominence in the eyes of the world. I'll make this simple by classifying most international film industries into different tiers (and for the sake of simplicity, the word 'film' in these contexts will encompass any kind of production involving moving images for long-form entertainment such as television shows, web series, et cetera):

• The almost non-existent film market: described as a country, city, or place where activity in creating original film content is almost absent or is not substantial enough to merit any kind of sustained attention in the international stratosphere of filmmakers and Hollywood. On the other hand, this tier does not necessarily exclude the country, city, or place from being used as a location, backdrop, or setting in a film production originating in a *different* country.

•   The growing film market: described as a country, city, or place where activity in creating original film content is growing at a rapid rate or growing so substantially that it has started to merit sporadic periods of sustained attention in the international stratosphere of filmmakers and Hollywood. Likewise, this tier does not necessarily include or exclude the country, city, or place from being a hotspot for film settings and backdrops in film productions organized by studios from *other* countries.

•   Near-Hollywood-level film market: described as a country, city, or place where activity in creating original film content is booming and thriving to the extent that it has warranted continuous interest and sustained attention in the international stratosphere of filmmakers and Hollywood. Again, this tier does not necessarily include or exclude the country, city, or place from being a hotspot for film settings and backdrops in film productions organized by studios from *other* countries. However, said market's booming original film content usually utilizes its own country, city, or place as a location in their own original productions, which naturally makes their country, city, or place a hotspot on the basis of its frequent use in its own locally produced content.

With those self-made tiers defined, let's start pegging a few countries to each tier – along with my justifications and explanations for why I believe these countries fall under each category.

- **Almost non-existent film markets**

  Basically, any other country that is not India (Bollywood), the United Kingdom (which has strong ties to Hollywood), Canada, South Korea, China, Spain, and to some extent Nigeria and South Africa. Now, before you get on my case on the European film industry – including France and Italy's film productions and a few other countries in that region – I'd like to emphasize that this tier is the 'almost non-existent film markets', it does not mean that the countries casually lumped into this category have completely nonexistent film markets. In fact, there have certainly been a few break-out films from France and Italy as well as other unmentioned countries that were internationally successful and remembered in the public consciousness; however, a few noteworthy films do not necessarily mean that the entire industry within that country itself has sustained international attention. Another easy way to look at it is the types of industries that generally first come to your mind whenever you think of a country. So, when I think of France, I think of the high fashion and cultural arts scenes; when I think of Italy, I think of architecture and food; when I think of the United States, I think of entrepreneurship and entertainment; when I think of Singapore, I think of finance and engineering. You see, sometimes these stereotypes of certain places actually live up to their public perception – and sometimes the simplest, top-of-mind answers are usually the right ones.

For example, if you were to name a random country like Samoa, I would probably not be able to tell you how its niche film industry is doing in terms of having its locally bred filmmakers and producers producing local content that would actually garner international acclaim or attention. However, I can say that Samoa serves the film industry in other ways, such as providing labor perhaps, or even being a good location for certain types of stories and narratives in productions organized by Hollywood or one of the other heavy content-producing countries. Again, non-existent film markets do not necessarily mean these countries and places cannot serve the global filmmaking community in other ways. I would also gladly add Singapore to this tier even though it has a substantially better-developed film community and industry compared to Samoa, mainly because most of Singapore's locally cultivated films or shows have only randomly garnered international attention that disappears from the limelight as soon as they enter it. Heck, I am sure you too, dear reader, are probably only aware of Singapore's existence through the film, *"Crazy Rich Asians."* And no, Singapore is not and never was part of China. On that note, let's be honest here: not every country *wants* or *needs* a thriving film industry of its own. Some of them simply serve as excellent film locations and in doing so bring the flow of investment into their countries. In other words, countries in this tier may get involved in the film industry by serving other film industries outside of their country. Anyway, how these non-existent film markets traditionally impact or add value to how the Hollywood community of filmmakers works as a whole is rather straightforward: they either offer up their countries as viable locations and settings in narratives through tax incentives and bonuses (whether they be applicable to foreign talent or locals only), provide cheap and inexpensive labor willing to learn the ropes from the pros storming in from larger entertainment capitals, or provide Hollywood with a loyal, somewhat-reliable movie-going audience for the type of content being created by the larger global film markets. This list is not exclusive.

As you can see, just because a country is deemed to have an under-developed or almost non-existent film market (based on my judging criteria) *does not* mean that the country's own locally produced films or shows are unwatchable outside of their local circle or that they are simply talentless and uncreative people. In fact, if you are looking for the right opportunities and actually happen to have a lot of experience from the second or third tier in the list, you could even seek to *be* that expert these countries may be seeking – helping to shape and grow these non-existent film markets into something respectable outside of their own country. Hey, you may even get the country's recognition and credit for it if you're *really* entrepreneurial. Again, countries that happened to be listed in this tier aren't inherently bad climates for filmmakers – they just have a lot of untapped potential to grow in ways that their own locals haven't thought of themselves yet. Until then, however, these places will continue to serve as important contributors to the global filmmaking machine through their fantastic locations, inexpensive or growth-oriented talent, or simply by supplying a couple hundred thousand movie-goers and supporters of traditional Western media.

- **Growing film markets**

Next up, we have our growing film markets of the world. Based on my analysis and understanding of their respective film markets from an outsider's perspective, I would personally place Canada, South Korea, Spain, Nigeria, and South Africa in this group (maybe Australia as well, though just barely inching it into this tier, in my opinion – please don't be offended if you're from Australia; I have my reasons). As examples, we'll focus specifically on Nigeria and South Korea. Now, you may perhaps be surprised by Canada's name being listed in this tier, but I'll explain why I have decided to list Canada as a growing film market rather than a near-Hollywood-level film market. First, let me ask you this: when was the last time you remembered an internationally acclaimed film being produced, created, and distributed *entirely* from the great country of Canada? If you had to use Google to find the answer to that question like I did, then chances are its *own local film industry* isn't at the Hollywood-level caliber yet. Sure, Canada has a *lot* of VFX houses and studios, is getting more and more production offices being based in Canada, and is also used *often and frequently* as locations for some of Hollywood's greatest films (the same can be said for Australia); however, as a standalone film industry of its own, you'd be hard-pressed to find many Canadian film titles that stand out in the international market. On the other hand, since Canada has amassed a lot of attention from the global filmmaking community in the recent decade as a film hub, ideal film location, and growing talent hub, it only makes sense that it deserves a place in this tier rather than the earlier tier of non-existent markets. One can definitely attribute Canada's growing recognition and attention in the international filmmaking space due to its influx of VFX and production personnel and increased establishment of production houses and bases in the heart of Canada, as well as a wildly popular usage of its unique environment for *thousands* of well-funded Hollywood productions. O Canada, o Canada – with all these resources, I wouldn't be surprised if locally-produced content and locally-bred filmmakers start taking advantage of them, elevating their country up into the next tier in some years ahead.

Now, let's move on to the film markets in Nigeria and South Korea, also known as Nollywood and Hallyuwood respectively (yes, the names, I know ...). Reader, perhaps you may be surprised by the latter (Hallyuwood) being placed in this tier rather than the next one, but hear me out. Just because several Korean films and shows made it out of their country and garnered (almost an instant) massive international appeal – including one film nabbing about four Oscars – doesn't mean that this group of productions are entirely representative of the entire string of productions being produced locally in South Korea at the moment. In fact, if we look at the history of South Korean films that have made it into the international limelight, it has only been in recent years (especially since Park Chan-wook's *"Oldboy"* in 2003) that South Korean films have started garnering significant international attention – and that was less than two decades ago (since the publication of this book). In addition, South Korea still only has a handful of local production companies – at least in comparison to the United States and even Canada – in spite of their growth, and though most film productions made in South Korea often feature locations in the country itself, you still rarely see an international film production organized by another country using South Korea as a backdrop for their narratives. Hence, even though it is evident that South Korea *does* produce great film content (heck, they already have a strong history and significant experience with the music and dance scene), it is these other factors (the low number of production houses, less international film productions on-location and perhaps fewer international collaborations) that keep South Korea in the tier of a growing film market. Now, is South Korea inching closer and closer to becoming the next Hollywood-level film market? Oh yes. In fact, I would actually rank South Korea as currently straddling in-between this tier and the final tier right now, but I am placing them in this group of growth until their development in other areas (that make a cohesive film market) prove to be sustainable over a longer period of time, in the eyes of the world.

Now, while Nigeria's film industry isn't as impressive as South Korea – at least not in the sense that they've had many films sustain international acclaim or attention – I am still placing Nigeria in this list as one to watch for potential exponential growth in the future. From what I've gathered from Nigerian intelligence (also known as people from Nigeria) and analyses, Nigerian films tend to appeal to local audiences, with their international reach being limited to mostly African communities spread out across the world. And while it has *way* fewer production houses compared to other countries in this tier, Nollywood actually produces *more* (that's right, more) films *per week*, surpassing even Hollywood themselves (only lagging behind Bollywood, which produces way more per week). It would appear that it is a numbers game to them, and that factor alone is likely to increase the chances that a handful of these productions may just make it into the international limelight and (hopefully) sustain long-term public interest. That being said, even though Nollywood has fewer production houses compared to places like Canada, the high output of productions per week means that they hire a *lot* of talent and create a *lot* of jobs for their people (which is a great indicator of a growing and robust industry). It also helps that their own Nigerian government takes their local film industry seriously and is championing its growth in addition to encouraging international collaboration with other film markets overseas. Looking forward, we can definitely expect to see more Nigerian landscapes, environments, and backdrops being featured in international productions – as I am sure you may have already seen one or two American reality television series featuring Nigeria or Nigerians. So, keep an eye out for Nollywood – there might just be plenty of opportunities on the horizon for their industry in the future.

So, I am sure that there are other growing film markets out there but hey, this is a book of insights and observations – including deep thoughts that first come to mind. So, if a market didn't come to me while writing this book, clearly it hasn't earned enough notoriety to get the top-of-mind awareness similar to most top consumer brands you would know. Just being frank and realistic.

- **Near-Hollywood-level film markets**

Finally, we have the film markets that are near-Hollywood-level caliber (perhaps even *at* Hollywood-level caliber) and these markets are as follows, in no particular order: India (Bollywood), the United Kingdom, and China. Now, the United Kingdom is kind of a no-brainer here in this group – not only has Hollywood and the UK formed strong industry ties in the sense that Hollywood tends to use *a lot* of British talent, resources, and reference material for their own show or movie replicas, they also have quite a number of studio bases set up in the UK as well (similar to the kind of setup they have going on with Canada). As a VFX artist, the UK is also a VFX haven with a notable number of VFX studios that were originally founded on UK soil such as Framestore and Double Negative. Of course, what makes the UK a noteworthy, near-Hollywood-level (or arguably *at* Hollywood-level) film market of its own also stems from the high-quality access to proper film education in the UK and, mainly, its plethora of UK-produced and distributed films that have captured or *continue* to capture international acclaim and public interest for a prolonged period of time (though some British critics argue that distribution success is largely due to their strong partnership with Hollywood and the fact that their films fundamentally go through America's distribution channels). Either way, look up famous films from the UK and you are sure to recognize most if not all of the titles displayed. In addition to the massive number of studios on the ground, the constant back-and-forth *and* numerous collaborations with Hollywood, the educated talent pool, and the success of its own locally produced content, the UK is *also* a hotspot as a film location (for both local and foreign-produced films) with a sizable movie-going audience to boot. Hands down, the UK deserves to be in this tier.

What about Bollywood and China then? Well, they're both just as respectable. Bollywood in fact ranks first in the world of filmmaking as the country that produces the *most* films per year (surpassing even Hollywood itself). Of course, when you look at their population count, this conferred title makes sense. Historically, we can trace Bollywood's first locally-produced film all the way back to 1913, kicking off a never-ending chain of locally produced content since. In addition to being a stronghold as a production hub of its own locally appealing content (with plenty of local production companies to boot), Bollywood's film industry rakes in *big* bucks for both its local and foreign films (such as imports from Hollywood). It was even claimed that Bollywood at one point (in the early 2000s or so) sold about 3.6 *billion* tickets worldwide for both locally produced and international films, a feat that even surpassed Hollywood's number of tickets sold; so yes, one could say that India provides a sizable audience that enjoys consuming its own movies as well as Hollywood's. In a similar way to the UK, India also has its fair share of film schools that appear to be teaching something right considering how much money Bollywood brings in for the Indian economy. Coupling robust education and a strong historical record of growth, it only makes sense to place Bollywood in this tier in spite of its local films having a mostly localized appeal and there not being many Indian films that have made the international limelight (unless it was an international collaboration with Hollywood). Given that fact, you might be wondering, shouldn't Bollywood be in the previous tier of growing film markets instead, seeing how not many Indian films have garnered sustained international attention and discussion? Well, cue in Netflix and other streaming platforms. With the advent and success of these streaming services (as well as virtual private networks) that allow for *any* content created *anywhere* to be easily accessed and discovered based on genre, preferences, et cetera, I would say that more and more Bollywood films (as well as other Asian or European independent or legacy films) are now even *more* discoverable in the global marketplace – perhaps making their once only-locally-known obscure films popular in the eyes of an international audience. With Bollywood's industry net worth, the number of jobs it creates for the local economy, its *thriving* VFX ecosystem (yes, if you look it up or if you happen to be from India, you know what I'm talking about), and its new opportunities to shine on well-known globalized platforms, I stand by my declaration that Bollywood is definitely a near-Hollywood-level (or at Hollywood-level) film titan of its own.

And last but certainly not least, we have China's film industry. Now, contrary to what the geopolitical climate has you believing, China's film industry actually has *very* strong ties to Hollywood and is actually one of Hollywood's largest supporters in terms of delivering the hordes of movie-goers in support of American cinema (in international ticket sales and grosses). We will actually dive a lot deeper into China's film scene next, so I'll keep this portion to its bare minimum for now. When it comes to VFX though, whilst you might think that India retains the bulk of VFX talent for Hollywood productions (albeit, as of the writing of this book, India's VFX scene is mostly limited to rotoscoping and scene layout tasks – basically, the more non-creative technical work), from my observations and conversations with people in Hollywood, it is actually China that gets the upper hand in gaining the more favorable creative talent transferred from Hollywood VFX studios. Now, why is this so? I wouldn't even begin to guess as it is out of the scope of this topic. Based on a few key conversations I've had with transferred – or about-to-be-transferred – veteran creative and technical supervisors I've met at studios along the way though, they have shared with me a little bit of insight as to why they were being transferred to China (mostly Beijing or Shanghai) and what their role is over there. With that kind of brain share going on between the Hollywood elite and China, one can only project that the Chinese film and VFX industry are working closely with Hollywood, which can only benefit their local cinema scene in the long run. We will talk specifically about how China's strong foundation and focus on these types of educational and learning opportunities benefit their film industry in the next sub-chapter. Now, from what I have also observed about China – other than their undeniably high box office revenue for domestic and international films (surpassing even Bollywood's), utility as a popular hotspot for story locations in a myriad of local and foreign productions, and their propensity to welcome certain types of international collaboration (especially when it comes to their VFX industry) – is that because there is such a good supply of production work coming in from local producers, some of these VFX studios (even the overseas branches of Hollywood VFX studios) also give local films a chance by taking up one or two well-funded productions that require impressive VFX. This gives local filmmakers a stab at acquiring Hollywood-caliber VFX work on well-funded productions, even though these VFX studios only do so with great selectivity. With a personal connection I have who worked at Huayi Brothers at the time (one of China's top multinational film production companies), I can definitely attest to the Chinese knowing how to deploy people on the ground in the United States to gather intelligence on how American productions are run – again, showing their fearless determination in boosting their own local film industry and productions. This contact I knew even enrolled in a producing class at the University of California, Los Angeles (UCLA), which only goes to show how serious and dedicated he was in honing and developing his craft – something that would eventually benefit his company and ripple into the development of a large majority of Chinese films in the nation.

With all that being said, China is definitely high on this shortlist of near or at Hollywood-level film markets, especially given the many equally fervent collaborations between Hollywood and China. Of course, this isn't to say that Bollywood or the UK's cinema falls short by any means. No, not at all. In fact, what makes these classifications so special is that there are no strict and definite terms that are meant to rank one film market over the other. Each country, location, and place ultimately supply their own unique factors in the creation, production, and distribution of both local and international films – it just depends on how far ahead specific countries are in terms of their relative strength in the global filmmaking community. Again, these are just my analyses, observations, and opinions – they are *not* science, they are *not* gospel, and you are free to agree or disagree with the way I have ranked certain countries based on my own reasoning and logic.

## China's growing influence and the Asian dominance

With the establishment of international film markets aside, there is one market in particular that – in the context of Hollywood – anyone even remotely interested in being involved in the film business should look at, and that is China's growing influence and dominance in film (and in general, their dominance across most fields nowadays). Now, I am not one for politics – being proudly apolitical – but you could say that the initial concerns the United States had about China were not unfounded. Having worked with people from Mainland China as well as personally knowing and meeting a few acquaintances who are from China (and are now in the United States), I have mainly this to say through my observations and long-term interactions with the Chinese: they are smarter than people give them credit for. They aren't only academically-savvy, they're streetwise as well (a deadly combination in any one individual). In fact, I find the majority of them to possess a knack for business strategy and reading people – especially if said people are of the more expressive sort (and, interestingly, those types of people tended to be people from the Western world). Again, just stating my observations here. I really miss the old days when you could state objective facts, opinions, and insights without being labeled something ridiculous out of polarized political spite – don't you? Anyway, I digress – I do hope you, dear reader, are not one of those politically-polarized people.

Now, back to the main point. To be honest, China has always had its hands in Hollywood in some way. Again, you don't need to be an active player in the industry in order to be involved in Hollywood. Just as places like Samoa serve the filmmaking world as a location, China serves Hollywood by providing the *largest* movie-going audience in the world through sheer numbers. That is because their population size *is* the largest in the world (as of the writing of this book anyway) – followed by India and then the

United States. Needless to say, whilst most films are made with the American movie-goer in mind, you can bet that big American studios are looking to make most of their bucks from international gross (also known as earnings) rather than domestic box office earnings. It's just the nature of the business – and in this case, it is a numbers game. Naturally, when you compare China's population of over 1.39 *billion* alone (ignoring the rest of the world for a second) to the United States' 330 million thereabouts, you'll have your global audiences – who usually have an idealized, starry-eyed vision of Hollywood and Western media – dominating your grosses. Now, this is cool and all, but know that international or domestic movie grosses do not apply to you, the aspiring VFX artist, or present VFX extraordinaire. In fact, you get paid like a regular office worker and you *don't* get a cut of the box office rewards and profits. This is normal and standard procedure. You, VFX person, *don't* get a cut just like the sound editor, colorist, and production designer *don't* get a cut. It's just the way it is – not all profits can be shared equally even if it appears your work carries the entire weight of the film.

Anyway, back to China – let's focus on their own film industry for a moment. Now, this perhaps might surprise you, but China was actually introduced to motion pictures in the very late 1800s and was considered one of the earliest countries to be exposed to this new medium of film. Historically, the first film in China could be said to have been made in the year 1905 (about two years after the first western film in the United States). ... And that's about all the history I am going to fill you in on in this book. From that brief glimpse of history alone, however, one can already tell that China has had a *very long* time to develop their cinema and filmmaking craft and, just as the United States released films representative of their era at the time, so did China. The main reason why we hadn't really heard or seen much of China's commercial film successes *globally* and *outside* of China (and outside of Asia, to a certain extent) is mainly because China was *initially* closed off to foreigners and foreign influence, only opening up in the late 1970s to early 1980s (which is considered fairly recent given the time it takes for domestic products and industries to establish themselves in the international scene). Aside from these facts and data points (which you can also look up on Google to verify or go deeper into the topic if it piques your interest), I do not claim to be an expert in any way on China's film industry as a whole, nor do I know of any more details about its specific market conditions. Similarly, you, dear reader (who perhaps doesn't really care about the nitty-gritty details either), should mainly take home one fact from that entire chunk of words above and that is this: as China continues to open itself up to the world, expect to see more actors from China in Hollywood hits, a stronger appeal to the Chinese movie-going audiences in Hollywood media, noteworthy and well-produced *heavy VFX* Chinese films, and even one or two random Chinese films that somehow made it to your local theaters wherever you are in the world (that also reasonably makes sense to Chinese distributors, of course). Now, whatever your individual stance is on China, China's influence in entertainment and film is growing in its consumers' spending power, its own locally cultured high-quality productions, and advancing knowledge in filmmaking and VFX. Multiply that effect by the number of people China has and you have an army of mass productions and activity going on in their film industry.

As someone who has ties to one of the top reputable Chinese education platforms in the field of VFX (and having been approached by various similar platforms from the Chinese market since), I can attest to the quality VFX education that is prevalent on an overwhelming majority of these platforms. From an incredibly detailed course curriculum to very realistic 3D models with industry-standard tools, had you seen what I have seen on these VFX online education platforms, any negative preconceived notion of China's education in VFX, video games, and animation would have been completely negated. Now, since I am on one of China's largest VFX education platforms, I'd like to think that I had and presently have a hand in contributing to China's advancing knowledge in filmmaking methods, VFX pipelines, workflows, and technical skills. Hey, you'll never know when one of these students who took my courses may end up changing the face of China's VFX industry – I was already told that there could potentially *already be* such a student in the midst, who took my VFX supervision course. Anyway, one can wish, and one can dream, ha.

On that note, however, it is important to shed some light on what the current buzz is with China these days – and believe me, filmmaking is most definitely *not* what will push China forward in the coming years. In my opinion, the industries that will make or break China essentially involve China's concentrated efforts and developments in technology (more specifically, artificial intelligence [AI]) and education. This is where China commands most of its power and influence on the world stage, which, by extension, enhances China's power and influence in Hollywood and the entertainment industry at large. Whilst I do acknowledge that China does have very, *very* lax laws on copyright infringement and intellectual property, it does not appear to stifle the entrepreneurial and innovative spirit of its locals – regardless of whether their ideas or entities were original or outright clones of existing brands from other countries. With China's ambitions in AI and an increasingly globalized take on their education, one can only speculate that the returns on these investments in better AI software, tools, and performance only serve to enhance the efficiency of local productions whilst spurring on new ideas of stories and narratives to be told (which may have originated from their AI-specific developments). I can only anticipate China playing a bigger role in Hollywood – whether that be as creators, collaborators, consumers, or suppliers – as their AI technology continues to forge ahead internationally; being aware that Hollywood commands the territory of entertainment in the eyes of the world, perhaps China is taking the route of advanced technology and technology education in order to claim a unique stake in entertainment (among other industries) in the future. This would be something to keep an eye on.

Going wider, let's delve deeper into the rising Asian dominance in Hollywood – namely, movie-goers from the region as well as active industry players who play a key role in creating 'Hollywood-caliber' original films and content. Now, as established in the previous sub-chapter, China and India (a part of Asia) form a large portion of the global demographic in box office ticket sales and international grosses. Again, it only makes sense because these two countries have the largest populations in the world. Whilst this isn't to say that the Hollywood moguls are designing their films to appeal to the Asian crowd, you can bet that they do factor in those numbers when it comes to getting a return on their film investment. Historically (and based on my personal observations and conversations with other Asians from various Asian countries), many Asian countries have always looked up to Hollywood films and Western media – it has been culturally-embedded into the consciousness of most Asian cultures and countries since the fascination with foreigners began. On that note, however, it would appear that an exception to this regional (and to a certain extent, worldwide) Hollywood-fascination is the country of Japan, who themselves have a strong animation (also known as anime) and film market of their own, with a style that strongly appeals to their own populace. Of course, when Hollywood decides to create content that was meant to be culturally appealing to any one specific Asian country, you can expect that they anticipate (and are probably excited to be) tapping into those box office numbers if their films are to be well-received by the target country. In addition to supplying Hollywood with revenue, however, more Asian-centric films, documentaries, and shows have been surfacing on streaming platforms and channels these days – and one can partially thank China for that. You see, with China's credibility as a powerful economy to be reckoned with as it is increasingly brought into the spotlight in Western media, it is likely that Hollywood has caught on to the trend; certain industry players – whether they be Asian or not – will highly likely be looking to take advantage of this opportunity to represent or showcase more of this oriental side of the world in Hollywood entertainment. From Asian-centric tales to an all-Asian cast or even an Asian lead in several independent films, I would partially chalk this up as an attempt to tap into a broader audience outside of the United States, seeing how most average citizens of China are also rapidly gaining wealth in recent years and that content from all parts of the world has only been made more accessible through online streaming services (with a virtual private network). Of course, as more films feature Asian storylines or jump on the Asian bandwagon, more Asian countries and places are also being utilized as film locations – leading to more Asian locals and production personnel being trained by Hollywood pros and, ultimately, more VFX branches being set up in Asian countries like India, China, or even Malaysia and Singapore (take a shot every time I use the word 'Asian' in this paragraph).

All in all, whether you are confident or ambivalent about China's standing in the place of film and VFX, China is one of the countries to watch for potential major shifts in consumer behavior and trends. After all, when you have a country with billions of citizens (particularly middle-income citizens) with rapidly increasing disposable incomes, access to better and more advanced technologies (contrary to what was depicted of China in old Hollywood movies), and an increasingly globalized outlook on education, you will soon have an army of highly-educated, semi-rich consumers who could either choose to remain as consumers (serving the entertainment industry as movie-goers) or become producers of their own local film content, in the context of filmmaking and entertainment. So long as China continues to forge ahead in the global marketplace, the Asian trend and dominance in film narratives and casting is most likely here to stay – at least for a while.

# 7

# GLOBAL ECONOMICS AND CONSUMERISM

From China to the world, it is important to understand that *all* industries will always be subject to the happenings of the world, the movements of economics, and the fundamental shifts of consumer behavior. Whenever major global events happen – such as a civil war, plague, or massive shifts in global corporate production practices – it impacts the economics of industries by either rapidly expediting opportunities of commercialization and production or completely halting industry activities in an instant. Sometimes, these events may be localized by geography or by the types of consumers relevant to the industry; whichever the case may be, I do believe that understanding economics and the movements of people (as well as their collective actions and behaviors in specific situations and industries) is important in making well-rounded decisions that fit *your* unique situation as a VFX artist of *any* position. This understanding is especially crucial for business owners. I do want to state once again that whilst I don't have a degree in economics nor did I study the subject fervently, a lot of the insights and observations provided in this chapter, in particular, are based on intellectual and psychological analyses of my experiences, others' experiences, an innate understanding of human behavior and of course, common sense (at least what I see as common sense). All I am saying is that we all – as artists, technicians, businessmen, or living beings in general – should be astute students of life, our surroundings, and human behavior. Although you don't *need* to know much (or anything for that matter) about economics and consumer behavior as an aspiring or existing VFX professional, I am including this chapter for people like me who like to know *a lot* about *a lot* of things. In the end, it doesn't hurt to learn something different – not everything has to be about VFX, VFX ... and VFX.

## Consumerism and the economy

Ok, consumerism and the economy. Where do I even begin with this one. I am definitely going to make a concerted effort to make this part of my treatise more interesting because honestly, which VFX artist *actually* cares about the details and fundamentals of economics? I know I don't. Again, I didn't actually study this so if you really want to get into specifics, feel free to pick up an economics book on the side; what I will be sharing here are my own observations and thoughts coming from an outsider with a non-economist's perspective on things. Alright then, let's begin with the very basics: consumerism is a driver for economic growth. Common sense ain't it, dear reader? I mean, clearly, the majority of consumers generally increase their spending whenever the economy is doing well (or when they *perceive* the economy to be doing well). I would actually attribute this generalized increased spending from the general masses as the process of being swept up in the tide of herd mentality. You see, most of you all have friends – ok, if that was an offensive statement to have indirectly classified you as one of the "masses" then switch that to *most people* have friends (do tell me what that is like in an email, ha) – and while one may or may not be aware of it, friends do have the tendency to influence your likes, interests, and behavior to a certain extent. Now, imagine if these friends are going out to have a party or to celebrate a special occasion with some drinks and movies. Depending on the individual personality and makeup of your friends – let's assume that you have one who is a popular extrovert with about ten thousand followers on Instagram or something – they have the tendency to be able to influence you and others around you to partake in the same thing. There's absolutely nothing wrong with that (plus, I am over-simplifying things in this example because nobody has that kind of time for individualized details). Now, imagine that scenario of influence multiplied by *each and every* consumer in the country of the United States – bingo, you have your hordes of consumers going out to spend, have a good time, or whatever. The emotionality, which fundamentally controls human behavior, is contagious to most typical human beings. People subconsciously pick up these cues and signals and – if they are typical human beings who like to go with the flow (which is absolutely normal) – these people will subconsciously re-enact or reflect similar emotional cues and behaviors back. That's how a trend of behavior starts spreading in crowds, pockets of populations, and eventually to the entire state or country – and with social media, it's becoming increasingly easier for emotion to spread like wildfire.

Now, I understand that it is a broad sweeping statement to claim that "all" consumers do this, but take a trip out of town to a mall on Black Friday and experience it for yourself. Perhaps an even better example is to go to an auction for art, real estate, or antique furniture. On that note, while not *all* consumers immediately partake in any spreading consumerist trend of the day, even the tiny sliver of consumers who *don't* get swept up in the spending spree when the economy is going well, and prices are at their peak aren't sufficient in numbers to completely derail or turn the trend around. Hence, you will normally have a strong uptrend in consumerist behaviors whenever an economy *is* or is *perceived to be* doing well. Likewise, the same could be said for when the economy is at its worst or is *perceived* to be doing poorly – most consumers, being naturally emotional and reactive, won't even consider tapping into their savings to make luxurious purchases (even though prices tend to be cheaper during economic downturns). Either way, who am I to judge their buying and selling behavior – I'm just a VFX artist.

Anyway, when it comes to consumerism and the economy, Hollywood *used* to be one of those industries that tend to be relied upon *heavily* during good economic times – defined as when people are willing to spend more on goods and services (including ancillary goods and services), when companies are taking advantage of increased consumerism (thereby creating more jobs), and when people are more-or-less happily employed (perhaps even getting raises due to the increased demand for certain goods and services by their employing companies). Nowadays, however, with the differentiated means by which entertainment can be accessed beyond the typical in-person cinemas, Hollywood has managed to tap into economic recessions as well – with most consumers not leaving their homes to purchase as often as they used to, leaving them mostly indoors to binge on Netflix, Hulu, or other similar channels. Needless to say, Hollywood still makes more during economic booms when consumers are more likely to want to invest the time and cash in purchasing movie tickets for the experience of watching a show or two at the cinema (usually accompanied by some friends or family). A great example to gauge how Hollywood is performing during less-than-desirable economic times is during the worldwide COVID-19 pandemic; with the majority of cinemas closed worldwide, frankly, it would *appear* that the film industry is taking a nose-dive similar to aviation. This isn't necessarily true. Sure, *actual* filmmaking and production activity may have been drastically reduced in some parts of the world (especially in the heart of Hollywood), but with the other distribution models at play – such as streaming services and online content – Hollywood will continue to see an uptick in revenue coming in from these channels to fund other activities for the industry. There have even been a few published reports of the revenue that's coming in from these online channels, showing that it has since increased exponentially due to the pandemic. Hence, hope is not all lost in Hollywood, even if it appears that the economy has come to a standstill.

Regardless of your own consumer behavior, reader, let's come to a consensus that consumers generally spend when they *perceive* the economy to be doing well and generally save when they *perceive* the economy to be contracting. If you would like to find out more about this subject, my suggestion is to seek out more information from our good friend Google – I am sure you will find plenty of supporting data and evidence on this massive topic. Either way, this herd mentality generated by masses and masses of consumers is generally applicable when it comes to driving people to decide whether to spend or to save, based on a collective subconscious sense and awareness of how the economy *seems* to be doing overall. Even those who claim to not subscribe to this herd mentality shift are simultaneously subscribing to the opposite wave of emotions (and a different, albeit less popular herd mentality) generated by the significant mass of consumers who chose to deliberately buck the trend. Wherever a consumer stands, they're bound to be caught in one wave or the other. It simply depends on which one is the stronger and larger behavioral trend at the time. It's just like surfing – most surfers will opt to ride the bigger wave.

## What makes a movie-goer

Now that we've established how each industry has its ups and downs and how during times of profitability people tend to spend more at the movies with their (hopefully) extra earnings, here comes my favorite part of this chapter: diving into the mindset of a movie-goer. Let's first remember, however, that people are complex creatures, and everyone is inherently unique and different from one another, blah, blah, blah. ... Ok, with that disclaimer out of the way, time to make some generic (but *applicable and true*) statements about what makes a movie-goer – regardless of their country of origin.

You see, when it comes to handling specific profiles of people, there is some truth in stereotypes and the types of people you may find in any one particular consumer niche. Let's use the legal industry as an example. Traditionally, when we think of attorneys and lawyers, the preconceived notion of them being smart, articulate, professional, and critical typically comes to mind. With that, we can extrapolate that lawyers tend to be rather disagreeable people, who are extremely obsessed with details and know how to mince their words such that they fit specific legal situations. Fair enough. Now, these traits don't exactly apply to *every single individual* lawyer out there (heck, some artists can also have all of the aforementioned traits) but you can guarantee that the chances of you yourself encountering a lawyer that fits this bill is extraordinarily high. The same can be said of consumers in any one specific niche. In this case, our movie-goer generally has a certain set of traits and expected behaviors that you and fellow filmmakers can come to expect whenever a film is released in theaters. Bear in mind that these traits and behaviors may not apply to viewers of online content – for, as far as I know, all bets are off on home-based viewers (especially since they could literally be anyone, anywhere in the world, with vastly different professional backgrounds and experiences).

Whilst it is crucial to note that there will also be subsets of movie-goers depending on the genre of the film in question (for example, horror films tend to attract a different crowd from those who fancy romantic comedies), here is what I would generally constitute as the psychosocial profile of a typical movie-goer, regardless of film genres:

• Young adults aged 18-to-29 with disposable incomes: you would expect to see *fewer* teenagers under the age of 18 as most of them tend to have been raised on streaming services and other more convenient means of accessing content such as YouTube, TikTok, et cetera.

• Tend to watch films in groups (with friends, family, or dates): by this account, movie-goers tend to have a higher tendency of enjoying the company of others more so than a solo movie-goer.

• Tend to lead somewhat active and extroverted lifestyles: this makes sense, especially when pairing this data point with the age group in question.

- Higher chance of their personality being casual, relaxed, and friendly: as most movie-goers take the time and money out of their day to physically go to a movie theater and enjoy a film, it is highly likely that movie-goers are less high-strung, less likely to be someone of a "Type A" personality, and less likely to take life too seriously.

- Tend to rely on word-of-mouth (from friends or family), a movie's online presence, and early reviews to determine whether or not to watch a movie: in other words, movie-goers tend to be more open to multiple channels of influence when it comes to deciding which film to watch, with the older crowds leaning more towards early reviews and multiple sources of influence.

- Will most likely be more liberal than conservative: again, this is entirely speculative though, seeing as most liberals tend to be more extroverted than conservatives, this is a targeted guess.

- Likely to go to the movies for the immersive experience of watching a movie in a dark cinema.

- Likely to watch a film because it stars a famous (usually attractive) actor: then again, this is standard behavior even for movies on streaming services.

- Going deeper, we can determine that movie-goers watch films in order to experience a form of catharsis outside the context of their present reality: psychologically, these individuals most enjoy the idea of being in a different reality and perhaps want to have a certain distance from their current identity in order to voyeuristically experience being another person through the lens of certain characters in a depicted film.

- Going deeper, we can also determine that movie-goers may see going to the movies as an important cultural and social construct: perhaps one that allows them to self-validate as having attained a certain degree of comfort in their lives in order to afford this privilege or routine.

- Going even deeper, we can also state that movie-goers may see going to the movies as a means of helping to solve or to avoid solving their own life's issues: again, this is entirely relative to the person but psychologically, we can speculate that some movie-goers use the experience as a means to rejuvenate themselves creatively or (on the negative side) use it as a means to temporarily avoid their problems by immersing themselves in a different reality.

The above is not an exhaustive list but you get the general gist of it.

As far as what a movie-goer looks for in the films they watch – again, psychosocial profile aside – all this would be subject to each individual's personal preferences, cultural upbringing, and life experiences thus far. For the typical movie-goer, we can anticipate that other than psychologically rewarding experiences and emotional payoffs, they might watch a film for simplistic reasons (perhaps to watch an attractive actor in action) to complex, higher-level reasons (such as to elevate their current understanding of spirituality and the cosmos). Of course, big names and big brands are a key component in any marketing of a film in order to attract eyeballs – both fans and haters alike will attend to watch their movies if you have an A-list actor the world knows about. Some movie-goers are also motivated by more basic human factors such as boredom or the desire to get out and escape their world for a while (just as some choose to escape via games, others do this through movies). Again, they're far too varied and subjective to conclude them all in this sub-chapter alone.

In general, we can conclude that our modern-day movie-goers are most likely people who have the extra income to spend and are open to being influenced by multiple sources (word-of-mouth, friends and familiars, social media campaigns, et cetera). After deciding on a film, these movie-goers will then pay for the experience of being in a dark cinema, living the narrative of a film with the rest of the audience. Honestly, while all this information is *completely* useless to the average VFX artist (sorry folks, but it's sort of true), for those of you who are considering opening up an entertainment-related business (or filmmaking studio), knowing exactly what your typical movie-goer is like as a persona is one of the keys to success. With their psychosocial profile pinned down, you and your producers can craft stories and narratives that deliberately home in and capitalize on some of your target audience's deeper psychological preferences to create films that are too addictive to turn away from. It's just the way business works, even when it comes to selling what some people might deem to be a non-essential product or "mindless" entertainment.

## Understanding macro seasonality

Now, as explained earlier, just as Hollywood has its ups and downs (even if it appears as if they don't), the economy does have its regular fluctuations – surprise, surprise – determined not only by economic booms and busts but also by activities performed by important regulatory bodies that sometimes supersede these very-controlled boom-and-bust cycles. Monetary policies (such as increasing money supply and controlling interest rates) and fiscal policies (such as government taxation and spending policies) enacted by central banks (in the United States, that would be your Federal Reserve – also known as the Fed) and the federal government, for example, also have the means to turn a large majority of the markets hawkish or dovish. And if any of these terms confuse you, you know what to do, dear reader. Now, I won't go into the nitty-gritty of the Federal Reserve, printing money, and adjustments of interest rates here as that is beyond the scope of this book, but what I will say is that when interest rates are lowered (also known as dovish or even bearish), depending on which side of the consumer-investor aisle you are on, a lower interest rate is usually an incentive to encourage consumers to go out and spend (and investors to invest, again, depending on which side of the deal you are on); when interest rates are raised (also known as going hawkish or even bullish), then it is a deliberate incentive to encourage consumers to save.

A real-time example you could use is your own bank account. If you check the historical trends of interest rates in your country and line that up with the timeline of your monthly interest earned from the cash sitting in your bank account – assuming you did not drastically withdraw or deposit significant sums of cash month-to-month – you will notice how your interest earned fluctuates in close alignment with any interest rate adjustments enacted by your country's central bank. Hence, if the central bank hikes up interest rates by one percent, for example, you will gain *a little bit more* in your earned interest based on your bank deposit; likewise, the opposite is true when it comes to the lowering of interest rates. Again, this is an easy indicator to quickly get a pulse on your local economy if you don't read the news or do anything else. Ultimately, it is all relative to whether you are a consumer, investor, business owner, bank, et cetera.

Now, I won't pretend to know the exact number of years when a cycle of inflation, stagflation, and deflation occurs but cycles *do* happen and *will* happen as the economy is regulated by market forces and central banks, among other important entities and human factors. There have been many camps in whether consumerist trends fundamentally influence fiscal and monetary policymaking or if it is the fiscal and monetary policies that determine consumer trends and behavior (sort of your chicken-or-egg dilemma) – whichever the case may be, markets ebb and flow and they surely have their seasons.

Anyway, about macro seasonality: like the four seasons, it does happen, and it will happen again. The economy has its cycles just as every industry has its cycles; some industries are more heavily affected by major shifts in broader markets whereas others tend to be inversely correlated to these shifts – flourishing during times of economic recession but floundering or maintaining at a lower volume in times of economic prosperity. The goal here is to determine what *your* niche industry seasons are and how they tie into the larger market and the broader movements of the local economy, followed by the global economy. For example, if you have the entertainment industry as a whole generally performing quite well in market net worth, expect that the sub-industries of film, themed entertainment, and games are also performing relatively well in comparison to one another. On the other hand, let's say a major catastrophe has struck the world of themed entertainment – perhaps a major supplier for theme park rides suddenly filed for bankruptcy out of nowhere – while this may negatively impact the industry of themed entertainment, the entire entertainment industry as a whole may not be as affected by this blip in one of its sub-industries. Hence, there may be events or developments that impact individual sub-industries – such as a nationwide recall of all roller coaster rides (I am clearly making this up as I go along) – that will most likely only impact the industry of themed entertainment but leave the film and games worlds untouched – yet still allow for the broader market and local economy to prosper as usual, and so on and so forth. Again, more specifics and complex scenarios can be found online if you are really interested in learning more about these correlations.

In the end, global economics does – to a certain extent – have power and control over the entertainment world, which in turn has control over Hollywood and ultimately the VFX industry – including people like you. There is only so much you can do or have control over when times are bad and there is only so much you can take on when times are booming – it all depends on the market and the macroeconomy. The key takeaway here is to focus on what you *can* control and let the market run its due course. You can't change the market (as a VFX professional), you can't change the economy (as a VFX professional), and you certainly can't control the ebb and flow of global production and seasons (as a VFX professional); what you can and should do to make the best use of your time (and your life) is to focus on priming yourself for opportunities when the time is ripe by timing the markets – which I will cover in the next sub-chapter. Ah, what a humbling moment it must be to imagine that ultimately – in the grand scheme of things – we VFX artists are nothing but tiny cogs in this machine called the 'global economy'.

## Market cycles exist in VFX too

Just as this is true with any industry, cycles exist in the VFX world. I am sure you saw that one coming given what I prefaced just a paragraph ago. Well, from my experience, there are certainly very specific months of the year when VFX jobs aggressively kick up a notch; this is usually during pilot season in television when a ton of pilots, new stories, and shows get picked up (or hope to get picked up) by cable and television networks. Occasionally, depending on the reputation of the VFX studio you are working for, you'll get one or two independent pilots that have yet to be picked up by a studio (but are actively pitching to studios) that apparently have sufficient funding to reach out to said VFX studio for their VFX services. Most of the time though, you'll have a bunch of new shows greenlit by television networks in hopes of those investments being able to bring in increased viewership (and consequently money from advertising revenue), whilst simultaneously improving their Nielsen ratings (look this up on Google if you're confused). Now, the reason why I am bringing up television as a prospect here – when I know most people who want to get into VFX prefer to work on feature films just because that's probably what they grew up watching – is because their VFX cycles are the *most obvious* to any person, even to outsiders looking in. Think about it for a second. Let's say a show like *"The Walking Dead"* typically airs twice a year – from what I recall, this is usually sometime in February and then later in the year in September or October. Now, if you trace back the steps from airtime to when production was wrapped, you'd get what would be the *general* period of time when post-production work would occur (including sound editing, color-grading, putting things in the edit, and of course, VFX work). Now, *most* cable television shows generally follow this split of airing twice a year with a huge break in-between. So, imagine that timeline, multiplied by over twenty networks or so with five or more shows each, and you'll have your peak period with a bunch of projects coming in. Again, if you can figure this out on your own, kudos to you – just remember what I said about things changing all the time. A classic example of this is the COVID-19 pandemic having shifted a lot of the typical television post-production cycles.

Now, for VFX in movies on other hand, I would say that there are usually at least three to five films going on during any particular period of the year. In fact, VFX for movies generally falls into a longer timeline (which makes sense given that long-form content tends to take a longer time anyway) and, depending on what VFX role you are involved in, a single cycle for you could be as long as a year or two on *one* production. Basically, if you choose to do VFX for movies rather than television, you could be set for a *long* period of time as peak-and-valley seasons tend not to exist in feature film productions. In essence, there's *always* going to be a film production for VFX artists to work on regardless of how Hollywood is doing as an economy (except in extraordinary circumstances, of course). This isn't to say that a path in television is inherently risky or that you are better off aiming for VFX projects that are features. Nah, no way. It just depends on what you prefer doing and the kind of pace that really excites you. When I was working in VFX for television, I can definitely say that the excitement of having a *lot* of shots to work on is rejuvenating just like the opportunity to work on *multiple projects* at one studio is refreshing. Does it have a tighter turnaround time? Yes, but you get to improve your skills at a much quicker rate than working on feature film projects alone. In fact, most television-only VFX artists and compositors I've met are not only talented but are also able to perform at *record speed* and deliver *tons* of shots in a day (an ideal for a lot of studios – even those that specialize only in feature films). Again, it all depends on who you are and your preferred modality of pacing. Ultimately, through my observations and experiences, it is typically *much* harder for a feature film VFX pro to adapt to a television schedule than for a television VFX pro to adapt to the pacing of a feature film production. Anyway, I digress.

As I have been all over the place in terms of studio hops, I must add that seasons *do* change from time to time. Personally, as someone who is too consumed by the job to keep track of these seasonal periods, I must confess that this is as much knowledge as I can share when it comes to identifying the *exact* peak periods in television VFX work (and in feature film work, to a certain extent). What I *do* know, however, is that there are usually *two* such lucrative seasons in any given year and this is usually how it goes in VFX (at least in television): you have a very hot season filled with new projects, pilots, and seasons for the year (note that just because I used the word 'new' does not *necessarily* mean that this surge of projects occurs at the beginning of every new year), followed by a lull (this is where most contractors are let go to find other projects elsewhere), followed by another surge of projects and then a lull period again – and the cycle repeats itself. There have also been times when these two surge seasons occur back-to-back, but from my experience, those are rare. Either way, you'll have to learn how to identify your own peak-and-lull periods once you get in as those tend to change slightly depending on the geography of your VFX market, among other factors.

In short, whether you are new to VFX or have been around the block for a while now, market cycles do exist in our industry whether you are aware of it or not. Now, I personally have not had any issues finding work (after I gained a significant amount of experience over time) during the dry seasons in VFX, but if you are just starting out, brace yourself for a potential lack of work coming in during those times. Unless you learn how to time the market accordingly (which you will only learn in due course – no single book is going to teach you that, to be honest), I advise having a significant portion of savings to ride you through the pockets of emptiness until the next peak season. That, or you could try entering the feature film niche in VFX (which is difficult as a beginner but not impossible, depending on what VFX role you are willing to take). Again, at the risk of sounding like a broken record, don't let this scare you if VFX is truly your passion. It is all about coming into it with a certain degree of market awareness (and hopefully some self-awareness as well) in order to know when to get the jobs and where. I'll say it again once more for those who weren't paying attention: a dry season in VFX work does not mean that there is *no work out there*, it just means that there is *less* work going around; but certainly, if you look hard enough and are qualified for the job, there will be work available throughout the entire year. It really depends on what your current position is in terms of your experience in handling VFX work.

## It's not you, it's just business

So, what if you have *just* lost a job doing VFX (and by losing a job, I mean your contract has ended, you weren't kept on the team for some reason, and you're now having problems finding work at another studio)? Well, if you want to blame anything, blame the economics of business (including the business of VFX, of course). You see, sometimes it all boils down to market cycles when artists who happen to be caught in the crossfire of the changing tides and seasons get let go or aren't retained by VFX studios as there simply isn't enough work coming in to go around. As a VFX professional, you should come to expect this so that you are less likely to be disappointed. As explained in excruciating detail in the earlier part of this chapter, sometimes market factors and external conditions of the economy *can* and *will* have a say in whether you get to keep the job or not; so, it is possible for you to actually blame the world for this (if you're that kind of person), ha. The sad truth is that just as certain roles in the filmmaking business are easily disposable and replaceable (like your technicians, grips, set decorators, et cetera), VFX artists, unfortunately, are just as disposable and replaceable as they come. So, if you don't suck at your job and you got let go of, it's *really* not your fault – and I really mean it when I say that (though who am I to speak, I've never had to experience being let go based on market factors unless it was part of my plan).

Let's start with a simple example to help shed some light on how market timing can actually dictate whether you stay or leave a studio (and get a subsequent job elsewhere thereafter). Let's say you work as a hired tour guide specifically for summer activities in Wyoming. The company that employs you specializes in summer fishing, boating, all those typical summer activities a family would do when they visit Wyoming. Fantastic. So, as a hired hand you do your job bringing tourists, adventurous locals, and the occasional new resident or two to Snake River to enjoy some fun under the sun – catching fish and then tossing them back, et cetera. Autumn comes rolling around and you are still doing fine at the Wyoming company – you're getting good tips, getting paid bi-weekly, all's well. Then the leaves soon empty the trees and here comes winter. Well, since the company (foolishly, from a business perspective) only does summer activities in Wyoming and it is now the winter season, the incoming tourists are no longer interested in booking the company's activities. Since there is not enough income coming in to pay you *and* keep the lights on for administration and so on, your contract ends, and you are let go as a tour guide for now. On that note, you'll have to look for another tour company (and perhaps if you have enough business sense, you'll work for one that has activities for all seasons of Wyoming). I hope that example helps in some sense.

Anyway, back to VFX. It really is just incoming business that is driving your VFX studios and their executive decisions. Just like the Wyoming tour company, when times are hard and dry with a lack of incoming work, contractors and some employees will be let go as the studio is simply unable to retain them (and even if they did, they would have nothing to do other than sit at their desks and accumulate unnecessary overhead for the company). Likewise, if it's the time of the year when new pilots and projects are coming in, you'll find that you not only have a *lot* more shots to work with, but you'll probably get to work on as many as seven to ten productions at once! Amazing difference, ain't it? With that in mind, of course, it's important to start planning ahead *before* you get let go of or your contract ends. For me, I find that having another contract already lined up serves in my best interests, regardless of whether or not I know that my contract at the current studio is going to be extended. While it surely is tempting to leave your fate in the hands of your employer, as an artist, know that *no one* is going to look after your best interests other than yourself. So, don't wait until you realize you are caught in a lull period to make your exit plan. Plan ahead, plan early, and cover your own hide – especially if you are one of those who have student loan debts and simply cannot afford a break in your earning history. If nothing else, let it be known that if you're let go of or your contract ends without being renewed, you shouldn't take it personally. It's just business and it's just Hollywood (and its market cycles). This is probably one of the only times when the phrase, "it's not you, it's me," is actually relevant. Sometimes, it *really* isn't you and it *really* is your studio (which means, it's the industry's market cycle). Tell *that* to your ex, ha (I'm joking, don't go and do that – that's a *terrible* idea!).

## A game of anticipation

Ultimately, if you want to thrive in the world of VFX and Hollywood, you've got to anticipate the peak periods and the struggling doldrums, as both will occur during your lifetime as a VFX artist. Not to scare you, dear reader, but if you are starting out as a VFX artist (*especially* if you are totally new to the United States as well) chances are that if you're not too careful, you may find yourself in a job rut if you don't know how to position yourself and time the VFX market. Again, as we established earlier in this chapter, there are no specific dates or set timeline for when peaks and valleys occur in VFX (let alone in most industries) as these timelines have the tendency to shift due to broader economic trends and changes, accompanied by any major anomalies such as a pandemic, for example. Thus, I would be doing you a personal *disservice* by pretending to know what these exact dates and timelines are (but hey, at least you are now aware that these cycles even *exist*) for peak periods. You'll have to experience them for yourself to make your own judgment call and come to your own conclusions (unless you are willing to pay someone a billion bucks for them to hold your hand and tell you all the answers – even then, their answers might not work for your unique situation). It is only through the route of personal exploration would you then *fully* understand how each market cycle works and how long each market cycle generally lasts. Keep in mind, of course, that it may be slightly different every year.

By anticipating the global consumer sentiment and herd mentality of movie-goers – and how that consequently impacts the megalodon that is Hollywood – you, reader, will be able to play the game reasonably well and get in (and out) of the industry when projects are ripe for the taking or falling short in supply. Going back full circle on this: do you *need* to know or understand the fundamentals of economics in order to get into or succeed in VFX? Absolutely not. Would it be useful general knowledge to know anyway in order for you to optimize yourself as a creative thinker in a creative industry? Yes. Again, understanding economics and consumer behavior is *not* a prerequisite in any endeavor in VFX or filmmaking – but it sure does help whenever you want to fine-tune your career or life strategy.

# 8

# WORD TRAVELS FAR

Man, oh man, was that a heavy load of information for you – especially if you, dear reader, are one of those who are solely focused on the creative arts and deliberately shun any subject (perhaps reminding you of your good ol' school days) that has traditionally been associated with being dry or dull like economics, mathematics, or perhaps even computer programming. Anyway, we are now out of that neck of the woods and can pick up where we left off with the life of a VFX artist and how the VFX industry works. If the earlier chapters focused on what makes the VFX industry as well as the different ways to be involved in the industry, this chapter goes specifically into how to get into the industry and, more importantly, how to *stay* in the industry. I remember one time when I went for an interview at Blur Studio (this was some years back) and spoke to the lady of

HR at the time, Monica. She gave me a quick tour around the Blur Studio block where artists work and where different departments and rooms are situated, yadda, yadda, eventually leading the two of us up into a quiet conference room for a quick, casual chat about upcoming works and projects. I believe I was seated on a really comfortable (but huge) couch (either way, that's not important) and Monica basically went over my résumé and asked me some questions. "So, when we received your name in our list that we collect from our job listing, what we do is basically shoot out an email to our connections at other studios we know to ask if anyone has had any experience or positive words to say about any individuals on this list, and then Mike (let's call him that) came back from [Studio Name Redacted] saying that he knows you and that we should definitely check you out, and that you're good," she said. "Oh? Really? Wow, I didn't expect him to do that," I replied in genuine surprise. "So, how long have you been working with Mike at [Studio Name Redacted]?" Monica continued. Now, the interesting thing about that situation is that I had actually *never* had the opportunity to work directly with Mike at [Studio Name Redacted]. In fact, what *did* happen was that I was also invited to tour his studio some time ago for an interview for another production but, as our schedules did not align, I did not have the opportunity to work with or under Mike at [Studio Name Redacted]. Shame. With that context established, however, I was actually *genuinely* surprised Mike recommended me without having ever worked with me because he was so impressed by what I could do even when we hadn't worked together. The point of the story is to show that hey, studios *do* talk with one another – even if they are in competition, in a manner of speaking, with one another – and word really *does* travel. Thus, in this chapter, I will break down how to get the word out about your work and yourself in the sense of breaking through a studio's barriers to entry, and then being so incredibly awesome that you will have gained your own Mike to help put in a good word for you (even if you two haven't even worked together yet). Oh, and if you want to know the ending to that story, I told Monica honestly that I hadn't worked with Mike before and of course, whilst she was surprised by that, needless to say, she was still impressed that Mike had such positive things to say even though we hadn't worked together yet. Honestly, I too was so surprised that I had to drop a note to Mike to thank him for that. Once again – thank you, Mike.

## Interviews, tests, and other checks

Now, I know I have covered this a little earlier in the book but, dear reader, I am certain you may be curious to know the *secrets* of how to ace that studio interview, test, et cetera. Well, I hate to break it to you (well, no, not really): there are *no* secrets. Yes, none. Zilch, nada, zero. It really is *just* another typical job or office interview so to that effect you ace it like any other job or office interview – you can even look up generic interview tips on Google and they will apply in the VFX world as well because our industry is no different from any other industry in that regard. What *does* make the interviews, tests, and other checks different from other industries is the extent to which VFX studios *love* to play it safe.

You see, VFX studios, much to your chagrin, are rather risk-averse. They'd much rather hire an old freelancer or returning returnlancer than have to deal with the uncertainties of a new hire. But of course, as established earlier in my treatise, new hires are a must – they're usually young, they've got that vitality and zest for life in them (before VFX drains the life out of them) and they're generally naive about important things like pay and overtime. Hence, VFX studios will still hire them but they will put these new hires through lots of tests – just like your insecure ex-girlfriend did when you two first started dating (or ex-boyfriend or whatever label you want to use). The trick here is to be able to ace these tests that studios will undoubtedly put you through even after you pass the interview stage and get selected for the job. First, let me break down the different barriers to entry you will typically encounter in the VFX world:

## 1. Job Interviews

Number one on this list is rather self-explanatory. You'd have to search *hard* for that needle in the haystack if you think that you could get a job in an industry without having to go through some sort of an interview – in such exceptional cases, it's usually because the employer has already had some prior experience with you or is choosing to "interview" you in other ways. It could even just be nepotism at play. Regardless of how you feel you would do at any sort of interview, expect studios that have had no experience with you personally or professionally to at least conduct some kind of interview. Now, this interview may be highly formal and standard (where you're asked questions on your performance, what you did in a shot, et cetera) to casual and relaxed (true story: a prospective boss once asked me whether I'd rather be a serial killer or a mass killer – yes, it happened and it was a legitimate casual interview question. No, I was not taken aback). From my recollection, most interviews were fairly informal and casual; the studios I have been with generally asked me about my availability and schedule, whether I knew person A from Singapore, or the kind of VR work I did at so-and-so startup. Again, very chill and relaxed. As for the few formal interviews I've had, the studios basically asked me about my experience working with a specific type of project, the other skills I have in my arsenal and of course, schedule and availability. Usually, these formal interviews will also be accompanied by a test or trial of some sort but don't make the mistake of thinking that casual interviewers aren't also testing you through an unspoken trial once you start your job.

As an aspiring VFX artist, you can generally expect these job interviews to lead to several outcomes: you get the job and are scheduled to do an at-home test shot of sorts; you get the job and are to do an in-house test shot live and with a set time limit (occasionally); you get the job and start the job the next day or on a scheduled day you both agreed upon (but you are secretly or being told outright that you are being trialed); you are told that the studio is just "putting out feelers" with their job advertisement and aren't actually looking to hire right now, which happens *very* frequently (so you don't get the job immediately, essentially); or you are told absolutely nothing (of which you should assume you didn't get the job). Now, if you are told absolutely nothing and *really* want to know the outcome of your interview, don't be too pushy. These studios are usually busy, and you should not pester them too much about the outcome of your interview (this is not like in school where you have free reign to pester for feedback until you get some). In fact, if I don't hear back from a VFX studio after an interview, test, or trial (or all of the above), I just move on. I don't even bother reaching out to them because I know it's not me – it's the market (see what I did there?). In all honesty though, it usually *is* the market and typically the case is that the studio has either found a better-suited candidate *or* they were really just looking to build up their database of artists and don't have any work available to bring you (or anyone else) on board. Either way, you shouldn't be offended or upset (I know I felt nothing), just move on to the next conquest as I did. It really *is* business, and it is *nothing* personal if you don't get the job at the time. Move on and move along.

### 2.   VFX In-House Demo or At-Home Test

Now, assuming you did well in the interview – the interviewer liked you or whatever work you showed – we now move along to the next barrier to entry of the VFX in-house demo or take-home test. It is exactly as it sounds: you do a shot live at the VFX studio's premises or you go back home and the coordinator, producer, whoever sends you a quick shot or image to work with. Frankly, I've done them all – from the take-home tests of compositing a still image in Nuke to compositing a screen replacement on captured footage of a cell phone, to even going all the way to Burbank via a three-hour public transportation trip to complete a VFX shot under pressure and under time constraints. Heck, that Burbank test was really fun though; it really felt like an examination room when I entered, as the VFX studio had set the in-house test up in such a way that multiple artists being tested showed up all at the same time to take the same test (but with different shots so that other artists could not "copy" from the rest). Even the computers were positioned in a way to prevent such "copying." How does *that* sound for an *actual* VFX studio examination? Either way, I was soon told after the intense (and timed) test that the studio was mainly just looking to add new artists to their database and that they weren't currently looking to hire someone immediately, so, that's what came of that. Now, you'll hear me mention this reason quite often (the fact that studios will put you through trial by fire only to tell you at the end of the day that they're just looking around to add to their artist database) because it is true that VFX studios do this a lot of the time. Don't be put off by it – they're just doing what VFX businesses would do when they are genuinely looking for new recruits – *in the future*. As you can already tell, VFX studios like to plan ahead (adding on to their well-known risk aversion).

As an aspiring VFX artist and depending on your level of experience when you encounter this barrier to entry, you needn't "study" or "prepare" ahead of time like an obsessive straight-A student in school. The test isn't really *that* serious. All you really need to know in advance is how to use the software and how to execute the task with utmost efficiency. Now, you technically won't know what the shot is (unless you are given an at-home test to complete), but this shouldn't be an issue if you are *genuinely* skilled and are confident in your VFX capabilities. Seriously, don't take these tests too seriously (I'm looking at all you Asians out there reading this, I know we tend to be incredibly hard on ourselves when it comes to anything with the word 'exam' or 'test'). Anyway, depending on the type of test you get as well as the position you are vying for, you'll generally encounter the following scenarios: you get a still image to be composited, modelled, textured, et cetera (depending on the VFX position you are aiming for) at home using the software they tell you to use (or whatever software you have, if they don't have a preference); you get captured footage to be used for the assignment to be completed at home (sometimes they may give you a time limit or ask you to track it in their temporary system); you have to travel to their studio location to complete a shot in-person with or without a time limit (though you can bet that they'll be curious to know how long you took to complete the task) and then leave the studio to await further instructions or next steps via email; or you travel to their studio location to do a "test day" performing on live shots for the day (with payment, of course) and then leaving the studio to await their next steps and follow-up via email (if the studio liked your performance that day). Again, the combination of scenarios is endless though you can bet that VFX studios are definitely getting more creative these days with their shot tests and assignments. The best preparation for these tests is to expect the unexpected and know your capabilities (as well as limitations) going in.

### 3. Trial Hire

Ok, so let's say you passed the interview, passed the in-house test, and are now onto the next phase. Now, this barrier to entry *may or may not* come right after your VFX shot test but trial hires nowadays are popular among plenty of VFX studios – especially since most of them generally skip the in-house assessment and would rather see you at their desk, performing and executing shots as a trial. Personally, I've been through plenty of trial hire phases with all of them concluding successfully. Some VFX studios (and even startups) like having a set number of days or weeks to "try you out" as an artist, whereas others are a bit more extreme and take to extending the trial period for as long as months (perhaps because they are too risk-averse or just can't find a vacant position for you but want to keep you around for some reason). Either way, I've been through it all: one-day trials, month-to-month trials, half-a-day trials – anything you can name, I've done it. It's funny because these studios will usually bring it up in the interview or meeting and they definitely have no shame in hiding the fact that they wanted to try me out first. I've heard everything from "Well, I'm not going to hire you full-time if I don't even know how you work" to "We're going to put you on a trial, and we'll see how it goes." Again, it's the way the industry is – just accept it (it's normal). As for what I've generally been tasked to do during trials, well, I really just see it as the start of my job. The only *real* difference between your actual contract work and trial work is that the word "trial" is being used instead of "contract" – other than that, there really is *no* difference between a trial period and actual "contract work." Again, this was my experience having done many, many trials – it is possible that things may have changed since then (though I highly doubt it). In essence, a trial is like a soft commitment to hiring you, and the chances of the VFX studio *not* hiring you after a trial are rare.

As an aspiring VFX artist, honestly, don't sweat too much about being a trial hire. Heck, if it seems like this whole time I've been telling you not to worry it's because, really, you *shouldn't* (if you are well-trained, can think for yourself, and have the VFX skills to boot to begin with). On the other hand, if you, dear reader, are an *aspiring* VFX artist and this is your first trial ever, then here is what I would suggest you do: definitely treat your trial period as the start of your official work, because you will surely be given *real* work from *real* productions. This isn't the time when studios give you fake shots, test shots, or shots from already-distributed movies to "try you out." Oh, no. This is the time when they *really* use you as the position that you applied for and put you to work. You'll be working on *real* shots, no doubt about it. Another aspect the studio would be watching you for is how you engage and interact with the supervisor and your team. After all, they're bringing you in as a trial hire for a reason – they do want to see how you work with others and how you communicate. Hence, if nothing else, make sure you're professional and at least communicating your needs and wants with regard to the shots you're working on. There's nothing worse than an artist who keeps to themselves and ends up wasting ten hours going in the wrong direction (and I've seen this happen at work many times with all sorts of artists and have often overhead supervisors complaining about these individuals at or after lunch). Ultimately, as long as you take your "trial" status seriously – and in my opinion, treat it as if you already *got* the job – you should breeze through this phase with little to no issues. Like I said, the chances of a studio *not* keeping you onboard after your trial period ends are rare; they'd probably only do that if you do something crazy like sharing the shot you're working on on Facebook (and then getting yourself fired and possibly blacklisted from the VFX industry forever).

## 4. Renewal-by-Continuous-Assessment

Now, this is sort of an extended version of a trial – I did hint at this earlier as the trial that continues month-to-month – so everything I had said about trials generally applies here with *one* exception: you are *constantly* on-trial. I admit this does seem a little extreme when applied in VFX (and thus far, the only encounter I've had of this nature was at a startup), but one can't really fault the VFX studio for being this extreme. From my communications and interactions with others in the industry, I've heard many horror stories of hires being unfit for the role or proving themselves to be the "wrong" hire after a certain period of time; either they lied about their portfolio (more on that later in the next chapter), lied in their résumés, cannot perform under pressure or are just plain nasty people to work with. VFX studios have since become increasingly cautious of hiring and turning freelancers into employees (which partially also explains why this industry is predominantly a freelancer's world). For the one instance that I was put through this renewal-by-continuous-assessment, it basically went down smoothly; I was first given a one-month trial, did my duties and performed my tasks dutifully, then met with the co-founders to discuss renewal or the extension of the contract. During that discussion, they simply said that they had wanted to try me out some more and so they did. My contract was extended for another three months (or possibly six months) when the termination clause had been changed from a stipulated date to "at-will" (meaning, I could terminate my own contract anytime on my own accord). This is basically another way of saying "you're hired, but we don't want to give you that false sense of security of being an employee, so we're going to still put you on trial (forever)," though I didn't have a problem with the situation per se. In the end, I was the one to end the contract as I simply was no longer stimulated by the work I was tasked to do at the startup – and that was the end of that.

As an aspiring VFX artist, expect this type of situation to be rare – *really* rare. In fact, I can assure you that the chances of you being placed on a renewal-by-continuous-assessment are much higher if you choose to work at startups instead of your standard VFX studios (no matter their size). Of course, with that being said, it doesn't mean that the "assessment" is necessarily over and done with once you pass their one-week or one-month trial period.

Remember that even if you did pass the trial, should you ever fail to perform or fail to keep up the charade from your trial days, then you will most likely be brought into HR and perhaps have your contract renegotiated or shortened. On the other hand, let's say on the off-chance that you do encounter this renewal-by-continuous-assessment scenario, you can generally expect the situation to pan out in the following ways: you pass the initial trial phase and get placed on a monthly contract that gets revisited every month and renewed on a monthly basis; you pass the initial trial phase and get placed on a "perpetual trial" contract that has a clause that allows for the contract to be revisited whenever it makes sense (so, you're basically an employee without being an employee); or, you pass the initial trial phase and are told to come back for the next week (and the subsequent weeks, and so on), with no official documentation to formalize your work period. As you can see, depending on the VFX studio you are dealing with, you may get all kinds of vagueness when it comes to whether you are staying and for how long. As long as you keep putting in your best effort – trial or no trial – you can reassure yourself that you're most definitely staying with the studio for the long haul until they tell you otherwise.

### 5.   Deliberately Vague Contract Terms

Ah yes, speaking of vagueness, we have vague contract terms. Don't we all love those? I hope you recognize my sarcasm. Anyway, this is simply one of the many strategies a VFX studio can employ to prevent themselves from hiring the "wrong" person. How does a vague contract help, you wonder? Quite simply, it allows VFX studios several out-clauses should a situation with a hire go awry. Whilst nothing this dire has personally happened in my career, I have actually encountered contracts with incredibly vague terms. Heck, some of them weren't even contracts at all but emails with a brief list of the role, pay, and work terms (even though, to be honest, that's pretty much all the information you need in order to start work at any VFX studio these days). Of course, once I got there, I had to sign a bunch of documents on confidentiality, sexual harassment, tax information, parking information (if applicable), but even then, I had no proper documentation or contract to stipulate the terms of my employment. Basically, all I had was the email consensus between the two of us (me and the producer at the studio at the time) and while this is usually more than enough to establish a work agreement between two parties, you have to be careful taking up too many of such "contracts" if your plan is for a reliable stream of work. In the end, I was right. Since we didn't have a proper work agreement, there was no means nor obligation to renew the "contract" to begin with; hence, I was there for about a week or less and had wrapped up and moved on to the next thing. Again, not a problem for me personally as I had anticipated that this was going to happen given that the only contract terms I had ever received were in an email and were only about four to five lines long.

As an aspiring VFX artist, receiving a deliberately vague contract might be a bit tricky, especially if you have already been through the trials and tribulations of interviewing for the job (or many other jobs) and getting tested all over the place. To this barrier to entry, I would advise you to use your own judgment to determine if the position (or project, if you happen to know what it will be) is worth the vague contract terms, because if you do decide to take the job and go past this barrier, know that the length of your employment may *always* be up in the air. In my opinion, a VFX studio that doesn't even have the time to draft out an official contract for its freelancers, employees, or new hires is either extremely disorganized, just starting out, or both. Again, I'll leave it up to you, as an aspiring VFX artist, to decide if you do indeed want to go past this gate, as it's entirely subjective to how you take to dealing with not exactly knowing where you stand with your employer. Just remember that if you *do* choose to go past this barrier and accept the deliberately vague contract terms, there is no one else to blame should you feel uncertain about your length of stay or if one day you find that you're told not to come in anymore (and that your "contract" had been ended for you because you're no longer needed). I recommend playing this by ear and always be looking out for *your* best interests. If you like having a proper schedule and a proper contract, ask for one; if the studio declines and says it's not their style, find a different studio to work at that suits you better.

### 6. Preliminary Background Checks and Surprise Reference Calls

Whilst I did bring this up in what feels like eons ago, in this chapter, we're specifically referring to how preliminary background checks (including drug tests and reference calls) sometimes act as an additional barrier to entry for the position you're vying for. Not a big deal if you know you're coming in clean and not abusing any substances – the only real kicker here is the part where the studio does a few reference checks by calling up your past employers. You see, one of the many traits of the majority of VFX people (at least those who stay in the industry for a good while) is that they have a tendency to be honest (whether that be to their benefit or not), so to that extent one of the many traits of the VFX industry is its propensity to be honest regardless of how it sounds. Heck, I wouldn't exactly pick a random VFX person to be a tactful diplomat, if you know what I mean. So, know this: should your prospective employer call up any of your past employers to ask about you, you bet that they'll tell the truth. After all, talent-poaching is not really a thing in VFX (a topic we will discuss later) so there really is no downside for your past employers to be telling the truth about you. Of course, most of the time, you won't even know who they called, so there really is no point in fretting over this part of the process. Trust that if you did a good job in the past and didn't step on anyone's toes with your abrasive or aggressive personality, your past employers will only have fantastic words to say about you. I am sure that at some point in my studio-hopping escapades I've had one or two studios dial up past employers on my résumé and asked about me (no question about it), though the fact that I still got the job anyway proves that, really, there is nothing to worry about with regard to those reference calls. It's just part of the process – and part of most processes in any other industry as well. As for background checks and drug tests, well ... let's just say that if you are an immigrant or foreigner coming into the industry, you *really* have nothing to worry about. And no, studios don't go all the way to your country to check your background or criminal record (it's just not that extreme, nor is the position worth the financial expenditure or effort). Unless you are being hired into the C-suite of a company, chances are that VFX studios won't try to dig up your overseas records if you are coming from another country. I mean, seriously, they're just hiring you as an artist – if they find something they didn't like, they'll just replace you with someone else. It's that simple.

As an aspiring VFX artist, know that going through background checks, reference checks, and in rare instances even drug tests is simply part of the process of being hired in *any* industry. As long as you didn't kill anyone (or commit an offense of moral turpitude, which will also impact your immigration status by the way) in the United States, you can expect to pass these background checks with flying colors. Drug tests in and of themselves are also exceedingly rare in VFX and I've only ever done one for this major conglomerate of a VFX studio; so, unless you are applying to one of the "bigs," I wouldn't necessarily fret over peeing in a cup and being tested for anabolic steroids or whatever it is kids take these days. The only real thing you have control over is how your reference calls end up sounding to your prospective VFX employer; to that, I recommend pre-empting negative recommendations by simply bringing your best to *every single* job you get – whether it's an internship, production assistant role or even working as a temporary barista at Starbucks. Don't think for a second that just because your previous job is in the food and beverage industry that VFX studios aren't going to call them up and ask about you. And of course, let me reemphasize that it is *highly unlikely* that a studio will try to call an *overseas* employer; time zone differences make that difficult enough, and depending on the position they are hiring for, sometimes, the studio will just take that risk and try you out for themselves. Of course, regardless of whether your résumé is mostly from your home country or whether you have been a waiter for five years before deciding to jump into VFX, never underestimate how word of mouth gets around and the fact that your prospective VFX employer can always use social media or email to reach your foreign employers if they're *really* serious about finding out about you.

### 7.   LinkedIn and Social Media Cross-Referencing

On that note, if there is any barrier to entry that you should *actually* be wary of, it's this one. Though I've never actually had an issue with LinkedIn and social media cross-referencing costing me a job (because back then my social media presence was practically and conveniently non-existent), I would generally tread lightly with this one. As proven in my earlier example of how studios talk, you can bet that VFX studios these days *will* look you up on LinkedIn to see if they have any mutual connections with people you both know. If they do, chances are they'll hit them up on LinkedIn (fairly easy to do nowadays, especially with read receipts) and ask about you as an artist and as a team player. If the HR person or producer looking you up on LinkedIn doesn't have any mutual connections (which is rare), then they'll proceed to find you on other social media platforms (think Facebook, Twitter, Instagram, and maybe YouTube) to see what you do *outside* of work, what your interests are, and, more importantly, if your *values* align with what they believe at the company. While VFX studios aren't necessarily as stringent when it comes to finding the "company-fit" compared to tech startups, they *do* care that you're at least not going around putting ten million close-up pictures of your butt, your alcoholic rampages, or your sexual escapades online. Ain't nobody who is serious about VFX work got the time nor tolerance to put up with that partying crap. Needless to say, the VFX industry is somewhat conservative in nature (and no, I *don't* mean politically), at least compared to industries like game development or even animation. Though there isn't necessarily a professional dress code (you don't have to wear formal office wear like a noob), they certainly have standards when it comes to attire, punctuality, and (of course) your behavior on-site (and to some extent, off-site as well). While I don't have my own personal anecdotes to share about this one, nor have I heard of any interesting stories from others, just know that VFX studios *do* look you up on social media even if they are being incredibly discreet about it (to the extent that there aren't even stories to tell on this topic).

As an aspiring VFX artist, the best way to pass this barrier to entry is to curate the content you put out on social media and on LinkedIn. Now, LinkedIn is a bit more forgivable as I have seen some VFX veterans and pros not update their profile in what appears to be more than a decade and they are still doing very well in the VFX industry (some of them are either senior artists or supervisors at this point). LinkedIn isn't going to be your main instigator of problems here. The *real* danger is on the more "casual" platforms like Facebook, Twitter, Instagram, Snapchat, and the like where your temptation to be authentic is *much* higher, emboldened by the fact that, "hey, everyone else is being real, so why shouldn't I?" Now, I am not saying that you should be fake, but you definitely want to be careful not to be too *extreme* in any one endeavor that has historically drawn the ire of the public. For example, if you work as a part-time stripper or escort ... maybe don't boast about it too much on social media if you're looking to get a desk job in VFX. If you're a hardcore Trump supporter ... maybe mellow that down a little as well if you're looking to jump into Hollywood VFX. You know what I mean. You can still be you, of course, just tone down the extremities a bit – you never know when a simple post or tweet may cost you a job at a Hollywood studio these days. Now, if you find it hard to control the content you put out for the world to see, then you could also consider setting your social media profiles to private, deleting them (I know this might be a *big* ask nowadays), or just pretending that these VFX studios (or any other employer which applies to you) are your parents – and by that, I mean, don't put anything out there that you wouldn't want your mother to see. All in all, LinkedIn and social media will usually be the last step in any company's verification and hiring process to reassure themselves that they've made the right choice in hiring you as a VFX person. Don't screw that up by not curating what you put out into the world. We live in a world today where others *will* judge you for your social media presence (or lack thereof), so rather than complaining about how biased and unfair that is (which it is), the best way to counter that is to play the game and ensure you're the winning player, regardless of what your personal feelings are about social media's role in employment.

Now that we have those barriers to entry done and dusted, let me walk you through how a typical smart person goes about the verification and recruitment process of being hired for a job in VFX. We begin first with the interview. Now, it should be common sense that in *any* interview for *any* job in *any* industry, companies will expect you to know the company you're applying to. Hence, a typical smart person will spend time researching the company, learning about their past works as well as the kind of VFX that is generally their specialty. From there, the smart person (let's call him Logan) will also know his own work and résumé *very* well – meaning, he will remember exactly what he did in that shot and how to verbally describe *how* he did it and with what software. Logan will also know how to answer basic interview questions that (surprisingly) tend to stumble a lot of people such as "Tell me about yourself" or "Where do you see yourself in X-number of years?" Of course, Logan being a smart dude will know that regardless of how you answer the question, the most important thing is to give the studio the answer you believe they would like to hear. For example, you don't necessarily want to tell the VFX studio that you plan to become an artist at Disney or Pixar when you are currently applying to Studio 123. I mean, why on Earth would they hire you then (why would anyone)? Now, you might be thinking: isn't that duplicitous? Maybe – it depends on how you see it. Does it work though? Yes. So, Logan makes sure that whilst he *is* honest, he is also *selective* in his honesty when it comes to his goals – especially if his goals would be in *direct* conflict with the VFX studio's goals when it comes to certain questions (essentially, don't tell your interviewer something that you believe will become a conflict of interest and prevent you from being hired in the first place). So, Logan passes the interview and the interviewer then proceeds to lead Logan to a room for an in-house demo (usually, the demo will be done *before* the interview just so that most of your energy is invested in doing the intense work first). Logan, knowing that such VFX tests have been implemented for a while and have gained popularity amongst studios, came prepared having done some practice shots at home earlier in the day. He goes in, completes the timed test, and then is told by the interviewer: "Ok! That's it for today. Good job. We will update you via email on our next steps." Logan goes home.

Now, on the studio's end (let's call this Studio 123), the interviewer (usually an HR person with zero VFX experience) will then get a senior artist or team lead to assess all in-house shots done – from their work files to the way the shot's results look; after getting the 'OK' from the assessor, the interviewer will then proceed to conduct other checks and prepare the onboarding documents for Logan. While the interviewer-recruiter does this, a few phone calls will be made to Logan's past employers on his résumé. "Hi, this is Allie from Studio 123, I'm calling about a Logan who used to work at your studio. Basically, we would kind of like to find out how he did as a 3D artist at your studio before we hire him." Logan's past studios, being honest and direct, will then share their experiences with and of Logan to Studio 123 accordingly; and of course, Logan, being the smart person that he is, already saw this coming, so he left all his previous jobs on a good note. His past employers had nothing to say but positive words. After this step of the process is done (usually amounting to two to three days), the interviewer will then follow up on Logan with an email requesting certain information and documents to be completed. These usually include mandatory background checks, tax information, a studio handbook (if applicable), and an official employment contract with terms. Logan looks them over, agrees to the background checks, and signs all documents; these documents are then processed by Studio 123. Within a week, Studio 123 has checked up on Logan's background and processed his documents and Logan is good to start the following Monday. Bada bing, bada boom – there goes Logan, the new trial-hire 3D artist at Studio 123. And that is just *one* of the many ways the recruitment process can pan out.

In summary, VFX studios are naturally risk-averse and can employ as many barriers to entry as they like depending on their reputation, their past experiences with hires, and industry trends of the day. The chances of them continuing to test you even after you get hired is quite high but that is the norm with almost any other company in any other industry out there today. These days the trend has shifted to more in-house testing and trial-hire contracts where interviews, which used to be seen as a significant barrier to entry, are now seen more as an ancillary step mainly used to collect basic information such as your schedule, availability, and the like. Reference calls and social media cross-referencing will continue to play a minor role (but a role nonetheless) in the hiring process so, no matter how much you *loathe* your working hours (honestly, you will get the same working hours no matter which studio you go to), your boss, or even just the lame snacks they serve up to artists, you *must* leave every job on a good note. Think of it this way: people are biased, and they will be biased – for better or worse. Wouldn't you rather have the studio you left be biased *for* you rather than against you? Keep in mind that your past performance and behavior at previous jobs may be requested by your prospective employer, so make sure you actually have the chops to begin with and *actually* worked at said studio on your résumé (a résumé is one of those things that just cannot be faked without dire consequences).

Now, on the off chance that you're actually a VFX studio reading this, well, you know how it goes. When it comes to reference calls, don't just call one studio on that résumé. If it applies, call multiple, randomly selected studios. And if you're dead-set serious or hiring someone for a *major* lead position, consider even dropping by said studio (though as a studio owner, I doubt you'll have the personal time to do this) and meeting up with the former boss of a prospective hire for lunch. You know what I mean. From the perspective of the employer, the more you get to verify someone or something with your *own* eyes and your *own* mind, the better. Oh, and make sure that your VFX shot tests *actually* reflect real-world scenarios. Don't be that guy that sends a prospective hire a 640 x 500-pixel still image comp test (it actually happened to me and it was the easiest test I had ever taken). Also, drug tests are ridiculously unnecessary and dumb. You're not organizing a natural bodybuilding competition, come on, let's be real here.

## These four walls speak

Following up on reference calls and inter-studio communications, let's talk office chat – namely, office gossip. Now, dear reader, let's say you've got in and made it – huzzah! You're officially on-contract (whether it's as a freelancer, employee, intern, or trial hire) and are now executing your tasks day-by-day, according to what the studio demands. Perfect. This section of the chapter is all about the unseen "communication" that tends to go on in typical office environments and enclosed spaces – namely, the unseen politics amongst your co-workers and amongst upper management. You see, while studios certainly *do* speak with other studios (what I would define as inter-studio communication) through reference checks or just random back-and-forth via collaborative productions, intra-studio communications occur more frequently than you may be aware of. Heck, there is a reason why this sub-chapter is titled 'These four walls speak' – because they certainly do, even if you never hear them directly. These walls speak outwardly (to other studios) and inwardly (within the studio walls). I'll cover the former in the next chapter which includes gossip, but for now, let's tackle how your studio walls bounce "information" across the room and through many, many ears.

Firstly, you should always be aware that regardless of how "creative" you believe your industry to be – whether it's working in filmmaking, graphic design, or visual effects – an office is an office is an office. A VFX studio is still an office, a production office is still an office, a creative advertising firm on the 11th floor of some fancy building is still ... you guessed it, an office. As such, you should treat offices like any typical corporate space where people congregate – where there is congregation, there will be group dynamics and politics involved. You *cannot* escape office politics no matter *where* you go or *where* you work. Human dynamics and consequently politics are an inherent part of human nature so they will continue to persist for as long as we exist (hey, that rhymed). The best way to deal with office politics is to navigate them with awareness and present yourself in a professional manner. In fact, you should assume that anything you say within these four walls *will* be audible, so if you have any negative thoughts or opinions (about the way things work, how certain people are, et cetera) that tend to go against the cultural or corporate norm of the studio you are currently working at, it's better to choose *not* to speak – even if you think you are alone. Of course, while most people in VFX aren't gossipy types by nature (though I notice that the ones who tend to be are mostly women in design or production roles), you shouldn't assume that people don't talk about you or about people. I have more fun examples of this in action in the next chapter but for now, let's just say that you should be careful of what you say and how you say things at your workplace (common sense, yes, but not necessarily common practice) – especially if you see yourself staying at said studio for the long haul; even if you don't like your work environment, remember those future reference calls your prospective employers could make. Access to your previous workplace records is only a phone call away.

Let me illustrate this with an incident that happened at one of the places I worked at. Now, this was a very small studio (almost micro in team size) with about two other artists, the founder, and an accountant-administrator person. I believe the studio had rented two rooms in this building, so quite a small set-up for a VFX studio. Interestingly enough, this studio has actually been around for several years but decided to keep their office space and upkeep small (and strategically, this is considered a good move when it comes to eliminating unnecessary overhead), so, due to the frugality of the situation, the two rooms are naturally connected to one another by a simple wall. Ok, nothing fancy there. Anyway, I remember at one point in my conversation with the two other VFX pros that one of them was discussing the manager's management style and how other freelancers had complained about the manager being a bit of a micromanager. Notice that this was the feedback shared by *other* freelancers of this manager. "Oh, really? That's interesting. Well, I don't really get that vibe from him," I replied. Honestly, I didn't actually get that vibe from the manager – and trust me, being somewhat of a control freak myself, I know a micromanager when I see one, and he wasn't it (at least, not by my standards). Either way, the conversation eventually trailed off and we continued working on our shots. About two hours later around lunchtime, the manager then popped by from the next room and asked everyone if they were planning to go to lunch (or something trivial like that), we all responded accordingly based on the shots we had on our plate at the time. After I responded, however, the manager randomly made it clear that he was working on being *less* of a micromanager these days before wrapping that thought up and walking off (I didn't even get a chance to respond). A classic case of how these four walls speak. Heck, I wasn't even the one who brought up the conversation *nor* had that opinion of him and yet somehow the conversation made it appear as if the opinions of all those other freelancers also applied to me. Now, I don't actually remember if I had corrected the manager on that misconception or not but what I will say is this: watch what you say and be careful of the conversations you *do* decide to partake in – especially if you are a new hire. Nothing is worse than having an innocent conversation be misconstrued in a way that could impact your relationship with your peers, your boss, or your future job prospects.

Now, while that incident didn't actually have an impact on my career whatsoever (because honestly, I didn't have that view of the manager being a micromanager to begin with), I can only imagine the potential detriment it *could* have caused had the conversation with the other co-workers been about anything else more damning or touchy (such as how the office was managed or topics on political movements and the like). As we all know, words get re-interpreted, paraphrased, and misinterpreted through each individual in all workplace gossip and banter, and while you can't avoid office politics and gossip, you can do your best to still be engaged with your peers by keeping your thoughts simple, concise and PG. After all, if they say that the hills have eyes (movie reference, anyone?), then trust that these walls have ears and mouths too.

### Good employees vs. great employees

Now, let's imagine you're the boss of a company for a moment. What would *you* personally see as a good versus a great employee? Stew on that for a moment and actually seriously ponder over it. Can you tell the difference? Notice that your opinion on what constitutes a good or great employee will ultimately depend on your life experiences, your own experiences, and views on your current or previous co-workers and managers, as well as your cultural and societal background (to a certain extent). Regardless of the conclusion you came to for that little exercise, you will find that there *are* in fact universally agreed-upon traits and qualities that separate good employees from great employees (at least based on research and studies put together by your top B-schools and various management consulting firms). Here is a quick breakdown of the traits and qualities that distinguish a great employee from a good employee (VFX artist or not):

- A good employee shows up on time.
  - o A great employee shows up early (though not in a showy kind of way).
- A good employee does as he or she is told and executes the task by meeting the bare minimum.
  - o A great employee goes above and beyond the task assigned and craves for more.
- A good employee does not socialize with co-workers that much and tends to focus on the job.
  - o A great employee makes an effort to appear approachable and shows an interest in the lives and activities of their co-workers beyond the job.
- A good employee hits their deadlines on time.
  - o A great employee finishes their tasks *way* before the deadline and asks for more work.
- A good employee is content with his or her current position at work.
  - o A great employee seeks for more responsibility where it makes sense.

- A good employee stays late because he or she was told to do so (and because it's required).
  - o A great employee stays late because he or she *wants* to contribute more to the team.
- A good employee meets a studio's expectations because it's part of the job.
  - o A great employee exceeds the expectations of what their job entails (and there is a way to do this in VFX as opposed to simply "overworking" or "over-massaging" the VFX in your shot).

Now, I am not here to give you the playbook on how to be an awesome employee – you will have to navigate that by yourself since the situation you find yourself in will be entirely unique to you (and the studio you're with) – but in general, you can expect that VFX studios are always going to search for valuable team players to add to their list of employees, even if VFX is one giant, gig-based economy. The reason for this is because VFX studios are still businesses and they still want to scale as businesses do. Most of the time, scaling up involves hiring and keeping the right team and one simply cannot do that if they're intending to remain as a small, lean VFX studio all year round by only hiring freelancers as needed. On that token, the VFX studio would need to recruit *and* keep competent loyalists. Of course, there are always going to be pros and cons associated with being a company loyalist through the decades versus living life as a freelancer, but I believe we've already covered some aspect of this earlier in the book (so, feel free to revert to that chapter on how the VFX industry works). What I do want to emphasize in this sub-chapter is that you don't necessarily *have* to be a great employee in VFX if your goal is to *not* be at that studio forever or to be a freelancer (or even a returnlancer). Surprised? Don't be. In fact, it is absolutely fine to just be a *good* employee in VFX and you'll still get a good word out from the employer after your contract ends (if your goal is to hit-it-and-move-on). Not everyone wants to be nor can be the greatest, so unless your intention is to become a mainstay employee and ascend through the ranks, you don't necessarily need to be a "great" employee in order to continue to get work in VFX (trust me on this one, I've seen *many* cases of other artists around me doing this).

If you're still not convinced, I invite you to take a look at the traits and qualities of a good employee alone (without the side-by-side comparison with what makes a great employee). Look at them *hard*. Notice how those traits alone already make you ... well, a good employee anywhere. Let me share a personal anecdote I know of one or two veteran VFX artists who have been with the same studio for what appears to be more than ten years (two people whom I would personally classify as fitting the classic "good employee" trope): our first story is of a senior VFX compositor by the name of Megan. I believe she has been with this studio for more than ten years (possibly even around the time the studio was founded) and she is most likely in her fifties (yes, senior women VFX artists *do* exist). Every day, without fail, Megan would show up on time, sit at her desk with her coffee (and salad for lunch), ignore everyone else and the conversations happening around her (for the most part), and work on her shots. She'd complete them as required and just waits for the next batch of shots to come in. What I noticed about Megan was that she rarely – if ever – went out to lunch with her other co-workers in the department and yet, she's still employed, still at the same studio after over a decade, and is even a senior compositor in the department (all by simply showing up and doing the work as your typical "good" employee). This is the same situation with the other senior compositor I know from the same studio by the name of Eric. Eric is a smart, tall, quiet guy who keeps to himself, rarely communicates with the other compositors unless working on teamed shots, rarely goes out to lunch with others, and, lo and behold, is still there at that very same studio after over a decade (possibly in that very same seat as well). All these two did was show up, do their jobs as *expected* of any good employee, and then finish their workdays (without much emotional commitment or loyalty to the studio's mission or vision itself). You see – it's totally fine to just be *good* in VFX (if your goal is *not* to rise to the upper echelons of some kind of general management).

All in all, VFX studios really only care that you can execute your tasks, stay overtime as required, and do not under-perform or fail to perform in whatever position you are in. You need not be a fanatic or company loyalist (like those Apple or Tesla fanatics you see on the news) in VFX in order to thrive in the industry if it simply does not meet your long-term goals. Would employers *love* to keep you for being a great employee for them? Sure – I am not saying just do the bare minimum if your default is to excel and be the best in everything. I'm just saying that you don't have to stress yourself out about it if, for example, your goal is to be a freelancer (hence, only working at a studio on a contract-only basis anyway) or even a returnlancer. In the end, studios only care that you do your job (just as any other employer cares that their employees do their job) and whether you choose to be good or great, the one important thing you mustn't do is suck at your job and you'll be fine. Not everything has to be about striving for perfection or excellence; allow me to remind you – just as those two fellow VFX veterans I knew have proven – that sometimes it's absolutely fine to just be *good* enough and still make it in the world of VFX.

## Returning returnlancers

And on that note, in case you have forgotten what a returnlancer is, it's a term that I will like to officially coin (you heard and read it here first, people) to denote freelancers who occasionally get called back to return to previous studios (or employers), over a long stretch of time, for various projects (with breaks in-between). We've already covered the basics of this position in an earlier chapter, so in this section, we will cover how returnlancers can be impacted by the politics involved at new and returning studios. Now, you might think, "Well, since I am just a freelancer, chances are these politics don't apply to me at all." Nope, they most certainly do impact you, because the first tip about politics is that they can occur *anywhere* and *everywhere* people congregate for an extended period of time (workplaces being one of these settings). There's nothing new to add with regard to handling company politics when entering a VFX studio for the first time – returnlancer or not – but as someone who leaves and then returns to the same studio again in the future, you have to be aware that company politics may have changed since you left (depending on how long ago your last stint at that same studio was). Heck, you may even be tasked or assigned to an entirely different team within the same studio and that alone could change the workplace dynamics for you as a returning artist. A good example of this happening to me was when I had returnlanced multiple times with two different studios: one was focused mainly on VFX for television, the other on VFX for features. For each of those occasions where I returned as a returnlancer, I was not only assigned to different types of shots and work but also on different productions; this usually meant that the team (especially on the feature film side of VFX) would most likely be an entirely new set of artists with a good majority of them (depending on the size of the studio itself) being people whom I've never met until that production. As such, with new people comes different group dynamics and modified politics that apply specifically to that team of people.

As a VFX returnlancer, how you manage your reputation as you return to a former VFX studio (or your previous client) for work is important in order to ensure that you continue to keep your foot in the door. Don't think for a second that just because the studio knows you and is familiar with your performance and reliability that it gives you free rein to do whatever you want in terms of participating in juicy office gossip or just being plain foolish (think of any foolish behavior you can imagine and insert them here). As I've described in my own personal experiences above, as a returnlancer you have to work to preserve your reputation as if you were a new artist coming into the VFX studio; with different productions, different types of shots, and different people in your potential team (who will usually be exposed to you as an artist for the very first time), you should treat your return as though you were a new hire all over again. In fact, it's probably better to see your returnlancing stints as simply maintaining administrative and environmental familiarity with the studio hiring protocols (of which you get to skip entirely whenever you return to a VFX studio that already has your records and data on file) and the studio building – in other words, you know where your department is at and, more importantly, where the snacks are, ha. Aside from those specific familiarities, bringing your A-game while entering the studio with your eyes and mind wide open when returnlancing is a must if you wish to continue to return to that same studio for work in the future. It sounds pretty obvious, but you'd be surprised at how many returnlancers (or just repeat artists in general) get complacent. You reading this right now – don't get complacent.

Speaking of familiarity, remember how I said that the VFX industry is fairly small? Well, if you are returnlancing often, you'll probably be bumping into other fellow frequent returnlancers at other studios as well. This actually happened to me fairly often. One time, even as I was working at a VR startup, a fellow freelancer I met at a *different* VFX studio happened to be doing a tour at this VR startup I was at. We exchanged pleasantries and carried on with our business of course, but not without first being pleasantly surprised to stumble upon one another at a VR startup of all places. Either way, you'll most likely experience this for yourself should you choose to become a returnlancer at *multiple* studios; honestly, it's also very fun to see familiar faces wherever I happen to be working at – it keeps the job enjoyable when we meet on those occasions and exchange stories about our various working experiences at the multitude of studios we've both been at. On that note, do keep in mind that apart from the familiarity of working with another artist you may have met and worked with from a prior studio, your working relationship with that person is entirely independent of the studio you are both presently at. Hence, what may have worked for the two of you at Studio A in January may be a bit different now that it's November and the team dynamics have been modified with a new supervisor. Always adapt to your present studio's dynamics and never assume that what had worked in the past will work today as far as the forms and types of "communication" happening within and outside your studio team are concerned. Treat your returns as fresh starts to adapting to the style of the current employees at any studio and you'll do fine as a returnlancer.

Again, returning to and working with a studio you have been with previously does not necessarily mean that all human elements remain unchanged; it all depends on the personalities of your new teammates as well as how much management has changed over the course of your absence. I've witnessed management change hands in as little as less than a year as well as the hiring and firing of people from winter to summer, so it would be safe to assume that the intricacies of company politics will have changed with these shifts in personnel. Of course, this book is not about politics and reading people – at least not entirely – so I'll leave those aspects for you to discover on your own. All in all, as returning returnlancers, complacency is your worst enemy when it comes to re-fitting yourself into a studio you have previously worked for. If you'd really like to continue making returnlancing your main schtick, needless to say, you should see each returnlancing gig with fresh eyes and always seek to clarify your previous assumptions about the production processes involved. Oh, and make sure you never step on the toes of other returnlancers; if you cross the wrong person, they'll take that view of you to other studios that you *both* happen to frequent often (generating negative word-of-mouth) and if the topic of you ever comes up or you coincidentally show up at that studio's door for a returning contract one day, well, it's not going to be a pleasant experience.

## The word-of-mouth phenomenon

Speaking of which, word of mouth has always played a vital role in any industry that has different "classes" – and I don't mean social classes, I mean classes of projects: from student and amateur films to mid-tier independents and major Hollywood blockbusters and TV shows. From my experience and personal observations congregating with all kinds of crowds at all levels of experience, the higher you get on the rungs of the Hollywood ladder (or on Hollywood-caliber projects and productions), the more important word of mouth becomes. What about social media, you may be wondering? Honestly, back when I first started out in VFX, I did not really have much of a social media presence – nor did any of the studios actually question or ask me about them. Even though social media certainly existed back when I first got into VFX, the industry hadn't exactly caught up (and frankly, me neither) with the trend of using social media to check up on or profile their potential hires. It was *purely* the word-of-mouth phenomenon at play and good or great artists were recycled and recirculated among the industry while those who were just starting out attempted to make a name for themselves. As I've reiterated multiple times, the majority of the VFX studios out there don't really care about your social life, political views, or religious beliefs – they only care that the person they hired shows up, performs their duties, and executes their VFX tasks. Of course, given the societal trends these days, it's hard to quantify just how many studios are starting to take notice of the social media profiles of their potential hires. For now, however, I can attest that word of mouth is going to continue to play a dominant role in keeping the VFX industry running for Hollywood.

Of course, reader, you may perhaps think that I somewhat contradicted myself in the book, having said that companies *do* look at your social media and yet at the same time don't actually *care* about your social media. Allow me to clarify: VFX studios mainly resort to looking you up on social media should they, for some reason, be *unable* to verify your character or work through past references, mutual connections on LinkedIn, or all of the above. In other words, if you are totally new to the industry, here is where your social media presence will play a bigger factor in determining whether a studio chooses to hire you or not – especially if it's your first gig in the VFX industry. Once you've established enough work history in VFX, social media becomes less important, and word of mouth starts to take over. Honestly though, VFX studios *really* don't care about your social media as much as you think. It's not like you're working in a government organization or for a big tech company where scrutiny over your projected values portrayed in your social media feed and followings is enhanced. Nah. This is just VFX – relax. It's really not a big deal.

On the other hand – especially given everything that has happened in recent years when it comes to societal consciousness – if I were to speculate trends that are starting to become more prevalent in VFX, I would say that social media is one of these trends to look out for. They most likely won't supersede the power of word of mouth but they will certainly gain a stronger footing in VFX studios and their HR departments as they start to catch on to the importance of hiring artists with the right values and character (in addition to being able to perform their tasks and do their job). If you have any desire to be involved in the broader spheres of Hollywood, especially on the production side of the craft (such as becoming a VFX supervisor or producer), your social media content has to be even *more* carefully curated as you're not only dealing with VFX professionals but also with people from the filmmaking world, who are as diverse as they come. What I have come to learn is that people on the production side of Hollywood (directors, producers, writers, designers, et cetera) are definitely more vocal and more likely to advocate for the idea of finding the "right cultural fit." In other words, you can bet that a young "woke" (ugh, I *hate* that word) producer these days will want to scour your social media profiles to ensure that the person they are bringing on board holds no "odd" or "controversial" views to their own. Stupid stuff like that. It's sad but it's definitely happening on the production side more so than in the niche market of VFX. If you are content with just playing a technical role in VFX however – be it as a compositor, 3D artist, programmer, or otherwise – you needn't necessarily worry about a raunchy tweet you posted seven years ago.

In the end, I cannot tell you how many times I have been to studios where a random compositor, artist, or supervisor would come up to introduce themselves to me, only to add "I've heard a lot about you" to the end of their introduction after a handshake. In fact, there have been way too many of these instances for me to even recall specific anecdotes to share with you, dear reader. Remember, there is great power in the word-of-mouth phenomenon. I have been asked once or twice how one should go about *trying* to generate their own word of mouth for themselves and, frankly, I don't have an answer for that as there are way too many variables out of your control in order to generate an artificial instance of the word-of-mouth. The way I see it, word of mouth happens organically, naturally, and usually *without* your intentional instigation or consent. You can neither control how word of mouth spreads *nor* what it entails, which is what makes this phenomenon so intriguing yet so potent. Depending on how the specific word-of-mouth began, it could either make or break your reputation in VFX and in the larger scheme of Hollywood (though through my observations, it has more of an impact in the latter than in VFX). As we've discussed, people are people and people will talk regardless of whether they are in VFX or film production. While you certainly have no control over how or when word of mouth starts to kick in for you, you can mitigate any unwarranted and unwanted murmurs about yourself as an artist (and as a person) by always bringing your best and always being professional. Whether you experience this phenomenon for yourself or not – even regardless of whether you like being the subject of these whispers or not – word of mouth is *still* king in VFX and in Hollywood.

## Debunking talent poaching

Now, about talent poaching in VFX. I was asked this question in an interview one time about the risks of talent being poached by other VFX studios when you have a *really* talented individual artist in high demand. Having worked in *both* the VFX and tech world, I would say that talent poaching is more common in the latter than in VFX. In other words, it just does not happen in an industry that relies on shared talent (and where companies do not offer many benefits or corporate perks compared to other companies to begin with). In fact, looking at the types of people drawn to tech startups versus VFX, I would even say that you'll mainly find those people who are susceptible to being poached in tech rather than in post-production VFX. This also makes sense as startups don't usually have the funding to offer high salaries and hence, must court viable employees and team players in other ways (through perks, benefits, and other corporate bonuses like stock options). Evidently, with all those promises of riches, solving the world's problems, and better, never-before-conceived credits, of course you would expect that power-hungry or ambitious (yet practical) people will leave and hop on over to other startups, willingly submitting themselves to being poached. This is absolutely normal and nothing to be disgusted or surprised by.

VFX, on the other hand, is a very niche and concentrated field and we generally do believe that a rising tide lifts all boats. Since most studios generally have to cooperate with other studios on any one major production anyway, talent poaching is just not a thing with us. It ultimately depends on how far an artist's reputation goes and who they choose to end up with for the long haul (if they choose to stay in the VFX industry for that long). The only things that *don't* get shared across VFX studios are systems, trade secrets specific to the business side of VFX studios, and connections to clients (for obvious reasons). Other than that, the VFX industry is renowned for its brain share and for its sharing of resources between studios that don't result in the detriment of another VFX studio's business. Heck, almost eighty percent or more of the studios I know use the industry-standard software Nuke and, likewise, the majority of these studios also use the same shot management software Shotgun. It's really the clientele and business-specific processes that *don't* get shared across studios in order for each VFX studio to compete against one another in the way most businesses do in any other industry. The fact that we have to share files, transfer clips, and shot temps (drafts) to other VFX studios involved in the same production already somewhat neutralizes that threat of sharing classified production information with an unspoken pact amongst studios tied to the same project; needless to say, worrying about their top talent John joining another VFX studio (that will most probably be working on the same production anyway) is the least of their concerns. Now, what the employees and artists say (or badmouth) about the other VFX company's work files and deliverables on the other hand tends to be a different story, but we'll touch on bad-mouthers in the next chapter. In general, cooperation and collaboration are the norms just as using Nuke for compositing tends to be the norm.

There was one time, for example, when I was working at this mid-sized boutique VFX studio specializing in post-visualization and we were at the stage where we would receive shots and temps (again, a temp is a draft, in VFX terms) from another VFX studio that also specializes in the same niche in VFX. Now, I happened to have *also* worked at that other VFX studio before (albeit on a different production in the past) but again, the fact that they too are working on the exact same production as I am whilst working at this particular VFX studio just proves that most VFX studios in the big leagues tend to work on the same productions anyway (and that talent-poaching is pointless to begin with). Basically, even if I were to be "poached" by this other post-visualization company, I would *still* be working on the same production as the other post-visualization company. Hence, talent-poaching is not only improbable but also pointless (and cannot feasibly exist without restructuring the way the entire VFX industry functions).

So, let's say you are freelancing and you are a VFX generalist (you're able to do both 3D and 2D tasks). Great. You may find yourself getting employed by Studio X as a 3D animator on Project Apple early in the summer and after that contract wraps, get a subsequent job at Studio V, *also* working on Project Apple but under a different capacity of a 2D compositor, let's say. A quick disclaimer that it is incredibly *rare* for an artist to do two completely separate and different roles back-to-back this way (as I've explained how the VFX industry loves pigeonholing and seeing a consistent track record in one niche), but again, this is just a simple illustration to show how poaching talent is just not feasible in VFX (with the majority of similar specialty studios most likely working on the same productions anyway).

Hence, it is entirely up to both the studio and you the artist to determine if you want to remain with the studio for the long haul or move on to a different studio by the time the production wraps. VFX studios don't generally make much of an effort to poach talent since they know that – depending on their reputations in the industry – they attract the best talent that their brand name can afford and thus, can afford to impose all the necessary barriers to entry by being selective in who they hire and how they hire. Of course, film production studios are a totally different game, and I am willing to bet that they have far more talent-poaching going on in the upper echelons of that realm compared to VFX (think executives and upper management people getting traded, bought, and sold amongst the big brand studios [with more going on behind the scenes]). Again, there's nothing wrong with that – it's just the way the game is played in the broader spheres of Hollywood.

## Your next gig rests on your previous, but ...

If you take nothing else from this entire chapter, know that your next gig as a freelancer or returnlancer may depend on how you performed at your previous job. "Yes, yes, yes, this is all common sense, Vicki," you may be thinking. But wait, I have not finished adding context yet. You see, while the chances of you getting your next gig depend on how you did at your previous, there is something to be said for a great, memorable portfolio. Since it is unlikely that you will be able to collect those shots you did at Studio A to place in your reel immediately, nor will you be allowed to (most of the time) disclose the titles of the productions you had worked on at Studio A to your next prospective Studio B, what really sells you a *continued* line of work is a great portfolio (at least until you get the chance to update it – and your IMDb profile – after the work done at Studio A has been released). A great, everlasting portfolio *still* triumphs all, no matter how you slice it. It will usually be the first and most important basis upon which you as an artist will be judged, with all else being equal (such as your character, punctuality, youth, newness to the industry, et cetera). Of course, if a studio has two equally competent options as artists (both with equally impressive portfolios) then they'll proceed to assess each artist's character, schedule, and experiences next, so it's important not to be wanting in those areas as well.

Even if you may have accidentally left a studio on odd or bad terms, however (I do not advise doing this but hey, sometimes it's easy when you know you don't plan on returning to that studio *ever* again), you actually don't have to worry too much about it. Having spoken to dozens of other artists who have shared their own experiences of working dead-end internships or temp positions (or even just artists who didn't like a particular studio for some reason), a pattern I've noted from these artists is that they simply exclude even mentioning that studio in their résumé. Now, I find that this tends to work best when you happen to be a fresh graduate out of college but not so much if you are already way into your career and will then have to explain why there is a gap in your résumé (though it's easy to explain this away if you're a freelancer). So, even if you, dear artist, for some reason decide to burn the bridges to one or two of the studios you have worked at (perhaps due to a bad experience or two), unless your prospective employer decides to question the gap on your résumé, an impressive portfolio will *still* win you that gig. Besides, most VFX studios won't go out of their way to destroy you and your future opportunities if you did unintentionally or deliberately (beats me why you would do it deliberately) leave on a bad note – even if they are being honest in reference calls from your prospective employer. It's just business and business as usual with these studios – and they know they can always find another artist that could fit their company culture a bit better.

This reminds me of what happened in 2017 when I was a business owner of my Singapore VR startup Seyenapse. We were in full swing when it came to hiring and building our team and I *most definitely* remembered the names and faces of the ones who had left the startup in the most unprofessional way possible (basically, disappearing without a word or any notice of leave). Objectively, however, if any of them *had* a good résumé or portfolio (in our case, the ones who had left abruptly were hired as marketing associates), they'd still be able to get a job at other companies in the future – even if they had clearly demonstrated poor communication skills by ghosting the team without so much as a word. And while we as a company had to find a replacement for these sudden (and unprofessional) dropouts, there is no denying the fact that we had to carry on with our business and leave them be. After all, only time (and karma) will tell if these individuals had a strong enough résumé to merit them other jobs in the future. Now, is that fair? If I were to look at this subjectively and personally, no. But we must all remember that life ain't fair and that yes, even if you've burned a few bridges throughout your VFX career, you can *still* get the next gig if your portfolio is really *that* good. Of course, don't be that idiot that goes around burning too many bridges just because you can, it'll probably weigh on your conscience at some point (and don't forget about karma). Hey, not to be all woo-woo here but I used to be a staunch *disbeliever* in karma until I learned that karma can certainly work on others (or you) in indirect and covert ways.

Anyway, while your portfolio and your performance at past gigs may determine whether or not you get the next gig, it is important to factor in the very human elements at play when it comes to breaking into and staying in the field of VFX. Yes, there are certainly elements within your control that you can manage – such as your social media presence (or lack thereof), the way you handle an interview, how you perform at a job, and even whether you choose to engage in odd conversations or gossip with your fellow co-workers – but perhaps what is most crucial is knowing how to anticipate and prepare for the forces that are organic and cannot be tamed (such as the power of word of mouth and studio office politics). Having been in the industry for close to a decade now, I have spoken to, worked with, and connected with all types of individuals, artists, and talent. I can definitely say that if you, dear reader, consider yourself to be more of an introvert or non-communicator, you can rest well knowing that you are in good company (for the majority of people working in technical VFX positions are somewhat introverted anyway). Heck, I would even go as far as to say that your introversion might be the insurance that you need to prevent you from saying dumb stuff at work that might get you into trouble – for if there is anything else you should note it's that these walls speak and they have ears. If nothing else, just remember the title of this chapter: word travels far, and I have met enough people from all walks of life to know that that assurance applies in *all* industries.

# 9

# THIEVES, FAKES, AND BAD EGGS

Human nature is quite universal. Bet you didn't expect that to be an opener, huh? But in all seriousness, that statement is true. People are pretty much the same and you can expect certain behavior from specific individuals or from people in specific fields. While I don't generally enjoy classifying people into simple black-and-white categories (except, perhaps, while ranting), there is much to be said about the good people that exist in *any* industry along with the bad ones. You see, just because you read or watch the news and see malicious Wall Street brokers and fund managers setting up Ponzi schemes does not mean that the entire industry is corrupt. It just means that those individuals are. Those individuals happened to all work in that particular industry, which happened to be publicized enough that it gave the entire industry a bad reputation. Trust me, I know a few investment bankers and Wall Street (or ex-Wall Street) traders myself, and most of them are really fun, jovial, and chill people. The point is that it is foolhardy to over-generalize without substantial, consistent, time-tested evidence. The argument of "well, it depends on the individual" will *always* win, *all* the time (and I don't use the word 'always' too often). With that premise established, how does this apply to our VFX fellows? While you most certainly won't hear of sensational news stories about a VFX dude who sets up a Ponzi scheme (because VFX just doesn't have the latitude to allow a scheme of that nature, technically speaking), there are *certainly* bad actors in the industry. I know this because I have met them, and they come in all shapes and sizes. Wonderful (no, not really). Now, if you've been dying for some stories and moments of drama, brace yourself, dear reader, as this part of the book will be a *really* exciting one; it won't be boring like those repetitive sections on economics, I swear.

## The "ugly" people of VFX

Ok, I do have to admit that I hate repeating myself, so I'll bypass the "through my many years of experience" opening clause. I am sure you've read enough of that. Anyway: "ugly" people. Let's just say that I have definitely met my fair share of ugly people in VFX – and I don't mean literal, physical ugliness (as we all know the cliché: beauty is in the eye of the beholder, yadda, yadda), I will actually get to that part later (though not in the way you're probably imagining). I mean ugly people as in the narcissistic, ostracizing, harassing, elitist, egotistical, and just plain mean and ignorant people in the VFX industry. Yes, those people *do* exist if you've worked long enough and at multiple different places. In fact, I could even list them all out for you; and you know what, for my own convenience, perhaps I will list them all out. As such, the following are *actual* instances of behavior or actions that I've personally experienced or observed that I would classify as bad behavior from bad actors in VFX:

- A politically insensitive remark about another person's country of origin.
- Talking smack (or gossip) of studios that the current studio is collaborating with.
- Talking smack of literally everyone – even co-workers – behind their backs.
- Unwarranted sexual advances (though to be fair, this usually comes from production or happens in VFX-related events outside of the studio workplace).
- Racially insensitive memes and jokes.
- Objectification of women as jokes.
- Exclusionary, cliquey behavior from specific groups of individuals.
- Obvious favoritism and employee bias.
- Singling out one employee for a mistake and blowing it out of proportion (a form of bullying).
- Passive-aggressive comments about a co-worker, usually in their presence.
- Unprovoked explosive and reactive outburst targeted at co-workers.

- Abuse of managerial powers in communications with an employee.
- Internalized misogyny in hiring practices or heeding of feedback.
- Conflict-avoidant managers who drop off from communication unexpectedly.
- The "you have to finish this shot or you are not going home" threat.
- The guy (or in my case, girl) who takes credit for your work in front of your boss.

Now, of course, the list is not exhaustive, though I am sure I have covered as much of it as I can remember. I would also like to add that I did not cover my experiences and observations working in the virtual reality space: that is a whole other can of worms right there. Perhaps I'll address that some other time.

On that note, I do like to add that just because I have experienced or observed these negative situations does *not* nullify or dull my passion and love for the craft and the field of VFX. Heck, having been bullied for ten years of my life, frankly, has built up some kind of resistance to some of these instances such that I was not really bothered by them (and am merely listing them here for record-keeping). As occurrences in and of themselves, these instances were really quite rare in the sense that if they were even listed above, it's because it happened only once or twice – and it happened to be memorable. That, and because I have an *impeccable* memory, so, I tend to remember a lot of things in most areas of life – like that one time a guy asked me if I played poker

... four different times ... spread out over a span of years (the answer was and is still no).

Alright, so, with that list above as clear as day, it is quite obvious that bad behavior can come in all different shades. You have your stereotypical issues that are familiar within highly male-dominated industries such as game development and construction work, for example, whilst simultaneously having issues that span across *all* industries (like annoying gossip, toxic co-workers or bosses, and sexual harassment). I will actually pick apart a few from the list above, especially the ones I found most prevalent based on my encounters and observations.

- **Talking smack (or gossip) of studios that the current studio is collaborating with – the Gossipers**

In spite of VFX being a male-dominated industry, you'd be surprised at how much men gossip in general. And yes, from all the instances I have recalled of this unsavory behavior occurring at almost *all* the workplaces I've been at, most of the gossip did come predominantly from men (only to the extent that it is because I am mostly surrounded by men and am working in a male-dominated industry). While this did not actually bother or perturb me as much as it annoyed me, I believe you, dear reader, should at least be aware that any environment or congregation of humans will ultimately result in some kind of gossip regardless. After all, it is only human to like to interact with others, albeit sometimes in an annoyingly scandalous manner. I cannot tell you how many times I've heard of a supervisor or lead artist complaining out loud about another studio's inefficient systems, shot slate, or working hours – and all this without the context of having *worked* at said studio. Of course, gossips aren't just limited to the collaborating studios: it could be about anything under the sun from a fellow co-worker to the boss that is cutting your paycheck.

I remember one particular instance when I was working at this small boutique studio with an all-male ensemble of artists and we happened to have a female boss. I observed these artists berate and criticize their boss like no other – even if she literally just stepped out of the room a few minutes before. "Oh, I could totally run rings around her," one proudly proclaimed with his legs crossed. "Yea, she isn't someone I would consider as good management," added another. While in hindsight I did see all the flaws and mistakes of her management (as astutely pointed out by her own employees), I still think it was in bad taste for them to be so blatantly critical of their boss every chance or moment alone they had. Honestly, if one really disdains their management *that* much, perhaps they should consider vacating the position for (hopefully) greener pastures. Either way, it isn't disruptive so much as it is annoying to have to constantly hear such critical remarks about someone who is supposedly paying you for your skills (not your opinion). So, as far as bad behaviors go, I'll give this one a pass if you can tolerate the barrage of complaints and maintain the neutrality of your judgment.

Now, what about you then? What can you do if you find yourself in this predicament as a VFX person? Well, as much as I don't like to be the bearer of bad news, I have to speak the truth.

There really is nothing much you can do if you really want to keep your job or complete your contract. You could, of course, listen to music and ignore your colleagues completely, though I wouldn't advise appearing too aloof just to avoid hearsay (lest you may find yourself being the subject of future office gossip). If you're in any way like me, reader, then I would simply accept the fact that gossip is an inherent part of office and group dynamics and build up a tolerance to it. It's *really* easy if you are naturally apathetic towards most typical human behaviors in general.

- **Exclusionary, cliquey behaviors from specific groups of individuals – the Discriminatory**

The next group of common bad or unsavory behaviors that you may encounter as a VFX artist (especially as one that freelances a lot at different studios) are the people I would like to call the 'Discriminatory'. As described, these individuals are usually a step beyond gossipers (although, sometimes, they are also the perpetuators of office gossip) and like to form little cliques within the work environment; you know, cliques akin to those you may have experienced and observed in your high school or primary school days: the cool kids hang out with other cool kids, the geeks prefer to congregate with the geeks, and the jocks buddy up with the jocks, and so on and so forth. While there is nothing inherently malignant about forming cliques in an office with over five hundred employees, for example, it does become a problem when said cliques deliberately use these group formations to show bias or favoritism towards specific individuals or artists – and I don't mean this in the "hey, I like you and am physically attracted to you," kind of way. I am talking about, for instance, the direct supervisor who deliberately chooses to only invite one of his same-time hires out to lunch while completely ignoring the other one (favoritism). Of course, other common discriminatory behaviors include ones that have actually been personally directed at me whilst I was in various work environments, including remarks that were politically ignorant, somewhat racist, and misogynistic. I'll spill the beans on *all* of them.

Now, I do want to premise that while some of these actions could be deemed offensive to the average person, personally for me, it was easy to get over them and they did not bother me as much as the biased cliquey behaviors did. I am simply bringing them up here for your awareness and attention, dear reader. So, let's start with the politically ignorant remark. I was at this mid-sized studio where we were tasked with a big project as a team. As a VFX artist, you don't necessarily need to meet or know every single person on the team (that's the supervisor's job) but in general, you'll soon get roughly acquainted with those you need to know, who happen to be working in the same room or cubicle as you (yes, cubicle, as in your typical office cubicle). It just so happened that this dude (Jeff or Jesse was his name) and I happened to be having a conversation about countries and where we're both from, of which I stated that I was from the country of Singapore. Nothing crazy there – just a normal conversation, right? Well, he then popped the question – that one *rare* question that rarely gets asked at VFX workplaces because, as I've said in an earlier chapter, VFX is just *not* that kind of environment: "Oh cool – what is the political system like in Singapore?" The room went quiet for a moment before I proceeded to answer his question, "Well, it's basically run by a single-party system so it's quite efficient," – or something to that effect. A few minutes later, a snarky voice from the other end of the room commented, "Heh, some people don't even know they're being led under a dictatorship."

... Wow. "Hah, I know right?" replied Jeff/Jesse. I honestly had nothing else to say in retaliation – and honestly, reader, if you were in this type of situation sometimes it would be better to just let it slide; after all, some human beings just aren't worth your energy. Anyway, not only was that comment from the red-haired, lanky, pasty Tony, Thomas, or Toby (not sure which it was but he was definitely a Tony/Thomas/Toby, from what I can remember) uncalled for, it was quite insensitive (and inaccurate) given that Tony/Thomas/Toby probably doesn't even know that Singapore is not and *never was* a part of China. No, no, no. Also, a *party* can't be a dictator because it's managed by a *group* of individuals. Moron. Either way, if you really want to find out more, feel free to look up Singapore's political system on Google – I assure you, it will most likely list it as being under a centrist-authoritarian leadership and the word 'dictator' will be nowhere in sight (unless used by dissidents and biased, disgruntled senior citizens of Singapore). And for Heaven's sake, I'd like to conclude once and for all that just because a country is in Asia doesn't mean it's run by a dictator or that it's a part of China. Sheesh.

Then, of course, there was this one instance where my identity as an Asian female was used as a bad joke. Now, to be frank, when I saw the joke, I was not offended, but I could tell that that joke was *meant* to be offensive. Interestingly enough, I happened to be working at the *exact same studio* where that political incident happened though this time the situation was caused by – drumroll please – a *woman* who worked in the production department of the film. Now, reader, this is the part where I encourage you *not* to go about randomly sharing information about yourself with your co-workers or colleagues unless asked. You'll see why shortly. So, I do admit that this entire situation could have been avoided had I been a bit more discerning in what I had revealed, but anyway, the VFX artist team went out for lunch as a group (as usual). The team was comprised of myself and three other guys. We happened to be on the topic of dating and were openly talking about our preferences. Interestingly enough, one of them was very vocal about his ethnic preference in women and how he does not date women of his own race. Long story short, I added in – as part of the conversation – about my own dating preferences and since we were on the topic of ethnicity, well, I added that in too. *Big mistake.* About an hour after lunch, I noticed the guys all huddled around the supervisor's computer screen laughing and snickering away at something, and out of curiosity, I went over. I was confused at first about what was so funny but then I soon caught on to the "joke." Basically, it was sent by a woman in the production department depicting Asian women in a less-than-positive light. She was, of course, not Asian herself, though I feel like that doesn't need to be said. A few hours later, this woman came up to me and made a big case about a shot I was working on that happened to feature an actor of a certain ethnicity. "Hey Vicki, would you date this guy?" she said in a tone that I sensed was meant to provoke me. "Uhh, no." "Why not? He's your type. See?" Again, this situation just proves that guys gossip as much as women (there really is no difference) and you really ought to be careful – even in *seemingly casual* conversations – about what you say or divulge to some people. You never know how they will interpret what you have just said – even if they said something somewhat similar just moments ago. Double standard? Yes.

Ok, those were really long exposés, but I felt like those stories needed to be shared and heard – especially if you, reader, are a woman yourself considering venturing into the world of VFX and are also coming from a country that is *not* the United States or Canada. Now, assuming you encountered or experienced a situation like this at your workplace (as unfortunate as that may be) – what could you possibly do to keep the peace while simultaneously continuing to perform and collaborate with your team productively and comfortably? Well, there is always human resources – though I recommend only escalating to this stage in the immediate if you *really* need to or if the remarks and/or insults become more of a pattern than a one-off incident. Thankfully, in both those instances I described, they were simply one-offs or one-day affairs. Plus, you should *always* remember that having thick skin really helps in these situations of provocation. If it is beneficial, I advise seeing those who offend you as ... how do I put this lightly ... not-so-intelligent beings (whether they'd be politically stupid or hypocritical tushes) who are not deserving of your enlightenment in these areas.

- **Unwarranted sexual advances – the Creeps**

With an industry that is heavily run and owned by men, this part should come as no surprise to you. Heck, I'd even pair the VFX industry with the game development industry as I have met, spoken, and interacted with numerous women who have not only complained about sexual harassment in games (as in, in the playing of games) but also in the development of games. Though it remains to be seen how bad this issue is in VFX – because to be absolutely candid with you, most of the issues I've had in this arena did *not* occur in my department (namely, the artists I worked alongside with) – I would imagine that how you appear and dress has a significant part to play in how much harassment you tend to receive. Thankfully, as I was largely androgynous-looking and didn't really put much effort into my looks at the time (zilch makeup, zilch hair-styling efforts), I did not actually experience *rampant* unwarranted sexual advances. I particularly want to emphasize, again, that almost all of the unwarranted sexual advances I have received came from *other* departments (like the production department) at studios, happened at VFX-related events, or were observed on film sets. I'll give you two crazy stories of such nature before we move on. Even if you are a dude reading this, be aware that guys can also be sexually harassed by *anyone* (man or woman). Of course, being in a male-dominated industry, the chances of that occurring are much lower.

Now, onto SIGGRAPH. You know SIGGRAPH – the premier computer graphics convention that occurs once a year. They even have a spin-off: SIGGRAPH Asia. Anyway, this was where one of the unwarranted sexual advances *started*. So, SIGGRAPH would usually have these networking mixers and little group meetings where, with the relevant entry pass, you can enter and mingle with your fellow conference attendees. As reflective of its industry and its nature, most of the conference attendees were men – with the exception of the majority of older women present coming strictly from the human resources and recruitment departments of their respective exhibiting studios. I believe this was in 2013 or 2015 (one of those years, possibly plus or minus a year) when I had attended one of these innocent mixers at SIGGRAPH. It was a spacious rectangular room with bright indoor lighting – typical of any convention space – with circular tables distributed randomly in the area. I strolled into the room, grabbed a glass of water, and then stationed myself – in typical Vicki fashion: silent and observant – at a random round table close to the entrance of the room. I believe I was just in a black T-shirt and some blue jeans at the time (I usually wear jeans anyway), so I wasn't wearing anything crazy or outlandish. Minutes of silence and observation passed by and then up comes this dude with jet-black hair and a blank expression on his face. His name was Joseph – I remember this because we exchanged numbers (more on that later). So, Joseph introduced himself as a 3D artist and he happened to have worked at several large VFX studios at the time. Either way, I don't actually remember what our entire conversation was about, and I only remember that we exchanged numbers and that he kept coming back to my table (maybe two separate times). I had a great time talking to whoever approached me – there were a few – but Joseph was the only one who kept checking in at my table. For the most part, I gave everyone or anyone my business card with my number (hey, that's the point of a mixer, right?) and I believe Joseph had one too and that was how we exchanged numbers. So, perhaps a day or several days later, after SIGGRAPH had wrapped, I got a message from Joseph that was, well, explicit and direct. Now, in his defense, it wasn't anything like an unsolicited picture or anything grotesque like that, but it was a message that went something like this: "Do you want to have sex sometime?"

Um, right. Now, you can imagine how awkward and odd it would be to receive that message without context – and from what I could recall, I *knew* that there was *nothing* sexual about our conversation at the SIGGRAPH mixer (it was really just typical networking talk: what do you do, oh that is cool, VFX studios you've worked at, and so on) – so I was definitely somewhat disgusted that this Joseph would think that I would be the kind of person open to doing that with a total stranger. Anyway, long story short, I declined his "offer" with (paraphrased): "No, I don't do that kind of thing," and he apologized (awkwardly) or something similar. It quickly became a short exchange and we never communicated again after that, *ever*. Now, is it possible that he could have misinterpreted any of my gestures or actions as interest? Possible. Is it also possible that he is just a socially awkward sexually aggressive dude who is extremely horny and wants to have sex with anyone that will agree to have sex with him? Very likely. I mean, to be honest, being a VFX artist can be a very lonely job, so, ha.

The next story is a little more flavorful than the last in terms of character. This time we're going on a film set – one that I was a part of but not credited for (so don't bother trying to look it up). Now, this individual isn't part of the VFX spheres per se but is a film director. In essence, I was involved in the production in a VFX-related capacity. On the day of the production at a green screen studio, I arrived on set with my supervisor kit and was actually quite early. The lights weren't even ready, the studio was just getting set up, and the only people there were the assistant director, producer, director, studio manager, and me. It took about thirty minutes to an hour for the rest of the crew to arrive and from what I had heard, they all were direct imports from New York. Apparently, the production had set up a collaboration partnership with a particular school (not the New York Film Academy or any notable film schools, just to clarify) in New York. Anyway, when they all arrived in one fell swoop, I very quickly picked up on a pattern: the entire crew were either young, attractive (in my opinion) girls or young, vulnerable-looking girls – with the latter giving off very strong "I am a damsel in distress" vibes when I observed them act and interact around others. Now, I hate to make this about movements and that sort of thing as I know it tends to get on people's sensitive side very quickly, but with the whole #MeToo movement going on, the decision to hire an all-female, young model-looking crew could either be seen as empowering or downright disturbing. In fact, the only men on that entire film set of about ten to fifteen people were the actor (he was old), director (he was old, in his sixties), director of photography (he was old, possibly also in his sixties), and the young assistant director (who was evidently on the homosexual side). I was then told that all crew members were personally hired by the director (the old guy in his early sixties) himself. Hmm. Anyway, if working on a set with potential Victoria's Secret models wasn't enough, I then observed how the director interacted with some of these young, college-aged girls – and he wasn't afraid to get handsy. Let's just say he had no issues moving these girls physically with his hands and grabbing their hands in the name of teaching them to "properly frame a shot in the mirror." "Oh, look at how cute we appear as a May-December couple," was the vibe I got when I observed this man in his sixties lean behind one of the young girls to physically show her how to frame a shot with both of them looking into the mirror. I saw her blush shyly too. Thankfully, I only had to work that one day on set – though having *also* been personally selected by the director to help with the VFX on set, I couldn't help but wonder if he had other intentions in the selection of his young, available, all-female crew (he did). Sigh. It's issues like these that make me really miss the old days when you could just hire based on competence rather than to fill or take advantage

WHY I DO VFX

of some ethnic or gender-related quota or movement. Anyway, I digress.

While the latter story wasn't an unwarranted sexual advance as it was more of a very disturbing situation and conclusion drawn from a clearly exploitative scenario, I understand that most readers of this book will categorically fall into the target demographic of the VFX niche: young or old male. I'd like to stress that just because these situations occurred to me and I happen to *not* be male, doesn't mean that you as men will be spared from any kind of unwarranted sexual advances. Frankly, I've not personally witnessed something of this nature happening to any guy I know who works in VFX, but hey, it's not like guys just willingly share this stuff if it does happen to them (although I would highly encourage anyone in this situation to share the burden – there is *nothing* to be ashamed of). And of course, always consult your HR department personnel: they're meant to remain the neutral and objective faces within any company so that employees and workers can feel safe reporting anything for them to review and take relevant action on.

Look, I understand that as human beings we do sometimes find people of the opposite sex attractive and vice versa (it doesn't even matter if you are attached or married as attraction is an innately human phenomenon that happens regardless of your legal marital status). The point I am trying to make is *not* that you *can't* flirt or banter with someone you find attractive at the workplace, but that unwarranted and unsolicited sexual advances are not okay. This part is definitely out of the scope of what the entire book is about but honestly, most people only find certain behaviors unwarranted if they *don't* secretly (or not so secretly) find you attractive, period (ok, ladies, don't get those pitchforks out – be honest with yourselves; you know this is largely true). So, learn to read the signals and if you are ever confused, perhaps just be upfront about your interest – again, this deserves a whole other book, or you could look up similar book titles on Google. Just saying.

- **The "you have to finish this shot or you are not going home" threat – the Bad Managers**

Last – though certainly not least – we have the bad managers. Now, bad managers exist anywhere people exist and congregate. It is almost impossible to eliminate them all and we don't really want to as those are the individuals who teach us the valuable lessons in life, such as how to *not* manage people and how to *not* be a bad manager. When it comes to these bad managers, though, there is no one-size-fits-all; as I have already listed above, bad managerial behavior can range anywhere from narcissistic bosses and supervisors to managers blatantly encouraging unhealthy competition through obvious favoritism to superiors who apply the Tinder concept of ghosting too seriously at work. Regardless of the type of bad manager you may encounter in VFX, you will eventually stumble across one. Again, the VFX industry is surprisingly small, so chances are that if you have been in the industry for a while you may even encounter the exact same bad manager I had. Yikes. As far as stories go, I definitely have more of these types of stories than those involving unwarranted sexual advances or discriminatory behavior – I'll share two of these stories that really left an impression on me in my line of work.

Let me take you eons back – it feels like a decade ago – to this one job I had at a major VFX studio. Now, this studio had over three hundred artists working on three projects simultaneously. I was definitely very excited seeing that it was my first big project as well as my first time working at a *big* studio. Spoiler alert: if you've heard any of my appearances on miscellaneous shows and podcasts, then prepare to be spoiled as I continue to unfold this story right here.

Anyway, back to the story. We eventually had to ramp up on massive overtime which wound up racking up to eighty hours a week, Monday through Sunday, with two shifts split between artists in all departments (being in the compositing department, however, I was mostly only aware of this shift-split being applied to us). Of course, this doesn't sound like anything bad or crazy (at least, not in my opinion) and again, it is absolutely normal for studios to require *some* overtime sometimes. And here's where it all went downhill. You see, bad managers don't necessarily even have to *be* the supervisor, producer, or head of the department. They can also be your co-workers who are only a level-up above you – and in this case, it was the team lead. He was also an executing artist (so he had his own shots to execute and deliver) but he was a team lead for the most part. At this company, it just so happened that the divided teams had scoreboards for which team performed and delivered the most shots that would then be approved by the director. The scoreboard would always be reflected on a display monitor in the center of the office. One time I was assigned a tough shot by the team lead; you'd think that would be the end of it, right? Well, not exactly. You see, this shot did not come with the layers that would normally be provided by a different collaborating studio – hence, the work was actually a lot tougher. With that period being crunch time (a casual slang for overtime), everyone was cranking away to get out shots and, as a beginner compositor at the time, I was having an issue delivering that shot in a way that it would be approved by the team lead. Instead of being helpful – as *any* team lead should – I would not only experience this individual constantly loitering around my cubicle to "check things out" with the shot but I was also subjected to degrading experiences like hearing him judge my eyesight as well as deliberately bringing up my delay (in a negative way – if you heard it, you would know what I mean) to the head of the department from a *reasonable* distance away from where I was definitely still able to hear what he said. At some point, I was not even allowed to end my shift until I got that shot *right* just the way the team lead wanted it. Honestly, this individual clearly ascended to being a lead for a reason, so he should have had some tips to share. However, instead of being helpful, he decided to be condescending (not a good trait to have in a team leader). In the end, that shot eventually got transferred to the lead of a different team because the director was *really* anxious to view it and that was that (something that perhaps should have been done a long time ago before any more time was spent on that shot, frankly). In the end, my contract was up, and I had a different contract lined up, so I just moved on. But I will never forget how unhelpful and unkind that team lead was (in all his great subtlety). Sneaky.

The next story I will share is one that involves a ghosting manager. A bit of a disclaimer: I was no longer working at his studio at the time of his vanishing act, but we definitely left on good terms when my contract ended (or rather, when I *chose* to do my own thing and decided *not* to continue working at the studio, which honestly is the reason why ninety-nine percent of my contracts end – because I *choose* to end them on *my* terms). This actually happened rather recently when I reached out to this person with a request – something I needed for something important. He replied rather quickly, and we had no issues from the get-go with regard to him assisting on this small matter and me putting in all the legwork in order to get this done and executed. I had the work done and had everything prepared in a week before sending it over to his email as agreed.

No response.

"Hmm, ok," I thought to myself. I gave it about two to three days before I decided to reach out to him on LinkedIn (the platform where we had our original conversation). ... Still no response and no read receipt. Interestingly, for someone who was initially so enthusiastic to assist on this matter, this guy – my ex-boss, a fellow *business owner*, and a manager of his own VFX studio – vanished without a trace. And while I managed to find a workaround for this inconvenience caused by his lack of courage in informing me that he was no longer interested, I truly believe that *any* business owner (in *any* industry) who does not have the balls to stand up, decline, and be upfront with their opinion has *no business running a business*. That action alone – completely ignoring all communication and efforts from me to reach out and have him proceed with the final steps on this particular issue – made me lose respect for him as a business owner, manager, and VFX professional. Then of course, about two months later I see him being active and posting on LinkedIn like everything is fine and dandy. Not an excuse to completely drop off from all communication when you had initially agreed to see something through – only terrible business owners and managers are conflict-avoidant, end of story. Dear reader, if you ever become or are currently a manager of sorts, don't you *ever* be afraid of conflict. If you have to decline something or plans have changed, mention it and decline whatever it is upfront – don't run away like a coward thinking that the person you were in communication with is going to forgive and forget that you ever did that to them. Take it from me, they won't. Think of your reputation and the reputation of your VFX studio if nothing else.

Of course, those aren't all the dramatic stories I have to share but I will have to save those for some other time, outside the context of this book, because I've certainly had enough of reading my own stories of bad people for one day. Heck, there was an even more dramatic story where this one particular boss (he was one of the founders) outwardly rejected a casual suggestion (on calendars) I made on the basis that he runs the company and that it is not a democracy (I believe he even used that word 'democracy' in our little chat online), *only* to take up that *same* suggestion when it was posed by a different artist who happened to be a dude. What a different outcome for an idea that originally came from me, hmm. But hey, as I said, I will only cover the stories that involve the VFX world – not the tech or VR spaces.

So, let's say you have stumbled across your garden-variety bad manager, whether you are new to the industry, a mid, or even a current manager yourself working alongside other managers, what are your options from here on out? While it is very tempting to confront your manager, this is not something I would personally advise. After all, your "bad manager" can *always* double down on his or her bad behaviors, further ostracizing you from the rest of the crowd in terms of bearing the brunt of their negative actions. What you *can* do (if you still want to work at that studio or if you don't have any other choice but to work there) is what I would also do if I were caught in the awkward situation of being a recipient of sexual harassment – gather evidence, gather allies, and *then* approach the relevant authorities within the studio (your neutral party, which should invariably be the HR department). You see, if you do the last step *before* gathering evidence and allies, even if you speak with HR anonymously, you are increasing the risk that this bad manager of yours will be able to identify you as the complainant (and hence, doubling down on their bad behavior towards you, if he or she *really* is *that* bad of a person or manager). Hence, I recommend gathering ammunition first in the form of evidence and allies who *may* have similar stories of their own encounters with this individual.

In conclusion, the number of these personalities you may be exposed to ultimately depends on your role. When I was a production assistant for example, yes, I did notice that I was treated very much like my 'racial stereotype'; even when I was an intern, I was definitely aware that I was being exploited in some areas. Heck, if you are an intern it is *highly likely* that you may even experience *more* unwarranted sexual advances since people *know* that there is a chance that your time at the studio is just a one-off, of sorts. Either way, my parting words for this sub-chapter would be to be cautious entering *any* industry. Certainly, don't let these ugly people deter you from VFX if it is your lifeblood and soul – hey, if you end up being *really* lucky, chances are you will never have to experience or meet any ugly person at all. Ultimately, people are people, and there will always be a spectrum of behaviors and actions one can tolerate. No human being is flawless.

## Spotting the occasional creepers

If I haven't shared enough stories about this, then let me reiterate here. The occasional creepers *do* exist – and in my experience, they mainly exist outside of the artist department; again, this isn't gospel, and you should use your discerning mind and eye to judge any awkward situation of said nature. In this section, I'll show you how I spot someone who is or could potentially be a creeper/sexual harasser. Though my insights below mainly benefit women, I know that men can also be subjected to creepers of all kinds. Alright, dear reader, this is the part where I say that this book is not *meant* to be about *"How to Catch a Predator"* (Chris Hansen reference anyone?) so if you really want to find out more, out of morbid curiosity, I recommend looking up such book titles on Google. I will keep these sections short and sweet as I'm honestly not too interested in going deep into such weird rabbit holes when we're supposed to be talking about VFX. So, even if this section is an odd deviation, here is how you can spot a potential creep at or outside your workplace (man or woman):

- **Assess their eyes and demeanor**

VFX tends to be a crowd that attracts more introverts than extroverts; more misanthropes and cynics than bubbly people-lovers; and more reserved individuals than boisterous noisemakers. However, I find that by assessing anybody's default demeanor you can determine whether they are *usually* a said way, or if they are acting out of their usual form. In addition, not many people can fake the glint in their eyes; the cliché of your eyes being the windows to your soul is surprisingly true. So, the next time you find yourself in a conversation with *anyone* whom you know you will either encounter or have to meet or work with again in the future, in some capacity, feel free to read what their eyes are saying while paying attention to whether their actions match their words. With untrained creeps, their actions and words do not usually line up. Even if they do, it's unlikely that their eyes will *ever* lie to you.

- **Track their actions around you and others
to determine patterns**

Following up on the above tip, the next actionable suggestion is to then track the way they behave around or with you in comparison to other co-workers. While it might sound a bit odd to compare this person's behavior towards you with how he or she behaves around others, it actually helps you to determine if the negative behavior in question is indeed isolated specifically to you or if it happens to be experienced by others as well. If the individual's actions are standard with almost everyone he or she meets, chances are, it's their default. If it's not, however, it's something to make a mental note of. Then you can determine whether the action is a one-off instance or *may* become a series of continuous actions (a pattern). Also, it helps to talk to others (in private) whom you feel have also had constant interactions with this person to determine if they may have experienced any interactions similar to the interactions you have endured with this individual (or potential creep). Remember, sometimes people behave differently in one-on-one situations when there is no one else around to observe or criticize their behavior.

- **Trust your gut instinct**

Our gut instinct or intuition often goes unheeded in today's society. Whether it's downplayed for being too illogical and impractical or simply lambasted as being hokey and overrated, there is actually a whole load of truth when it comes to your natural intuition about people, situations, or things. In fact, there was a time when I ignored my gut instinct regarding a certain individual to the detriment of my own safety and life – and in doing so, I *almost* lost my life when this person tried to strangle me in the bathroom of a rented Airbnb home. I'll save that story for another time. In short, if your gut is telling you that there is something not quite right about a specific person, listen to it and heed your intuition. No, you are not being paranoid, you are being cautious for *your* sake.

Now, you may be in a situation where you have spotted and successfully identified a creeper and he or she happens to be your co-worker or team member – what can you do then? Well, in cases like these, it usually ends up being a "he said, she said" scenario, so the best thing you can do is to start collecting evidence if he or she continues to persist in any unsavory actions towards you. You can also confront this person privately and inform them – in a professional, unemotional manner – of your concerns before potentially escalating the issue to the relevant authorities at your studio. First things first: protect yourself by collecting evidence that will help your case.

All in all, as I've said before: where there be humans, there be drama and sometimes creepers too. Being a creep is not industry-specific and creeps certainly do exist in *all* industries out there. Name any industry and you'll usually find one or two creeps walking around. And yes, female creepers exist too – in my opinion, they're just rare. The closest example I have encountered happened to have been involved with the VR industry; she was arrested in Northern California for stalking (and other sorts of similar activity, I don't remember in detail) an ex-boyfriend of hers – and there is even a mugshot of this woman online. Funny how some people turn out to be more hostile than they initially appear.

## Nasty men and women

Now, I am not even going to pretend that I am an expert on knowing what to do with nasty men and women, but I do want to preface by stating that nasty men and women exist in *all* industries (I am sure you already knew that). They may be your driver of negative company politics, your credit-takers and stealers, your annoying obsequious bootlickers, all kinds. These people make the gossipers and creeps look like innocent children in comparison with their narcissistic attitudes and highly toxic gameplay at the workplace – though to be honest, I have yet to meet one who could best Machiavelli at his own game. Perhaps I am just lucky or was able to detect these entities or individuals before they could do irreparable damage to me. I've certainly dealt with and met nasty men and women, sure, but none that I would consider as being at the upper echelons of Machiavellianism. Either way, if you have not already caught on to the varying degrees of nastiness in the earlier sections of this chapter, be prepared to be amazed by the nastiness of the people in this one. Again, if this type of subject just seems way out of left field when it comes to VFX, well reader, you can simply skip this entire portion. On the other hand, if the seedy underbelly of these dark personalities and morbid undercurrents of humanity have always been intriguing to you (which is absolutely normal as we are only human), then I advise you to proceed through this sub-section with caution.

Firstly, I'd like to disclose that these examples are from what I have gathered either through my own stories (and this time, I am including my entire work history, even at tech startups and my ventures into VR), others' retelling of their stories or through careful observation, analysis and piecing together of fragments of a story to put together a more complete narrative of what went down. Alright then, here goes.

Our first story comes from a veteran in the VFX industry. For his sake, I am not disclosing his identity. Now, he and I were quite close, and I could safely classify him as a friend or at least one of the closer acquaintances I know in the field of VFX. I had enlisted him to help on a particular contract work, of which he delivered successfully and skillfully. Absolutely brilliant. Either way, he was driving me to lunch that day and we wound up talking about one of the top – what shall we call him – "content producers" in the field of VFX. In fact, if I mentioned his full name, you would know him, if you were in the field of VFX. Anyway, this person (who is also a veteran of a similar age or so) had actually started out in a similar position as he was way back several decades ago at a small company. Interestingly, according to his purported experience with this individual, he was not only a really bad artist, but he basically did little to no usable work at this studio, yet somehow managed to claim credit for the work. According to my veteran friend, this person continued to do the same thing at various other studios before he ended up releasing his own content and making himself known as the go-to person in this area. Based on my analysis and observation of my friend's facial expression (et cetera), I could tell that his frustrations were genuine and that he really *did* feel ripped off and cheated by this person he used to work with. Again, even today, this person is *still* a well-known figure in this particular niche of VFX who, according to my friend, did absolutely nothing but take credit for others' work.

The next couple of stories stem from hearsay (yes, yes, I know...) from fellow co-workers at a mid-sized studio. Now, for the record, none of the people who shared these tales with me actually worked at this studio, but they were direct connections to artists who worked or continued to work at this particular studio. "Yeah, you know what? I heard that [Studio Name Redacted] actually tracks your mouse movement before they pay you. Like, I know someone who worked there, and he told me that even when he went to the restroom, he had to ask his friend sitting beside him to move his mouse to show that he was working. That's crazy, man," explained my co-worker at the time. As a beginner compositor back then (and pretty much a new entrant into the VFX world), I didn't really have the bravado nor enough of an understanding of the situation to garner a reply to that, but I do remember thinking how intense (and psychopathic) that studio's management must have been to enforce such an unnecessarily strict tracking system on their artists in order to *determine* payment. And back then, their studio *was* actually one of the more well-known brands in the VFX world. Today – or at least as of the writing of this book – after looking up this studio online, one can already see the after-effects their negative, controlling management style has had on their business (from being a somewhat recognizable brand in the VFX industry to becoming a hollow shell of what they used to be). Heck, even their website now has the "Not secure" notification – meaning, they were either trying to save money on their site due to the decline in cash flow or have really given up on setting up proper security connections on their site (which makes the site less credible, which probably also means they are not presently seeking to tend to their reputation and online profile as other more pressing matters may be afoot). Last I checked, their social media channels have all been inactive since mid-2019, so it's safe to say that they've definitely fallen from their prime back in the heydays. Another similar example is a studio owned by the brother of a VFX veteran friend I know. I have met the brother only once and I don't personally know him, but my first impression of the dude is that he definitely had somewhat of a scummy business owner vibe to him (shhh, don't tell my friend I wrote this, ha); in other words, I get the sense that if he could take a dime or two away from you without you knowing, he would. So, of course, what invariably ended up happening a year or two later after casually meeting this brother who owned this VFX studio (which was somewhat reputable in name but not as well-known as the first studio in this paragraph) was that the studio ended up laying everyone off all of a sudden and had to close. Now, I don't know the specifics of what went down, but from the looks of it, it didn't seem like the brother had lost anything significant in its closure. Again, I don't know anything else other than what I have mentioned, but I would say that I have a powerful intuition for these kinds of things – and it is highly possible that the brother *did* leave that business behind unscathed.

Of course, businesses fail and close all the time, and this is no different in VFX. However, it is the *way* they close or where they wound up today that signals whether a business is inherently run by nasty men or women or if they genuinely failed due to market factors. There was another infamous example of a *big* VFX studio (one I had actually worked for at one point) that laid off more than half of its over three hundred employees after everyone stood up, clapped their hands, and celebrated the completion of a few major productions. It didn't happen to me, but someone who had been with this company for almost a decade at the time told me that this happened and that it made *many* people upset (and I can see why they would be). From what I heard, there may even have been a class action lawsuit against this corporation – not surprising, seeing how they ruthlessly sacked their employees after they were done with using them to complete their VFX productions. In fact, back in the day, mass retrenchments of staff were actually (and sadly) the norm; they were such a norm that studios making school tours even went around talking about it all the time (I remember being in school when one or two studios talked about just that). Now, businesses in and of themselves *cannot* be nasty. They are inherently neutral entities and, ultimately, it is the people owning and running them who turn these businesses into nasty or great places to work at. Hence, if you want to pin the blame on anyone for a business' lackluster performance or toxic work culture in today's market, don't fault the business itself, fault the *people* who run them.

The final story that I will be sharing with you, reader, in this sub-chapter involves my work in the VR space. To be frank, the tech space definitely has its fair share of employment woes and nasty men and women. Sometimes, these nasty men and women even date one another, leading to a toxic coupling akin to the likes of Bonnie and Clyde or Myra Hindley and Ian Brady, though perhaps less macabre. From being intentionally misclassified as a freelancer (in order for the startup to avoid providing certain benefits) to deliberately overworking employees and underpaying them, many tech startups are notorious for exploiting the goodwill and enthusiasm of wide-eyed technicians or programmers, thinking that they can get away with many misdeeds in the name of being the driving force for their mission. Well, not so fast there, bucko: not *everyone* is completely blind to your devious ways. Sometimes, all it takes is just one misstep, one wrong move, to get yourselves exposed as nothing more than exploitative, nasty startup founders. This is a true story that happened to me in the VR space. You see, nasty men and women sometimes aren't so easy to spot. In this case, the female co-founder was definitely the bigger instigator of what went down. So, I was recruited and paid a meager rate to help this VR startup develop an innovative stereoscopic conversion workflow, that did not exist at the time, for a project the team was planning to pitch to Oculus. You see, back in the early days of VR, solving stereoscopic issues through conversion or stereoscopic VR shoots was a big deal. I believe I was only there for a few weeks (or less than a couple of months) before I successfully developed this novel stereoscopic conversion workflow in the popular software After Effects for them to use in their VR series. Of course, rather than celebrating this victory as a team, what happened next was simply astonishing. I was basically let go from my position while the startup went ahead to pitch their production to Oculus without me. I was offended but was even more enraged by what came after. One fine day, I happened to stumble across an article on Fast Company about a VR startup who wanted to get the jump on a new VR camera system, touting their innovative in-house stereoscopic conversion workflow. Hmm, that sounded familiar. I read the full article and was in complete disbelief with the words I saw coming out of the co-founder's mouth (paraphrased): "Yea, we have our own in-house workflow that we invented, but it still has some kinks to work out," she proudly stated in the interview article. There was *zero* mention of my single-handed contribution to that development and that startup basically claimed the *entire* workflow as their own innovation – something I knew was not only a lie but also *not possible* given that both co-founders were nothing but performing clowns (or, more objectively, theatrical actors) with *zero* background in computer programming or even post-production VFX. Basically, I was *not only* underpaid, but I was also *not* given the *credit I deserved and earned* for single-handedly developing that workflow for *their* VR startup. Now,

240

I did email and confront this woman about it, and we ended up meeting up at some place where I casually brought up the article and accusation with tact (I will keep all other details regarding this meeting to myself for now), but nothing changed and, of course, it was too late to do anything about the article at that point. Even the writer of the article wasn't interested in hearing my story. From what I know today – if I even bother to look up these two scumbags (which I don't as it is not a productive use of my time [or yours for that matter, reader]) – they have possibly divorced or are having issues with their marriage (and rightfully so). No offense, but your wife was and is a treacherous b ...

Ahem, excuse me (I'll censor myself, no worries). Let's move on.

To my surprise, my case was not the only instance of this type of behavior happening in the VR industry. There was another VFX professional by the name of Joe who was also hired and then fired after he had helped set up and establish some fundamental protocols and systems for *another* VR startup (one that, in my opinion, was even bigger than the one I had slaved away for). At least that was the story I got from another friend and acquaintance I've worked with in VFX who also does VR development. We exchanged woes and he told me about what happened to his friend Joe. From what I could recall of that conversation, Joe was also visibly upset and felt betrayed by the entire incident as he too was *not* given *due credit* for his work and contributions at that other VR startup.

As you can see, with people stealing credit (whether it's a VFX shot or an entire workflow) from people, VFX businesses being run by bad eggs, and VFX people getting ripped off by bad actors (or literal actors) at VR startups, these people *really, really* bother me to the core – so much that I get incredibly and intensely enraged every time I am forced to think about it (or in this case, write about it). And yet, the interesting thing about these nasty men and women is that they could be *anyone* – your peer, your supervisor, a random person in production, or even a couple of stage performers. Everyone is suspect. Now, how does one look out for these types of people though? Well, remember that earlier sub-chapter on spotting those occasional creepers? The same steps apply, for the most part. Sometimes, however, the best gauge is to use your intuition – on that front, I find that my intuition on people is usually right about ninety percent of the time, and you'll gain more experience as you cache different profiles, signatures, and behaviors of people in your mental database. Always be seeking to enhance and improve your natural intuition on people, situations, and things – *always.*

The really funny thing about that VR incident, however, was this one car ride I had with the female co-founder one night. You see, they were the sort of couple who are quite into spirituality, horoscopes, and the "speaking from beyond the grave" kind of thing – I am not for or against it, it just isn't my style. So, during that car ride (and this was before she sacked me a few weeks later, of course), we somehow ended up on the topic of horoscopes; she then asked me about my sun sign and moon sign from the natal chart (you know, those sun signs, moon signs, planets, et cetera). Oh, and if just *reading* about horoscopes irrationally angers you to oblivion then my suggestion is to skip this bit. Anyway, as I happened to be *forced* (yes, forced) to know what mine were – in other words, I didn't have a choice when an old guy decided to do a horoscope analysis on me for free (on his dime and time) – I told her that I was a Scorpio Moon (Pisces Sun, if you're curious about my answer to her other question). Now, from what I was told and have read about this particular moon sign, well, let's just say that if she actually took horoscopes *that* seriously to begin with, then she should have known from that very moment I answered that question (the most important lesson of that entire car ride): you don't *ever* mess with a Scorpio Moon – *ever*.

Non sequitur aside, folks, just be aware and be careful out there. I think it's becoming redundant for me to repeat the phrase "XYZ people exist in *all* industries" as I am assuming you, dear reader, are smart enough to know that already (even if I haven't hammered that line home incessantly enough). As such, all I can say at this juncture without sounding repetitive is that life can certainly throw you a bunch of curveballs in the form of crooked players – your best plan of action is to take them all head-on and use them to empower you rather than hinder you. There will be bad players everywhere: don't fear them, *use* them.

## Portfolio, reel, and résumé thieves

Moving on. Now, this one is hilarious because I actually caught an "acquaintance" of mine who did this – faked his résumé by wholesale ripping off my résumé section on VFX skills. Heck, it's even listed in the *exact* same order I used. Hilarious. Now, I did not confront him about it as I didn't see the point; after all, he wasn't exactly *in* the industry in any capacity (not even as a legitimate filmmaker), so I let it go. In the end, the one that ends up getting damaged is he himself if he was actually recruited for an industry VFX job and ends up being unable to perform due to the lack of experience and skills he purported to have in his résumé. Aside from that one case, however, I have yet to experience this type of thievery coming from anyone who is actually *in* the industry, so take everything I say here as conjecture until proven otherwise. Anyway, let's first get onto the case of portfolio and demo reel thieves.

From the stories I've heard from other co-workers, portfolio and demo reel stealing are actually *quite* common in more ways than one. Of course, it hasn't happened to me (or at least, not that I am aware of), but it did happen to one or two of my work colleagues and even one of my bosses. Stealing can come in many forms. There is, of course, the direct way of stealing somebody's body of work by downloading them off their site or ripping off their reel from YouTube and claiming that as your own, et cetera, but then there's the even more *sneaky* way of stealing that these thieves commit as well. Let me illuminate that with a story. So, I had been with this mid-sized studio for a while now – and by a while, I mean as a returnlancer on various productions – and with that came the perks of knowing almost everyone at the studio, including the boss (or one of the bosses anyway). One day, on my final day of work, I ended up having a casual conversation with this boss and we wound up on the topic of demo reels and getting footage for my reel (something I normally ask for and prepare in advance before I officially wrap up on my contract). He was jovial and, of course, obliged to my reasonable request and agreed to have someone supply me with the raw clips once they're released, though he did add on an interesting tidbit of information, which made me go "Oh, wow ... didn't know that that was a thing."

"You know, one time I was working with this gentleman and we were both at the same studio. A few years later I discovered that he had used some of my shots as his own and didn't give me credit for them, especially when he only did a small portion of the work on those shots." "Oh wow, yea that sounds shady," I replied, before we proceeded to wrap up our conversation with other thoughtful words, with me then leaving his office and the studio for the day. Very quickly, you can already tell that stealing can also come in the form of using another person's shot and claiming that you did the majority of the legwork on it. For example, if you were a rotoscope artist who only did the rotoscoping on a hero shot whereas somebody else was the lead compositor on the shot (coupled with one or two other secondary compositors), claiming that *you* (the rotoscope artist) did the *entire* shot on your own as a compositor – or worse, not even listing what you *did do* in that shot in your reel by deliberately leaving it vague – *is* stealing. Even if you had simply forgotten to add in your contributions as a side note, it still makes you look like a thief (intentional or not). Hence, word to the wise, always be *honest* with your work and always make it known what your *actual* contributions were in the shots on your reel. You don't want to end up stealing somebody's hard work by accident or omission.

Next up: résumé thieves. They are not as common as portfolio and reel thieves but as with my earlier example in the first paragraph of this sub-chapter – they *do* exist. Now, I have not been told of such cases through the stories I've heard from friends and co-workers in VFX, but I find that the ones who tend to duplicate others' résumés or "steal" them are generally *not* already in the industry. In other words, if you happen to have broken into VFX, chances are that you will not *need* to steal somebody else's résumé. Of course, there are those who steal another artist's site, formatting, or the design of their résumés, but that is a whole other topic right there, which I will cover in a later sub-section of this chapter. Now, are there people who steal *both* résumés *and* demo reels? Yes, yes, and yes; I just haven't had the misfortune of meeting, knowing, or discovering such people (yet).

In the end, as an aspiring or entering artist in VFX, you need not worry about this as these individuals eventually get called out, found out, or just proved to their hiring studios that they never had the skill set to begin with (and that their entire résumé and shots in their reels were stolen). And while you won't be able to stop their actions nor prevent them from stealing – especially if you end up becoming someone worth stealing from – you most certainly won't be able to catch *all* the thieves without some extensive help (and I am also of the opinion that you should not even bother trying to catch them, frankly). Thankfully, there are fraud-prevention tactics employed by most significant studios these days to ascertain whether the artist they are intending to hire is legitimate and *did* do the said work he or she claimed in their interview (we've covered this in an earlier chapter) so your best action – if this has happened to you – is to ignore them and trust in the intelligence of these studios as well as their process of due diligence. What goes around comes around. Know that studios know what to do to fact-check and verify their incoming potential artists – especially if said studios are one of the VFX giants in film or television.

## The ones who fake their résumés or titles

On that note, while stealing another person's résumé is definitely wrong, faking one is just as unethical. Nothing is more untruthful than pure and outright fabrication out of thin air; whether this be the fabrication of résumés or fictitious titles and positions at a company, there is something to be said of *any* individual who is willing to deliberately beef up their résumé with false titles, projects, credits, and work periods. Look, I get that we all want to get those fanciful titles at work, we all want to be known as the lead or boss of something (anything), and we all want to add those delicious film credits to our name (it strokes the ego and healthy narcissism that most people innately have). However, faking a résumé or position not only does yourself (as an artist) a disservice, but it also deceives the businesses that hired you and trusted you to deliver. Fake it till you make it only applies if you're an actor, not if you're responsible for executing and delivering technical work like VFX shots and sequences. While most might think faking a title here and a credit there is a victimless act, it actually has consequences that may affect the broader industry as a whole. In this sub-section, I'll show you why.

Let's say John is a fresh graduate out of art school. He went to a notable art school in Florida, let's say, and studied computer animation. All good. Now, he's having a bit of an issue finding a job in the industry and not because he isn't skilled or resourceful but because employers keep telling him that they are looking for someone with more experience at this time. So, John (our fictitious, mysterious, and mischievous John), decides to do the unthinkable and fakes his résumé to add at least one or two years of non-existent experience under his belt along with some fake credentials of having worked on a few popular independent films in his area. John applies for a job in Los Angeles and gets it – hurray! So, John goes to Los Angeles and starts working at Studio 123 (fictitious Studio 123, for your information) as a 3D animator. However, because John *lied* about his résumé and past (non-existent) positions, the studio soon realizes that John is *clearly* out of his depth, way overpaid, and lied to them about what he was capable of (which ended up costing the studio more money to keep and retain him as talent). The studio could then decide to either terminate his contract or let him wrap up and whimper out silently. Studio 123, from that moment forward, will not only tighten up their regulations and vetting processes for *all* future incoming contractors and employees, but they will also most likely be willing to share their *candid and honest* experience of John from Florida, leading other VFX studios of the same caliber to *also* apply more discernment and caution in their hiring processes, causing a ripple effect of reputational damage to John that could follow him for the rest of his short-lived career (at least in Los Angeles and to a certain extent, California). Get the picture?

Interestingly, it is usually the actions of the brilliant or the bad that lead an industry to make big and dramatic changes for better or worse. In the case of fake résumés, fake credits, and fake positions though, the few individuals who do this end up inadvertently causing a massive shift in VFX hiring processes from being quite open to outsiders and new entrants (with proven demo reels, of course), to being *more* selective and word-of-mouth based. So, dear reader, if you have been trying to break into the industry for a *long* time and are wondering why it is so difficult to get in, you can partially pin the blame on the ones who faked their résumés, job titles, and credits, burning the trust of the wrong (but very well-connected) VFX studios. Now, should you personally make it your life's mission to pay attention to the people who do this just to get a job in VFX? No, not really – it's not a good use of your time. Unless you are the owner of a VFX studio intending to hire a few artists for a project, it really is neither your moral nor individual responsibility to give a toss. All you can and should do is ensure that *you yourself* do *not* fake any aspect of your résumé, your titles, or your credits. That would be my best bet on the best plan of action to take against those who fake and lie.

In the end, we are not here to discuss how to uncover the truth behind résumés and lies (unless you are an employer, then see the previous chapter on how employers currently recruit and hire artists), we are here to understand the types of ugly people you will most likely encounter throughout your career as a VFX artist. In addition, you can most definitely find solace in the fact that what goes around comes around and know that VFX circles are surprisingly small (in spite of VFX being so international and global). These fakes and liars eventually get found out or caught so all you can do as an individual is to stand by and watch as the lies implode on these people. Harsh, sure, but they get what they deserve. As for titles, well, to be honest, not many people in the VFX world actually even care about them (even if they happen to be fake). It only really matters when the lying applicant is seeking to jump from a technical position to a supervisory position, but aside from those types of instances, most people in the VFX world are more concerned with a résumé or credit that was faked rather than a position or title.

Ultimately, VFX is a world that, for the most part, rewards the truly talented hard workers. The ones who sacrifice hours in overtime at the studio, the ones who *actually* do what they said they could, and the ones who are able to perform on time and on budget according to the wishes of their studios. I've said it before, and I'll say it again: fake it till you make it is a *lie* in the world of technical and creative VFX work. If anyone strongly believes in that spiel, then please become a Hollywood actor or performer instead.

## The surprising number of ...

Button-pushers. Yep, button-pushers. Of course, everything requires context, and while your capacity to utilize your creativity is entirely dependent on what your specific role in VFX is, not *every* position allows you to utilize your creativity (or your brain, for that matter). Over my many years in this industry, I can definitely attest to having met some of these individuals – some of them are just *really* dismal thinkers and problem-solvers in general, which also explains why most of these people self-select themselves out of the VFX industry eventually, after less than a year or a few months. Now, I have nothing against button-pushers in VFX; in fact, we *need* some of these roles in VFX for specific tasks that tend to be labeled as mindless such as rotoscoping, layout, rigging, and to a certain extent tracking work. The problem arises when some of these artists eventually, for some reason, get selected to do more creative tasks such as 3D modeling or lighting, of which they sometimes struggle to excel at just because they were so used to not doing much mental work before. Don't get me wrong, there *are* successful artists who have managed to transition from rotoscoping to compositing, rigging to animating, and so on, it's just that some of them end up doing terrible jobs in their new niche, which then require somebody else at the studio to pick up the slack (and usually they will be doing it on their overtime too).

If you have always had this preconceived notion that VFX is all fun, all creative work, and all awesomeness, well I'm sorry to disappoint you, but there *are* roles, work, and tasks that *are* mind-numbing and soul-crushing (such as the few mentioned above).

The sad truth is that sometimes these individuals just get stuck doing these mind-numbing tasks and *never* get out of that vicious cycle because the other more "creative" tasks are already occupied by existing artists (or there is already a lot of competition for those types of roles to begin with). On that note, reader, you may be wondering if there is any way to *not* end up being pigeonholed as a button-pusher. Well, a wise man (or a very young man with the nerdiest-looking glasses) once told me, "You've just got to stop accepting that type of work." That was it – plain and simple. For added context, he was sharing his experience on transitioning from a compositor to a VFX supervisor *on set* (one of the highly coveted routes *many* compositors honestly aspire to embark on – myself included at one point in time), and he basically said that all he did was *not* take any more compositing work. Now, it is difficult for many to just do this (for many reasons subjective to your own life and priorities) but it definitely worked for him as verified by the résumé I saw.

Now, is there anything negative about being a button-pusher? Well, it depends on who you are and what you are looking for. If you happen to stumble across a button-pusher at a studio should you avoid them like the plague? No. They're still people and they really won't do you any harm. The only reason why they're even in this chapter is because I am just letting you know that they exist and that you'll probably know a few (or plenty) of them when entering the world of VFX. So, if your goal is to *not* work a mindless job coming into VFX, at least you now know what to do and what some of these types of tasks tend to be. What you wish to do next with this information is entirely up to you.

To a lesser extent, there is also a surprising number of copycat artists in the industry – and when I say copycat, I mean someone who literally wholesale copies the design of your site, the way you display your work, your personal style, et cetera. Not to brag but over the course of my life thus far I've encountered way too many copycats. In fact, I've encountered so many that I've developed a sixth sense for even the slightest of infringements (like the design of a wallpaper for art class in high school, or the design of a thumbnail for a free VFX online course that also happened to have a suspiciously similar format and content). Not saying that I am right all the time, but I would say my sixth sense is surprisingly *quite* accurate in figuring out my copycats in any endeavor, style, or medium. Heck, I remember when I was schooling at SCAD that there would be one or two students *per class* who would try to copy my work style, my interview answers, or even – and this *actually* happened – decided to completely change tracks and *also* become a compositor because *I* was a compositor (when he was initially interested in becoming a lighting artist). While I totally understand that guys and girls of *all* ages might potentially copy someone because they are inspired by that person's awesomeness (or perhaps the guys possibly even liked me at one point), I personally don't find it flattering. Sorry, but it's annoying to have your identity or parts of your style, personality, content, or work so mindlessly duplicated.

Anyway, personal grievances against copycats aside, I am sure you are not here to hear me rant (you could follow me on Twitter for that ... or not, ha) – we're here to talk about those who try to make their reels, website or even branding very, *very* similar to yours as a fellow VFX artist in order to, oh I don't know, take your clients away from you perhaps. And while I have debunked how the VFX industry works and how talent poaching is *not* a thing in VFX, it doesn't mean that you should settle when someone blatantly steals parts of your website, reel style, or résumé design.

Sometimes, waiting for the laws to catch up to modernized forms of stealing, copying, and copycatting (yes, this is actually a legitimate word) isn't going to cut it either – it takes way too long and there is such a thing as the statute of limitations. As such, here is what I suggest you do should you find yourself being a victim of copycatting: collect all the evidence and store it away for future use or reference, and then confront them (if you can). Meaning, actually start a dialogue with this copycat and see if you can resolve it that way (just be sure to take all the pictures and store all the evidence away first). Now, if you happen to have a ghost as a copycat (like what happened in my case) where the only way to contact this person is to *pay* for something of theirs, well, don't do it. Direct confrontations aside, there really is nothing much you *can* do if you end up finding a copycat of yours with no social media (at least, without them being able to *also* collect your contact information in return) or direct means of contact in this instance (though I wouldn't necessarily be all doom-and-gloom about the situation).

You see, the personality of copycats in *any* endeavor is quite straightforward. These individuals either lack the creativity to think for themselves (in fact, I wouldn't be surprised to find some copycats as button-pushers and vice versa, which partially explains why they work button-pushing jobs to begin with), the courage to develop their *own* style, or methods or think that by imitating *somebody else's* work or successes that it too would generate the same results. I guarantee you it does not and *never* does in the long run. For that reason, I encourage you to trust in the system and in the process of how VFX studios (or other design companies) choose and keep their talent (I don't know about you, but it was definitely *very* tempting for me to go ape on the copycat, so even I have to rein myself in sometimes, to trust in the process). *Trust* that the VFX studios and vendors are *smart* and *discerning* enough to know a fraud or a copycat when they see one (especially if their actual work, style, and performance don't even match up with the depicted view and style of their site and branding). Of course, while we do have to trust them, let's be real (and realistic) here: sometimes these people *do* get away with copycatting and sometimes studios really are *that* blind or apathetic to the situation (perhaps deciding to turn a blind eye even). Life is inherently unfair and unjust (even if we'd like to believe otherwise), so the best plan of action going forward is to then learn how to play the game *better* than your copycat (and one-up them in ways they will *never* expect and can *never* replicate).

On that note, whether you just meet a bunch of button-pushers, end up becoming a button-pusher (if that is not what you want), or have a personal copycat relentlessly on your tail (or in my case, several copycats), remember that life is in its very nature unfair and unjust. Know that and you are less likely to be surprised or disappointed by its cruelty, allowing you to then be as clinically objective as possible. Being as clinically objective as possible then allows you to *turn the tide* of these perceived negative events into positives that work tremendously in your favor – alas, something I will only go into deeper, dear reader, outside of this book perhaps. At the end of the day, it is all in the perspective. If nothing else, just remember this: if you are currently a button-pusher and don't want to be, you can choose to stop being a button-pusher (if you really think hard enough about the workarounds for your specific situation). If you have a copycat on your tail, it means you are successful, they suck, and you are someone they see as being *ahead of* and *better than* them. Own that greatness – and use that to *snuff the living life out of them* by gaming them in other ways.

## Obesity over the years

Now, I don't know about you, dear reader, but after rehashing all that I have above you may be thinking that that should pretty much be it with the ugly people in VFX right? Well, not so fast. Now, if you identify as obese or overweight at the point of reading this (and are extremely sensitive and thin-skinned), feel free to skip ahead. If you are fine with this sensitive topic though, then I'd like to set the record straight with the brutally honest truth for a *large* majority of VFX professionals or aspiring VFX professionals. Once you enter the industry, chances are you *will* gain weight. Now, to be clear, you may not become the specimen of obesity overnight, but you will *definitely* look chubbier and meatier than you were coming in. You see, the VFX industry has the habit of laying it on thick (pun intended) and with the stress of deadlines (if you experience stress), free office snacks, and drinks galore, as well as long hours of constant sitting (though sometimes, standing desks aren't any better), it is inevitable that you *will* gain weight working a profession in VFX. Of course, with human biology at play with sarcopenia (muscle loss with aging) and the ease with which our bodies store body fat as we get older, you should not be surprised with – or even expect – weight gain. Not body-shaming anyone, just stating the facts as they are.

Through my studio-hops, I have worked and sat alongside skinny guys, small obese men, large obese men, skinny-fat dudes (also known as guys who look thin on the outside but probably have less-than-optimal guts sticking out; look this up on Google if you need more examples) – and everything in-between on the spectrum of physiques *except* the muscular or athlete-level fit type of dude. Even the women I've worked alongside are on the plumper side or, at the very least, skinny fat. With that being said, even without scientific literature and studies in this niche topic, I can confidently and unilaterally state that there is a growing number of fat and skinny-fat people in VFX *and* game development. It really is because our jobs make it *easy* for us to put on weight in those undesirable places; sitting for prolonged periods of time also has a negative impact on the body and tends to contribute to weight gain (though, please don't quote me on this

– look it up on Google if you are really keen on the scientific research and supporting data). Now, I'm thankful that I pretty much look the same (underweight or skinny) as back when I first entered the industry, even though I didn't have a gym membership that I actually used until about 2018 or 2019 (understanding why or how I was able to stay in shape prior to 2018/2019 is hence completely out of my depth here). Then again, there was a time when I *could* have been one of those thicker girls if I were not too careful with my snacking behavior. I mean, hey, I was happily enjoying those free office snacks whilst studio-hopping from place to place, after all. In fact, one time I was at a startup and literally devoured up to seven or eight packets of chips *per day*, *every* day. Yes, I was that aggressive on those chips – so much that the executive assistant chick had to put a sign reading, "Take one only! Thank you!!" I ignored it, of course. Still, after many months at that startup with my tech supervisor pointing out just how much chips I had devoured, I still left all that weight behind when my projects were wrapped.

Honestly, you would *hardly* find an artist – male or female – who is in rockin' good shape. Now, of course, what constitutes a fit and healthy body in good shape is entirely relative, contrary to what the fitness industry will have you believe. Judging with my critical eye though, I have yet to meet someone who is actually in the "shape of their lives" who is also a post-production VFX professional. The closest "fit" people I see are your VFX on-set supervisors – and that's mainly because they get a lot of activity done running around on and off set. Heck, even your post-production supervisors are unfit – sometimes even more than your regular artists. The obesity statistics are probably worse in the game development industry (though I do know that the animation industry is much more forgiving on that front, at least when it comes to having a large proportion of overweight artists and professionals).

Heck, there was one big studio I used to work at where the supervisors, HR personnel, and an overwhelming majority of the heads of department were overweight or skinny fat – and some of these individuals have been with the company for over ten years! Amazing what time does to your body if you don't take care of it.

Of course, this isn't to say that you will *definitely* become obese in VFX. Nah. I am also not here to bring down those who happen to *be* obese who *are* in VFX, no. Like I've said, I have also met those who were underweight or too skinny for their height (even though a large majority of the supervisors and senior artists were in the obese or skinny-fat group) – they're just more uncommon in a world where sitting for long periods of time is the norm. Being incredibly observant, I did notice that the ones who do maintain something of a semblance of a fit body and healthy appearance whilst working in VFX are either business owners of VFX studios or those who freelance *a lot* and take regular breaks in-between freelance gigs. Anyway, the point is that if you aren't too careful working in VFX (or games), if you just sit in front of the computer all day and all of the night (The Kinks reference anyone?), if you continue to binge on the free office snacks provided at any respectable studio worth their salt, then you *will* most definitely gain some unflattering pounds. I mean, not to make this into a joke, but wouldn't it be annoying to you every time you stalk a person on LinkedIn – fellow VFX artists, supervisors, and others who work in VFX in any capacity – to see them use a clearly decade-old profile picture on their bio, only to have met them in person for them to look, well, *much* chubbier (and older) than their profile pictures portray? And you would think this kind of thing only happens on dating apps and sites. Heck no. I for one *detest* using old profile pictures of myself, so I cannot tolerate people who do this (especially if they are now sixty and their profile picture clearly has them de-aged by about twenty years – I have seen this numerous times). So, if you don't want to be in that embarrassing (and annoying) situation of using an old headshot of yourself yet appearing like your Aunt Liza or Uncle Bob in person, work on yourself to stay in shape (or have the guts to be confident in your own *authentic* skin by using an up-to-date profile picture). Just putting that out there.

Mini-rant aside, what you should take away from this sub-chapter (and technically, the entire chapter as a whole) is that the VFX industry definitely does have its dark side, unspoken issues, and bad eggs. Be a part of *any* industry for a while and you will soon discover that they, too, have their unspoken issues and dark side. From thieves to fakes, button-pushers to bad eggs, it is what one can expect when it comes to the dark side of human nature and any kind of congregation of people in general. All you can do is be prepared for when you may encounter these individuals – and do your very best to avoid becoming one yourself. After all, to be armed with knowledge is your first line of defense. Aside from this potentially bleak and dark chapter, dear reader, VFX is *really* and *genuinely* a great field to work in if you're looking to develop your creative and technical skills – I just wouldn't necessarily recommend VFX to anyone who wants to have any semblance of a life (family or otherwise) or business (outside of the VFX niche), neither would I recommend it to anyone who wants to look like a ripped bodybuilder. But hey, this is Hollywood after all, which is why I am also not surprised when some locals colloquially refer to our world of filmmaking and entertainment as 'Hollyweird'.

# 10

# PREDICTIONS ON VFX, FILM, AND ENTERTAINMENT

Ugh. I bet you are glad that we are now past that chapter. Elaborating on all those bad eggs and actors really does get tiresome and disgusting (mainly because these individuals are tiresome and disgusting). Anyway, let's move on to something more positive like the future of VFX, film, and entertainment – or more accurately, my predictions and foresight in this arena. As you are most likely aware, technology changes *very* quickly, sometimes even at an exponential rate. This is no different for certain aspects of VFX, film, and – to a certain extent – entertainment. Changing technologies change the hardware of our industry, which then forces the software (the human aspects of VFX) to catch up and adapt to the advancement or detriment of certain positions in the market. In this chapter, I will give you my *best* – using my many years of experience in the field (and outside of the field) as well as my many years of experience observing, analyzing, and understanding the broad strokes and commonalities in human behavior – in predicting where VFX as an industry is organically headed in its processes, available positions, and trends, as well as where the broader market of film and entertainment are moving towards in terms of its desired talent pool and other areas. As usual, I will be approaching this with a realistic bent based on my interpretation of recent developments in the space and with the world at large (basically, telling you what you need to hear rather than what you want to hear). As much as we all want to live in an ideal fantasy world where everyone comes out unscathed and alive at the end whenever changes happen in industry or society, let's leave those ideal fantasy worlds to the movies. The real world is definitely less flowery and pretty than it seems (even reverse nihilism won't spare you from the realities of life and living). Anyway, by reading on you'll find that it's not *all* bad and I am certainly not here to be a downer for no reason; after all, change is usually a *good thing* for the industry – whether or not we as a people take to said changes is a different story altogether. ... Now, why did that feel like I totally went off-tangent there? Anyway, let's get to it.

## Understanding past trends and patterns

In order to predict the future, we must first look to the past. Of course, life is a lot more complex than this and there is certainly a lot more that goes into predictions than simply embodying the overused and abused quotes of "past behavior is the best predictor of future behavior" or "history repeats itself" – or its market equivalent. For the context of this book, however, we are going to take on the historical records of development in the field of filmmaking and technology (whether the latter applies to animation and visual effects or not). Now, it is true to a certain extent that sometimes history repeats itself, sure, but I find that this mainly happens in the context of human psychology and broader societal movements and trends. While human behavior and psychology do affect the developments within certain industries at times, these industries shift and change based on factors beyond the people. We will have to dissect these factors individually though by understanding the past in general, we can more reliably predict future trends and patterns in VFX, film, and entertainment. Just to reiterate, I won't go into detail about the history of VFX. As I already mentioned at some other point in this book, if you really want to know, please go ahead and look it up on Google instead; my book is not meant to be a mindless regurgitation of history that has already been widely publicized online and elsewhere. Anyway, we begin with the propensity for efficiency.

You see, we humans have a tendency to take the path of least resistance. In essence, we desire to keep things simple yet efficient in terms of our day-to-day or common activities. This is no different when it comes to how VFX has developed historically when it all began with the power of the film camera. Heck, a savvy supervisor would usually recommend doing as many effects or as much prep work on-camera rather than in post-production, where feasibly possible. In fact, past trends in development have shown this to be the case in our industry as VFX advances alongside available technology and the age of the Internet, continuously making things more efficient in terms of dividing labor up into specialized, concentrated roles (just stating this as an example) in order to expedite the process of post-production VFX. Think of your manufacturing days when factories hired groups of people to do only one specific task in the chain of manufacturing – the same concept applies in VFX with these specialized niche positions in production and post-production. From matte paintings that were done by hand and then displayed in film to digital matte paintings of today, VFX has historically been one of the early adopters of (at the time) new technology as it's only natural for an industry that relies heavily on output to attempt to find the means to expedite its work processes.

On that note, another obvious historical pattern to take note of is VFX's transition from analog to digital forms of production execution. As with the matte painting example, work and crafts that were initially done manually in analog form have now mostly been digitized and streamlined via tools and software – another sector within the VFX industry that generates massive growth, revenue, and jobs in the VFX market as a whole. Back then, even the release of *"Toy Story"* was all the rage mainly based on the declaration that it was the first-ever computer-animated feature film; based on that alone, you can tell just how far we've come since. It only makes logical sense that the VFX industry will continue to forge ahead with its use of technology all in the name of serving creators, storytellers, and filmmakers.

Another thing we can take away from the earlier decades of VFX is how the VFX kingpins of those days technically still remain the kingpins of today through their innovation and forward-thinking. Industrial Light & Magic and Digital Domain (being ahead of their time) are but a few of these longstanding brand names that not only established themselves as leaders in the field of VFX back then but are some of the companies that still continue to reign today. While it is true that companies that had once founded or dominated industries may not necessarily continue to do so in today's society, in the case of VFX, these titans have continued to innovate; hence, they still "own" the lion's share of the VFX market when it comes to delivering feature film projects and progressive, immersive content. In addition to this, back in the day, international artists and international work systems weren't really a thing until the VFX industry slowly spread abroad, defying the confines of Hollywood as the Internet brought the world closer to everyone's feet. Again, this is the industry's attempt to make itself more efficient through globalization. By offshoring specific tasks to cheaper countries (or countries with tax incentives), the VFX industry has managed to make itself more efficient by minimizing overall expenditure (through foreign labor) and maximizing output.

All in all, we can summarize the past trends and patterns of VFX as all for making things efficient for increased output and results. If you were too lazy and didn't read, here's a list for you:

- VFX was usually done on-camera where possible, only transitioning or utilizing technology if they had proven to deliver better or desirable results.
- VFX as an industry had the tendency to be innovators, trailblazers, or early adopters of advent technology and techniques of doing things.
- With its embrace of technology, the VFX industry soon developed its own niche market in the development of software and tools specific to serving the needs of the VFX and animation industries.
- VFX historically has had a trend of transitioning from analog to digital in the name of better results and increasing efficiency.
- The sharing of resources and knowledge by going offshore and globalizing VFX was mostly done not to benefit other economies but to optimize production through cheaper or more accessible labor, division of labor, and the effective utilization of time zones to establish a 24-hour production cycle.
- Innovative studios that established themselves at the time still reign today and will most likely continue to do so with the right management, direction, and technological leadership.

And that should pretty much be it as far as past trends and patterns go. If I had to sum up the history of VFX's past, it would be one of innovation and learning. Efficiency has also always been the name of the game, especially in VFX.

## Understanding present-day

Given the delays that come with publishing a book (though to be honest, this timeline has been drastically reduced given the rise of different forms and takes on publishing), one can reasonably expect that the data points mentioned in *most* books out there today tend to be outdated, especially if they're talking about technology. That being said, most of those books were written over a span of *years* (sometimes decades), so you should forgive the writer on that front; I am sure he or she had a lot of other things going on in their life that led to the lengthened timeline. Thankfully, reader, you have me: this crazy VFX artist who decided to go all-in on writing this book within a reasonable time frame – cramming all my nine to ten years of experience into this one book with high speed, high accuracy, and high dedication. Heck, I even self-isolated like a hermit in my room with no social life and no other activity beyond writing and lifting so that this book wouldn't take five years. Hurray. Now, back to the point on the present-day times and well-being of the VFX industry; if we have established VFX's past as one of innovation, progression, learning, and making things efficient, today's modern VFX world is all about that *and more*. Meaning, not only are the VFX innovators (your kingpin VFX entities mentioned previously, for example) still continuing to innovate, make progress and contributions to their companies (and consequently to the industry as a whole), and learn, they are also pushing the boundaries of what it means to be "optimized and efficient" to a whole other level. The trend in the 2020s for VFX (give or take several years) is real-time, live-time, and ideally *all* the time. Let me break that down for you.

So, there are a few organizations and positions out there that support filmmakers and Hollywood, the somewhat "unglamorous" and unspoken side of what makes Hollywood movies Hollywood spectaculars: these are your technologists and motion picture engineers. While I've always found this group to be underrated and hidden away like a long-lost key to a wardrobe that leads to a secret world, these engineers are actually what make certain modern-day technologies possible for high-end Hollywood productions. From your Sony Electronics to Canon and Panasonic, these engineering conglomerates create the technology that serves as the foundation on which filmmakers and creatives could build their stories upon. Then, of course, there's the RED camera that everyone loves, hands-down. Anyway, my point is that this sub-industry of Hollywood (the engineers) will soon play an equally important role as the VFX innovators in the VFX industry when it comes to how the market is doing today. Of course, developing and manufacturing actual tools and equipment themselves takes time, and just like the legal system, sometimes these manufacturers can take years before they finally catch up to the ambition of modern-day filmmakers. Not all filmmakers care about 8K, UHD, 3D television, or even HDR, and to be brutally honest, some of these professionals – having met several of these motion picture engineers – could be helped by having a bit of a pulse on what is actually desired and needed by filmmakers rather than simply iterating resolutions to oblivion. Here's where it appears that the technologists and engineers who have crossed over to the VFX side (or who were originally talent from the VFX side of Hollywood) have got it right by focusing on solving the right problems and actually speaking to the right (usually well-known) filmmakers. Hence, today, the VFX headlines are no longer going on about (technically, they *never* were going on about those) fancy 8Ks, 12Ks (and in case this part is confusing to the layman, I am referring to film resolutions here), stereoscopy or even high-dynamic-range imagery (HDR/HDRI) – they're targeting more on-set VFX action and more live-production VFX execution. Real-time, live-time, all the time.

Let's think about it for a second. What more could we ask for in terms of getting close to the ultimate efficiency desired? Having *real-time* VFX delivered directly on-set or to the cameras as realistically rendered as possible. That, and eventually morphing from real-time to autonomous real-time would be the next phase, but I've got to hold my tongue for this section because we're focusing on the present day right now. Still, I'm already seeing some automation (albeit still accompanied by some manual input or adjustment) going on when it comes to motion or object capture systems, setting up production sets and sound stages (yes, those are starting to become automated – don't ask me how I know), and specific VFX post-production processes and tools. On the note of tools, more and more tools are being developed by studio developers with pure efficiency and automation in mind. I've personally seen the automation of keying and shot design, and, of course, After Effects has certainly made great headway with the initial introduction of the Roto Brush tool (which is now going to be powered by AI). Soon, you'll need fewer and fewer rotoscoping artists with these AI-driven tools at play, which could be good news or bad news depending on where you are at and your current position on the VFX job spectrum. Either way, we'll get to that part later.

What I found most fascinating, however, is that the initial shift from analog to digital of VFX's past is interestingly transitioning *back* from digital to analog (more specifically, from digital to live on-set) – an interesting reversal, if you ask me. I am sure you, dear reader, may have seen some recent (well, maybe not so recent by the time you read this) behind-the-scenes looks into how LED screens were used in the direct *replacement* of green screens through the virtual production on *"The Mandalorian"* – where virtual sets would literally be "projected" and captured live on-camera through walls and walls of LED displays. Again, another classic example of how the transition to computers is now being reversed by bringing these technologies back on set. Another type of production to look out for would be volumetric-based capture systems – another close contender to virtual productions if done and executed right (and if the use case for these systems is justified). On that front, we already have a few companies out there attempting to create a system that works for Hollywood – if you look this up on Google, sometimes it is bundled under the umbrella term of XR (extended reality).

Needless to say, we know how interconnected our world is today, and the VFX industry has most likely optimized the globalization of its production processes as best as it could ages ago; we technically could have VFX created non-stop, day and night, without any pause in production at all (talk about the ultimate form of productivity). To take this global optimization one step further, remote working is also starting to become an important working modality in VFX – for obvious reasons that you should know as well, by the time this book is published. If major events like the COVID-19 pandemic hadn't pushed remote working to the forefront, the VFX industry would have eventually (give it several years to adjust) taken to the trend of allowing its artists and technicians to deliver results from the comfort of their homes. The main reason why remote working was not adopted sooner in VFX (and in Hollywood in general) is mainly due to the strict NDAs, confidentiality agreements, and trust issues. Of course, given that almost every industry has been pushed to this option in 2020, Hollywood and VFX are forced to adapt and have *some* trust in their hired hands and employees – of which they'll soon learn that trust is the best gift any employee could receive from an employer (no matter the industry). After consulting and catching up with some acquaintances and veterans in the VFX industry recently – as I write this book – it is safe to say that remote working is and will soon become a norm for VFX artists all over the world; and once you allow artists *all over the world* to work from *anywhere, anytime* and on *any project* from *any country*, other than the work visa, employment, and tax legalities (all of which will be forced to play catch-up to try to contain potential widespread, global "illegal employment across borders"), Hollywood will soon be able to tap into global talent without even having to ever meet said talent face-to-face. Ladies and gentlemen, the largest worldwide competition for talent is happening right here and right now. If you thought you were competing against the world five years ago, remote working has brought us here today.

In short, today's VFX world is all about real-time, live-time, *all the time* – a step forward in achieving efficiency yet again. And of course, to those who were too lazy and didn't read, here's another pretty list for you:

- VFX innovators have closer access to filmmakers; hence, engineers in this space are more accurately able to determine and enact technological developments that actually matter to filmmakers.
- Artificial intelligence is starting to (and will continue to) make its way into VFX tools, software, and systems, if they weren't already attempted by programmers and developers seeking to automate specific tasks and processes.
- What was once about moving analog tasks to digital, today's VFX market is about bringing the digital back to the analog by merging digital sets and environments with on-set camera capture systems or projecting digital assets into actual reality.
- Virtual productions, volumetric camera systems, and tools that fall under the XR umbrella are starting to pick up steam and attention in VFX as efficient and effective means of VFX execution.

- On the subject of XR and real-time virtual productions, game engines have started becoming commonplace in VFX studios as several game engines allow for plenty of customizations and lend themselves as better facilitators of real-time feeds and streams.

- Remote working is becoming a widely accepted means for artists to work on and contribute to projects today compared to VFX in the past, opening the flood gates to true global competition.

- With the enabling of remote working, potential tax and employment laws may be. unintentionally or deliberately broken by studios; laws will have some years to catch up in legality to attempt to control rampant cross-border remote employment of workers.

- Even present-day developments (that included more frames and larger resolutions) are all about making things more efficient and optimized for a better, more desirable result.

And that's what we have and what we are presently seeing in today's VFX market (give or take a couple of years). Remember the mantra: real-time, live-time, *all the time*. Either way, it's still all about efficiency and optimization.

## The process of elimination & simplification

Before proceeding to predict the future of VFX in the next few segments, I thought it would be important to impress upon you, dear reader, one of the biggest patterns drawn from the past and present of the VFX industry – the process of elimination and simplification. As we've conclusively drawn from the past decades spent in VFX, hand-drawn, manual crafts were simplified via digital tools and execution. This can even be seen in the entirety of the post-production space in general; what once required a literal projection, cutting, and splicing of shots to constitute what was then known as editing is now mostly done in a non-linear editing suite such as Final Cut Pro or Adobe Premiere Pro. Even post-production sound has been simplified tremendously. Moving on to the present, all this simplification has in fact eliminated the tedium involved in certain tasks (such as in our manual cutting-and-splicing example), simplifying them tenfold whilst expediting the output per man-hour.

Of course, with said elimination and simplification comes the elimination of unnecessary roles and artists. Glass matte painters had to adapt to the new normal of digital matte painting and pick up new tools along the way should they wish to remain relevant and employable in VFX (the same with most other positions). Hey, remember the videocassette recorder (VCR) and how that died out to give way to DVDs and CDs? And remember how those were then eliminated by the Blu-ray (even though that didn't catch on as much as it was hyped up to be), which subsequently got decimated by tiny (but powerful) flash drives that too got destroyed by having data in the cloud? Heck, who even owns a VCR, DVD, CD, or Blu-Ray Disc player these days? We've eliminated and simplified so much of our data and content such that they're not even physically tangible as they get presented to us via data over the cloud through streaming (for the most part).

This process of elimination and simplification is the same trend our VFX industry has taken since its inception decades ago; whether you personally like the displacement that occurs with this process, it has happened before, is happening right now, and will continue to happen much into the future of this industry.

In general, most of us can come to a consensus that the more you can possibly capture what you need live, in real-time, and on-set, the easier things become (in addition to making it much, much simpler and cheaper in post-production). If today we're seeing digital set extensions being modified, adjusted, and enhanced in real-time, live on camera, and just by a handful of VFX artists on set, it is likely possible that we will be seeing actual 3D characters and models projected *live, in real-time*, and captured on set in the future – utterly bypassing the slow rendering process typically involved with computer-generated imagery (CGI). And no, I don't mean this in the "Tupac hologram" kind of way.

By eliminating outdated methods and simplifying execution alongside technological developments, the VFX industry has effectively achieved as much optimization prowess as it can, given the limitations of current technology. As a VFX artist, you may always find yourself being caught in the crossfire of such developments as the VFX industry forges ahead with changes to existing ways of doing things or existing means of execution. The best strategy you could employ is to keep up with the times and adapt to the VFX market. Who knows, the next phase in their process of elimination and simplification may just find you terminated from a VFX position or have your role or specialty completely simplified and taken over by smart technologies. If you're not too careful, you could eventually be eliminated from a job (if your goal *is* to get a *job* in VFX, that is).

## Specific predictions on the revamping of VFX roles in post-production

Now, I admit that throughout this entire book I've enjoyed writing so much that sometimes you may be wondering why I don't just cut to the chase rather than use fanciful words to enhance my vanity metric (also known as my word count). Well, here is that moment where having me divulge incessantly may be to your delight; after all, there's only so much conjecture one could surmise about the future of anything – a topic where, if one gets it wrong, they'll be laughed out of the building and yet if one does get it right, it'll be shrugged off as beginner's luck. Either way, reader, predictors don't win; so, I'm just as curious myself as to how many insights and inductions I can incorporate into the next few sub-chapters. With that, let's get straight to it. Here are my specific predictions on the revamping of VFX roles in *post-production*:

- **Singular specialized roles will soon be eliminated**

I hate to break it to you (actually, no, not really) but it does appear that the industry is heading towards a form of consolidation where specialized roles may very well be discarded. Don't get me wrong, we *do* still need experts and people who are *exceptionally* good at one specific thing – it's just that being good in that *one specific thing* is no longer going to cut it once the VFX industry evolves with the technology to allow most of those specialized roles to be completely replaced by AI or machine learning. Of course, there will always be that fallback guy or gal whom studios will rely on should the AI be incorrect, but even those positions will soon be nullified once programmers and developers fine-tune their AI to account for those deviations and human errors. To be more specific, roles such as rotoscoping artists, pure compositors, 3D modelers, and the like have a high chance of being displaced and replaced by advanced developments in the post-production world in general. The displacement will first begin with elementary roles that involve preparing a shot or setting things up (such as the likes of rotoscoping, texturing, et cetera) before eventually moving on to the next rung of potential displacements or role modifications; this next rung of roles will primarily involve secondary, slightly advanced creative roles like compositors, lighters, and animators, who may find that while their roles may not be completely eliminated from existence, they most certainly will be in less demand than they are today. Honestly, just as my 2016 TED talk had predicted what is presently happening today (as I write this treatise), it would no longer be sufficient to simply be good at *one* thing and *one* thing alone.

- **Generalists will play a bigger role in VFX**

On that note, the decline and eventual dismissal of a large proportion of single-niche specialists will pave the way for strong, multi-talented generalists to rise to the bountiful opportunities that will be available to them. Following suit with how VFX post-production is becoming more of an on-set endeavor, these generalists will be able to apply an assortment of their skills live, on-set, and in real-time; hence, possessing a sharp wit and ability to make decisions quickly will also be essential in addition to simply possessing the skills in 2D, 3D, animation, painting, et cetera. It is also highly likely that generalists will *not only* have to be generalists on the creative side of the spectrum but will also have to possess some degree of proficiency with code and programming as well (definitely a harder combination to find in most talent). Of course, this isn't to say that arts generalists are essentially less valuable to studios in the future – I am sure they'll serve their purposes at a myriad of other places – it's just that with new tools being driven and controlled predominantly by code, AI, and developers, it definitely pays more for a generalist to live up to their namesake and actually be *real* generalists (in every sense of the word). Then again, linking back to the VFX industry's propensity to be very forgiving and very open in who they let in, I am sure the highly sought-after creative technologist combination will still be years ahead (and creative generalists will most likely be the first types of talent that the industry will go for once the shift in VFX post-production starts to set in).

- **VFX post-production artists will become more entwined with on-set production work**

With that being said, we are already seeing the early beginnings of this shift in post-production: the shift from post-production work and roles to on-set, live, and real-time VFX work. VFX jobs in post-production will soon be expected to show up on set to perform their duties live and possibly cooperate with the other crew members as well (though of course, through the VFX supervisor of the production – you don't want to bypass his or her authority on set). Technically, we've already had this type of role in the form of the previs or techvis artist position (depending on the visualization studio you are dealing with, these two roles could be combined) but I am predicting that a wider variety of multi-talented artists will soon be brought onto set (with the VFX supervisor) to perform quick and perfunctory creative tasks with whatever post-production tools are at the production's disposal. Again, game engines are becoming exceptionally common for such productions and positions, so if any post-production VFX artists are going to be brought on they'd most likely be a couple of expert or master generalists who are able to work game engines like a boss. It'll most likely start from there as the VFX industry revamps itself to exclude single-niche specialists in favor of these true generalists who can do a bit of everything masterfully. After all, it's most likely cost-effective this way and may result in less studio and production overhead overall.

- **VFX studios may be in favor of hiring a leaner team of a few expert generalists versus an army of specialized skills labor**

Speaking of cost-effectiveness, it is highly probable that VFX roles are not only going to be redistributed amongst existing artists in the industry but that there are also likely to be fewer of these newer or revamped VFX positions available for the mass pool of talented (and untalented) artists out there. Frankly, we shouldn't forget that art and VFX-concentrated schools pump out hordes of new competition every year (some of them twice a year even) so the existing talent pool will also be competing against the newcomers attempting to break into Hollywood VFX. Of course, you can also bet that as VFX studios revamp their traditional post-production roles, they'll most likely only be interested in existing, mid, or senior-level artists who will be able to fit these roles given their current experiences; basically, you shouldn't worry about the throngs of new VFX graduates being pumped out of schools (*yet*). Anyway, back to the point: the trend of hiring a leaner team will most likely start first in Hollywood's filmmaking industry – the place where some productions force their grips to be the gaffer/production designer/production assistant/caterer/truck driver/assistant camera person and so on. Heck, why not start with Hollywood filmmaking since they're already infamous for forcing a lot of hats onto a lot of its crew members. With that, you'll soon see the VFX industry following suit with their preference for a leaner team consisting of multihyphenates, trending away from their past history of hiring thousands of special skills workers for

3D, for example. The rate at which this change will take hold in VFX depends on the rate at which AI and highly advanced technologies are adopted by the VFX industry to deliver high-quality results in certain tent-pole productions. In the end, I've noticed that all the industry really needs is one *really good* (and lucrative) case study production to prove a point before the technology is eventually assimilated into other major (and subsequently minor) studios in VFX. This is true of most industries – for better or worse.

- **Repetitive or perfunctory roles will be replaced by AI programmed and controlled by a few**

Now, if I haven't already made clear the types of roles that are *bound* to be destroyed by AI a few paragraphs ago, here is me reiterating that point again: repetitive and basic roles will eventually be replaced by AI, which will be developed and controlled by a mere handful of AI developers working in the VFX industry (and trust me, AI developers are already quite *rare* in VFX – though bountiful in the game development spheres). Your basic VFX tasks like texturing, rotoscoping, rigging, and perhaps even modeling may be at risk of being automated or taken over by hyper-intelligent AI tools or technologies (basically, any task that involves setting things up or performing basic preparations for a shot); from the better-developed AI-automated unwrapping of UVs to instant rotoscoping tools (and no, I am not just talking about the Roto Brush), these types of tasks – which sometimes don't require much mental acuity to begin with – will be the first types of tasks to be sent to the chopping block when AI becomes more commonplace and more powerful in the VFX world. I mean, let's be honest, who doesn't want to kill themselves whenever they're forced to rotoscope hair strands of some blonde chick being blown by the wind? As such, as the AI industry propels itself further in its overall development and progress (in robotics, the Internet of Things, and whatnot), that development will eventually trickle down into other industries that utilize AI – including VFX. As an artist, dear reader, you should anticipate that these changes are coming and that they are inevitable. AI is here to help make many, many industries more efficient; if it comes at the cost of many other jobs, then it is what it is (you can't have the best of both worlds in matters like these).

I'm expecting VFX post-production to undergo the biggest reform in terms of the types of artist-type roles that will be available in the future. Regardless of where you believe you fall in this major shift (that is already happening right now, *but* most *sustainable* changes usually take a while to fully flip an industry, so you can breathe a sigh of relief if you were concerned), take note that there will *always* be several other smaller or boutique studios out there that will still be running on older business models or older technologies in VFX. Hence, even if these predictions were to come true and a huge majority of the VFX studios in the market shift to adopt the stance of employing master generalists, there will always be those several laggards in the industry who still have access to enough available work for single-niche VFX specialists. Really, it's not the end of the world – just be prepared for change when it happens *to* you.

## Specific predictions on the revamping of VFX roles in production

Moving backward from post-production, here are my specific predictions on the revamping of VFX roles in *production*. Now, most of them are just points re-affirming or overlapping with what I mentioned in the previous sub-chapter but nevertheless, this just goes to show how VFX production and post-production are only becoming more and more intertwined with one another. Some of these points are common sense (or at least they seem like common sense to me) and really shouldn't surprise you if you yourself have been keeping abreast with what is currently going on in the VFX space (in terms of the new tools and present means of production). Well then, here we go:

- **VFX supervisors on set will continue to play an important role in bridging post-production and production VFX**

Needless to say, VFX supervisors have always played a crucial role in bridging VFX teams and filmmakers. As you may well be aware, dear reader, not *every* filmmaker is exactly tuned in to how VFX works (nor do some of them seem to care – especially those indie filmmakers) and the same goes for the VFX team – not every VFX artist or person out there is tuned in to what goes on and how things work on set in terms of camera data, specifics, and whatnot.

Hence, irrespective of how the VFX industry evolves over time, on-set VFX supervisors will continue to play a key role regardless of how much technology revamps the entire post-production side of our world. If anything, VFX supervisors themselves *must also* evolve with these technologies and become multitalented generalists; technically, to be an on-set supervisor one must already be some kind of a generalist and have a strong understanding of both the film and VFX worlds, but predicting ahead, I am saying that the few VFX supervisors who do *live up* to being those master generalists themselves will continue to dominate the sets of Hollywood. Heck, I wouldn't be surprised if these VFX supervisors will soon be expected to be multitalented swiss army knives *and* whizzes with real-time game engines (coupled with programming know-how). One thing's for sure, if the pressure is on in post-production to keep the team lean and filled with superbly talented master generalists, you can expect that same pressure (multiplied by ten) to be placed on the VFX supervisors themselves to be extraordinarily well-equipped and skilled.

- **Post-production artists will start to gain more access on set as live-recorded or live CGI become dynamically integrated with footage captured in real-time**

As already mentioned in the previous sub-chapter, not only are traditionally specialized artist roles starting to be exchanged for highly talented generalists, post-production artists will also soon find themselves leaving their seats behind computer screens more and more as the VFX work slowly becomes integrated with real-time, on-camera VFX. Since a set can only (and only wish to) accommodate so many cast and crew members before it gets expensive, it naturally only makes sense that only a select few of these VFX artists get to go on set to perform their tasks. Hence my prediction on the contraction of roles from specialization to master generalization – basically, a jack-of-all-trades *and* a *master of all trades*. Now, dear reader, you may be wondering if becoming a master of all trades in *any* industry is even possible and to that I'll confidently tell you, "yes." In fact, I do happen to know several generalists who at least appear to be good in several aspects of VFX (except for the programming side) and I *especially* know at least one woman who is *exceptionally good* in both the creative aspects of VFX *and* in all types of computer programming – and I know this person *really* well. Anyway, I digress, the point is that you can certainly expect several hand-picked post-production artists – who are multitalented and skilled in more than just one VFX niche – to be brought on set with the VFX supervisor in order to perform live, real-time VFX post-production; although, I'm not sure if we can still call it post-production if the work is to be done during production itself. Hmm ... Perhaps it could even be known as the VFX live-production or on-production team. Who knows, but I know one thing's for sure: the VFX industry doesn't care about titles or ranks other than to make it easier to categorize groups of people in the studio pipeline.

- **New roles may emerge through a merger of existing singular-niche roles in VFX**

So, I will actually dive deeper into my speculations of these potential new roles in a later section of this chapter, but as a cursory descriptor to this point for now, I will say that you can definitely expect new roles to appear as post-production roles get displaced and combined to form leaner, meaner (no, not literally) teams. The same goes for traditional VFX production roles where a VFX production assistant or data wrangler – traditionally common roles in most major VFX productions – may also be merged into these VFX master generalists they bring onto set. The surfacing of new roles will also apply to the broader industry of filmmaking where, with the newer technologies available that may potentially overrule prior tools and outdated ways of doing things, several roles involving gathering data just for data's sake may be combined or replaced by someone from the on-production VFX team instead. In other words, singular-niche roles in filmmaking may also be lost alongside the evolution of the VFX team on set. Of course, if you are an aspiring artist or even a mid, I wouldn't necessarily worry about the potential merger of niche roles in VFX. Until that happens, the studios that saw this coming will most likely preempt this by sending the few *selected* artists on their team for some kind of retraining and re-skilling. Note, however, that this will probably only happen if you are a mainstay *employee* at that company – if you're a freelancer, you'll have to do it on your own time (which again, is not necessarily a negative).

- **New roles may arise based on the new tools and technologies incorporated into VFX**

Following up on new roles being formed on the basis of merging existing roles and transforming specialists into generalists, new roles may also arise based on the new tools and technologies that will have been incorporated into VFX. Again, I will dive into specifics later in the chapter but for now, let's just say that the contraction of roles will most likely be equivalently matched with the creation of new roles and jobs arising from the use of these newer tools in VFX. From advanced virtual production to volumetric capture and projections (with the latter being a stretch but still likely possible in the distant future of VFX), it isn't all doom and gloom when change happens in any industry. Reader, I am quite certain you may have read or heard of the AI scare where certain jobs are going to *inevitably* be replaced by machines, but let me tell you that that is certainly only *one side* of the story. With destruction comes creation and usually what AI will replace (which is already being done *terribly* by people anyway – think of your always-late postal worker or bad-tempered customer service operator) AI will also create by generating different *kinds* of human work and jobs that were not possible before. Honestly, don't we wish that those horrendously unreliable postal workers and inattentive waiters who may mess up your orders be completely displaced anyway? I know I do. In the end, it's survival of the fittest, and the ones who adapt to newer technologies and the upgraded economy are ultimately the ones who have earned their place (and their jobs) in their respective industries. The same concept applies in VFX, so just because several repetitive tasks may soon be replaced by smarter tools and AI does not mean that other, different, newer opportunities will not be created in the process. Again, it is all about maintaining perspective. One thing's for sure however, most of these new roles will most likely be popping up in the production phase of any VFX project – again, shifting focus away from post-production, after-thought editing to live, on-camera, and real-time VFX manipulation.

- **Generalists will be preferred over specialists except when it comes to programming and development-related tasks**

Moving on from VFX roles in production, now, this is something I have already mentioned above but for emphasis I am stating it here again (because this also applies in the production phase of any film project) – generalists will become the norm over specialists with the *exception* of programmers and developers in the field. And while it is important to state what could change in the future, I believe it is just as important to specify what will most likely stay the same with said changes – and this factor is certainly one of them. You see, programmers and developers earn their worth and increase their value as they "age" into their fields and focus on one or two highly specialized niches. Of course, a rare and talented programmer is one who is a master of all things programming but even then, those are rare finds and might come across as inexperienced to studios looking solely for a game engine developer specialist for instance; honestly, we can't blame them, the public consensus has always been that programmers and developers who have been around the block for at least a decade definitely have much more experience to bring to the table – and I doubt that that perspective is going to change (even with new tools and technologies being made available). Thus, dear reader, if you happen to be one of these developers or programmers looking to get involved in the VFX industry in the future but are afraid that new trends and changes might put you out of work – you really have nothing much to worry about. Work on your people skills and continue concentrating on those relevant areas when it comes to programming for VFX, and I can almost assure you that your position will still be in demand even if all you do is develop tools for Autodesk Maya. Really, programmers and developers are incredibly valuable in almost *any* industry regardless of how specialized or concentrated your programming focus is.

Typically, when we think of VFX, we think of post-production tools, post-production behind-the-scenes, and post-production people. Overall, my anticipation of the future of VFX in production is that it will become the new focus of what the VFX pipeline represents and embodies. No longer will post-production be the emphasis in most behind-the-scenes work of your latest and greatest blockbuster hits. Instead, we can expect to see more VFX artists walking around on set on par with the director, cast, and crew. Now, if you've been following the VFX world for a while,

I know this vision might be hard to take in seeing how VFX has always been a very "behind-the-screens" kind of job where you can expect to be seated comfortably in an air-conditioned room rather than sweat it out with all the muck on a film set; but hey, I am just speculating here (though I honestly wouldn't be surprised if VFX in the future starts to have on-set work overriding post-production behind-the-scenes). Either way, our industry likely has many, many more years ahead of us before we reach this fulcrum – and once we get there, don't say I didn't tell you so. If there is anything else that I know *for certain* it's that change is usually just around the corner – it all depends on how many corners the industry takes.

## New emphasis on supporting skills

Remember some pages ago when I said that if you have any additional skills (VFX or not), those supporting skills will *not* be utilized and are as good as non-existent? Well, surprise, surprise – I am now here to officially contradict my previous statement on the basis of predicting the *future* of VFX. Again, this doesn't nullify what I said earlier – that fact still stands *today* – however, I *strongly believe* that the future is certainly going to look a lot brighter for those who indeed possess those extra ancillary skills but are unable to put them to use at their specialist VFX jobs. Supporting skills such as knowing how to rig and animate (assuming those roles themselves still exist in the future) or even knowing how to read balance sheets and create python scripts for miscellaneous tasks, while not important today (if your job simply requires you to be a matte painter, for example), will eventually gain traction and significance as the VFX industry starts to fuse several singular-niche tasks to create more well-rounded generalist-type roles. Again, the merger and creation of these generalist roles are mostly for the primary purpose of having versatile artists be brought on set to manhandle new tools and technologies that will inevitably become commonplace on major productions; as also mentioned, keeping these types of teams lean is important in order to not extract unnecessary dollars from production for people who do not *need* to be on set at all. With all those factors enmeshed, it seems certain that a new (or renewed, depending on your perspective) emphasis on having supporting skills in addition to your primary skill sets will be crucial in the future years of VFX.

Based on my boots on the ground and having access to several pairs of eyes and ears "working for me" on my behalf, observations and experiences have proven that we are already starting to see generalists rise in importance as several major niche VFX studios – such as those that handle previs/postvis in filmmaking – are primarily *only* hiring multitalented master generalists (VFX artists who can model, texture, rig, animate, track, light, and composite – at record speed). It is my belief that generalists will continue to become more important as VFX and technology develop over time. Heck, I already know of some of these types of generalists who get to go on set *and* work on the post-production of several major productions while your specialist finalist compositor gets pushed into one corner of a dark room to work like a machine on what would, in the end, be very similar types of shots and problems to solve. Again, the preference for generalists has begun and I'm only predicting that it'll eventually become the norm for the VFX industry as a whole. Then it's bye-bye animator/compositor/3D modeler.

Of course, a new emphasis on supporting skills is not *just* limited to VFX skills alone. Oh, no. I've also had the privilege of experiencing the early beginnings of a special type of attention being paid to people with *both* a prowess in the creative arts *and* in programming and scripting. In fact, it is highly likely that the future of VFX will involve a higher priority being placed on artists with programming skills over pure artists (who either loathe code or don't want to learn how to code). Look, this isn't me saying that you *must* learn programming in order to get into VFX – nah, I know *plenty* of artists who are pure artists (in fact, about 9.5 in every 10 artists I meet are pure artists with zero programming skills – the 0.5 is to emphasize how *rare* this combination is that it doesn't even merit a full person); but, when it comes to the future of VFX, these types of supporting skills that tie in closely to the increased use of game engines will, of course, become a deal-sealer when it comes to studios making their hires. Don't get me wrong, they'll still accept you if you happen to be a pure creative VFX generalist, but studios will *love* you if you happen to be a true generalist in the arts and the sciences (sometimes also known as a creative technologist).

While supporting skills in today's VFX market aren't necessary (nor coveted) as someone who strictly specializes and excels in *one* particular niche, recent developments in technology and in the industry prove that certain markets aren't only congealing together – such as the harmonious interlocking between VFX and the game development industries (as I predicted in my 2016 TED talk) – they're also creating new opportunities for new types of talent to thrive. While there is no certainty in things panning out the way I am predicting in this treatise (obviously), as a fellow VFX artist myself, I can only say that I have witnessed and observed generalists starting to become the center of most VFX productions (with specialist VFX artists being relegated to the sidelines) and I won't be surprised if this seed continues to grow like an unstoppable rhizome in the future. So, if you're concerned that everything you have learned in art school about animating, texturing, and lighting will be rendered useless by the time you enter the workforce as a rotoscoping artist – I wouldn't be too disappointed years down the road.

## Predicted potential new roles

At long last, the moment you have all been waiting for (I am guessing), here are my predicted *potential* new roles as they pertain to the speculated future direction the VFX industry is going. On the basis that *advanced* mixed reality is starting to emerge on major Hollywood production sets and AI programs are becoming more sophisticated as we breathe, I reckon the following new roles will surface by the time VFX hits 2030-ish (possibly a little earlier than that – plus or minus a couple of years):

- **VFX on-set generalists (or XR artists/virtual production artists)**

Sometimes these positions may also be known as technical artists (at least as it applies today). I am listing this as a new role mainly because it is likely that the emphasis and utility of XR tools and the like may become commonplace in the future, such that it warrants the creation (or merger of existing artist roles) of an artist solely dedicated to the execution of on-set VFX. On the other hand, it is also possible that the work involved in on-set VFX may be rather fluid, meaning there really is no "definitive" job scope for this type of position (other than flexibility and versatility of a diverse range of applicable skills). Still, if I had to pin down a few types of tasks this position will be doing, it would generally involve real-time modeling, animating, lighting, and compositing all at once, live on-camera, and at record speed (and accuracy). They *may* be involved in wrangling technical data as well, but it is possible that this will be assigned to a dedicated data wrangler on bigger productions that are clearly able to afford the expense (and the XR tools). VFX on-set generalists, XR artists, or virtual production artists will very likely be reporting to the on-set VFX supervisor or the next predicted role in this list.

- **XR supervisors/specialists**

Possibly doubling up as VFX supervisors on-set, the XR supervisors or XR specialists may be possible new roles in the future given the direction VFX is heading. The reason why it would *likely* be a different person from the VFX supervisor will ultimately depend on the complexity of the tools involved in the production, the budget, and how much work the VFX supervisor has on his or her plate. Naturally, a VFX supervisor is going to be *the busiest* VFX person on set, hence, having a separate XR supervisor may help lighten that load as the XR supervisor or specialist focuses specifically on the management, direction, and delivery of all XR tools involved. Just as we have 3D supervisors, creature supervisors, and compositing supervisors today, having a separate XR person-in-charge on and off set is a natural progression from having XR artists in the future VFX pipeline. I imagine this person will have to work closely with the VFX supervisor in order to execute the director's vision while leveraging the technologies available to the production. My speculation is that the XR supervisor/specialist and VFX supervisor combo will make a deadly duo on whichever production they end up on; expect lots of brain share to occur between these two, which will only lead to more innovation and progress in the future. XR supervisors or XR specialists will, of course, share leadership over the team of on-set VFX generalists or XR artists alongside the VFX supervisor (if the two are separate individuals).

- **Volumetric data wrangler-editor**

Depending on how widespread volumetric capture systems become in the future of VFX – which honestly still remains to be seen – the probability of there being a data wrangler-editor type of person when it comes to handling heavy-duty volumetric data is a high possibility. Having dealt with some degree of volumetric footage before at Intel, those few shots alone contained a *lot* of data to work with in post-production. Of course, knowing that these existing systems that I had worked with would most likely have progressed years into the future of VFX, it is possible that volumetric data will eventually be streamlined when being ingested into proprietary software or systems. Until then, I would imagine that a volumetric data wrangler and/or editor would become necessary to not only handle, manage, and sort through all that data but also potentially discard noisy/useless data for the VFX generalists to work with in post-production (or otherwise). They may even have a nickname in the future like tweakers, modification artists, or a new type of VFX "editors" who in essence are simply people who tweak existing data captured through sophisticated systems; they may very well even be generalists who also function as a higher-level type of compositor or "editor" from what we have today. Either way, I would imagine that this person will have to be extremely meticulous – and will most likely be direct personnel supplied by the company of the volumetric system itself – and also require a certain efficiency of speed and accuracy in order to make the available relevant data ready for the next artist in line. Volumetric data wranglers and editors will most likely be reporting to their company's supervisor and occasionally be communicating with the assistant director and VFX supervisor on-set on basic issues such as the time required to ingest data, how the data is looking in real-time, and anything that may impact moving on to the next shot set-up.

- **AI VFX developers**

Ah yes, the wonderful world of AI. I am personally excited for this potential new role prediction as I have seen the wonders of AI and how it can really make or break humanity in terms of expediting progress and accelerating the efficiency and effectiveness of many, many things. I am anticipating AI VFX developers to be all the rage in the future as more advanced proprietary tools soon require more advanced developers to tackle and develop reusable solutions for – and this is *not* just your run-of-the-mill python or expressions in After Effects or Nuke. Depending on the type of AI required by the production – as you may or may not know, there are many different *types* of AI (AI is simply an umbrella category) – a studio will require a handful of extremely talented AI developers with a special background in VFX (or at least a history of working with a few VFX studios and projects involving entertainment). Just as tasks in VFX post-production range from production to production, I anticipate an AI VFX developer to have a plethora of tasks involving crafting, training, and skilling an AI system specially designed for that one particular studio or production. Again, if you are really curious about the different types of AI and their potential in VFX, I highly suggest doing your own independent research on this topic – I most certainly do not claim to be an expert in AI whatsoever. Either way, AI VFX developers would clearly be expected to deliver systems that work and that are designed to work *without* their continuous presence or input. Depending on how each studio structures its hierarchy, you would typically expect to find your

AI VFX developers either working independently or reporting directly to whoever was meant to be in charge of the particular project (perhaps a technology supervisor, technical director [TD], or even the founder of the studio).

- **Game developers (or game engine developers)**

  So, this isn't exactly a new role in and of itself, but it is a role coming in from the game development industry to VFX. Game developers, once circling only amongst the development of video games and the like, will soon find plenty more opportunities to venture into other forms of entertainment as game developers become the next coveted "app developer" type role; remember when being an Android and iPhone app developer was such a huge (and lucrative) deal? Well, brace yourselves for these game developers to become the next "app developers" for many decades to come. Not only are game developers industry-agnostic – you can have a game developer developing games and interactive experiences for the medical industries, hospitality, and so on (beyond *just* consumable entertainment) – they have also begun to play an important role in VFX productions as game engines like Unity and Unreal (mostly the latter, frankly) get used on major and minor film productions alike. Of course, game *engine* developers could also be a huge hit in the future as more innovative VFX studios are requesting heavy customization of existing game engines in order to suit their VFX production needs. In fact, I was even part of such an endeavor when I was at a VR startup in Los Angeles – of course, I wasn't a game *engine* developer by any stretch of the imagination and I definitely know my limits in programming and developing. Either way, I would speculate that not much will change in terms of the expected job scope requirements for both the game developer or game engine developer, whether or not they are specializing in games or VFX (or both); a typical assignment of most game developers would be to assess and promptly develop and execute an interactive or immersive experience (game or not) and I would expect the same for game engine developers, where it would be an expectation to modify market or proprietary game engines to help deliver those results in a production. Like the AI VFX developers, it is highly likely that these developers will be tasked to work independently or work with a separate unit formed within a VFX studio that caters to all developers alike – it depends on the studio.

It goes without saying that the above is not an exhaustive list – they're simply roles that are top-of-mind whilst I write this book (which could also say a lot about the importance of these roles). Clearly, we are trending towards a state of pervasive AI and mixed reality mediums in many aspects of our society – this is no different in respective industries such as VFX. From on-set VFX generalists (in fact, this role is already starting to come into existence, popularized by *"The Mandalorian"* production) to AI VFX developers, roles in the future of VFX are being highly concentrated into the talent and innovation of a few singular individuals who can do many things effectively and proficiently. Of course, as I have stressed many times above, this isn't to say that you *have* to be excellent at multiple things in order to thrive in VFX in the future. Truly, it is my belief that the VFX industry will continue to remain robust as it stretches and flexes with developing technologies and trends of the time; wherever one presently fits today, it is highly likely that there will always be a role that will fit a passionate artist. As I said, this list is not the end of it all. I am sure there will be plenty of new and differentiated roles popping up in the future of the VFX industry; for now, we can only speculate and anticipate given all the data we have available to us today.

## Roles likely to be long-term stays (with caveats)

Now, even if changes abound, there will most certainly be several roles that exist in the VFX industry today that will continue to exist and persist into the future. After all, machines can only take us so far and sometimes certain areas simply require human intervention and interference. The following are my predictions as to the roles that will likely be long-term stays in the foreseeable future of the VFX industry (with *some* caveats, of course). Now please note that I am not a walking encyclopedia of *all* possible VFX roles so this list is definitely not a complete one (there will, for sure, be a few positions that exist in our industry but are not specified here for no other reason other than the lack of top-of-mind awareness):

- **VFX supervisors**

This really needs no explanation, nor should it come as a surprise – VFX supervisors on-set are definitely here to stay and will most likely continue to stay long into the future. Now, I believe this staying power only applies to the on-set VFX supervisory role and not so much for singular-niche VFX supervisors (except, perhaps, those who are there to supervise the *other* future-proof positions also in this list). With the obvious reason of several of these singular-niche type artist positions fading or merging into new roles, one wouldn't *need* these singular-niche post-production VFX supervisors either (after all, what's to supervise if you have no artists working under you?). Either way, regardless of how developed and transformed the VFX industry becomes in the future, a feature film, television production, or even a high-end commercial is *always* going to need some kind of expert in terms of executing, meeting, and delivering the visual magic and results expected for those productions. This person happens to be the VFX supervisor, and this VFX supervisor is very likely going to continue to be in equal or greater demand as the VFX industry forges ahead with its embrace of innovative technology and tools. Essentially, production roles are not going away in the future and neither are creative supervisory positions like production or project-based VFX supervisors. Dear reader, if there is a *safe, bankable* position you'd want to make in staying in the VFX industry for the long game (if that is indeed your intention), being an *on-set* VFX supervisor is one of the ways to go.

- **VFX producers**

Following hot on the heels of the on-set VFX supervisors are your VFX producers of today (and tomorrow). Just as productions get more and more complex (logistically), VFX producers are needed to balance out the prevailing VFX supervisors on set. With novel and innovative technology comes more administrative, budgetary, and logistical issues to manage on behalf of the production – here's where your all-too-important VFX producers step in as long-term stays in the VFX industry. Honestly, I do not foresee these VFX producers going away any time soon, even if the VFX industry somehow finds a way to regulate itself logistically, on-budget, and instantaneously. VFX is a complex process that involves modified or custom pipelines that usually work better when sorted and managed by a human than a machine; as such, VFX producers are here to stay. Now, they'll probably need to adapt to understanding the new tools and systems involved with XR and so on (just like the VFX supervisors on set, if they're not working with an XR specialist) but I would imagine that – having known several mid and veteran VFX producers myself – these individuals have no problem getting acquainted with new data and learning new stuff along the lines of their work. Yet again, dear reader, another bankable position, if being on a film set every day is not something you fancy.

- **VFX coordinators/administrators**

So, this is one of those "with caveat" roles where it really depends on how VFX studios decide to morph or keep these positions. Don't get me wrong, VFX coordinators and administrators are important in keeping most of the happenings at VFX studios organized, but frankly, I have experienced and witnessed several studios combine this position with a generalist or VFX producer and they're doing fine thus far. Of course, depending on how heavy or massive productions get at any one studio, having a few VFX coordinators around is a wise investment in maintaining some semblance of order when juggling multiple projects of various sizes. This also leaves the VFX producers free to do what they do best – produce *for* VFX.

Either way, the real caveat here with this position depends on how VFX studios modify their workflow when it comes to the number of incoming XR-heavy productions. Whilst these tools have the *potential* for becoming commonplace in bigger, high-budget productions, it remains to be seen how frequent these projects will become – hence, a traditional VFX coordinator may be a role that will continue to persist into the future even if it *seems* like a role you'd want to replace with an AI system. If you know anything about VFX coordinating, reader, you'll know that it involves *more* than just organizing, including a load of communication and phone calls with people *outside* the VFX studio as well. Ultimately, most VFX coordinators I know end up leveling up to VFX producers – so, we've got to have that entry-level position for VFX producers somehow.

- **Technical directors**

Technical directors are a tricky one, and their ability to be a long-term stay really depends on several factors such as the technology involved with their positions, the type of artists required per production, and what these TDs ultimately end up doing or contributing to the production. As such, it is hard to say how many of these TDs will continue into the indefinite future without being dependent on so many variables. Their roles may also be defined entirely by the VFX studio in question (or perhaps, even by the production itself) so it is highly likely that the TD position will become increasingly flexible and fluid over time as it adapts to the changing times in VFX. While I do know a few TDs in my network, the majority of them are niche-specific (dealing with animation, creature FX, or lighting for example) and, again, the chances of TDs persisting into the future will depend highly on how many of these sub-niches still remain in VFX (that's the caveat here). For now, however, TDs are likely to be long-term stays in the VFX industry since there will always be a need for some technical direction when it comes to a large majority of VFX productions; let's also not forget that not all studios in the VFX market can afford to upgrade or uplift their entire VFX business model on the basis of prevailing technologies of the day – there will always be a market for doing VFX the traditional way, even if the projects you get to work on aren't as glamorous or "cool-sounding" as those major Hollywood blockbusters.

- **Previs/postvis artists**

Having been a postvis artist myself on many occasions, the previs and postvis artists have my vote on artist positions that exist today and will continue to exist way into the future. Presently, these positions still function as an important segue to envisioning something off the script to a preliminary form in post-production. Of course, this will definitely be a position that has a major caveat in terms of its longevity in the industry: it depends on how advanced and multitalented our VFX on-set generalists get (which remains to be seen). As much as we would like to imagine that there are plenty of talented people in the world (not just in VFX, but in all communities), the truth is that *real* talent is hard to find and as rare as a freakin' unicorn. Last I checked, unicorns don't actually exist, period. So, on that note, it truly does remain to be seen how many *super-talented* on-set VFX generalists exist in the future, as it will definitely cut into the need for the existence of the previs or postvis artist to begin with. You see, as the VFX on-set generalists perform tasks typically done by a techvis team, there is a high possibility that these future on-set VFX generalists will also be able to double and triple up to take over the previs and postvis work as well (again, if anything I have said sounds confusing to you – use Google). Hence, while I would peg this role as something that will last into the future as VFX continues to adapt and adopt new technologies to expedite its efficiencies, the *number* of previs and postvis artists *needed* in the industry may ultimately dwindle depending on the growing number and proficiency of our future on-set VFX generalists; thus, it really depends on how *that* goes first, so we'll just have to sit this out and wait and see.

- **3D generalists**

Ah yes, 3D generalists. They'll last and they'll be around for a very long time. Similar to your on-set VFX generalists, my prediction for 3D generalists is that they'll likely be the pool where our future on-set VFX generalists arise. This isn't to say that all on-set VFX generalists *are* 3D generalists – since the on-set generalists will require non-3D skills to excel in their positions as well – but being a 3D generalist is definitely a good starting point for anyone looking to get ahead in becoming a *future* on-set generalist pro. That being said, being a 3D generalist is actually also a very desirable prerequisite to being a previs or postvis artist, and artists can technically dip their hands into both these pots as skilled 3D generalists. As we deal with more 3D (and even 4D) data and volumetric cloud capture systems, working directly with depth and 3D data is only going to become *more* important as we march forward into the future of technology and VFX. So, dear reader, if you are ever on the fence about what niche to specialize in today when it comes to VFX – being a 3D generalist is as good as being an engineer in the real world. You really can't go wrong when you know how to model, texture, light, and animate – among other things – in VFX. The demand is there today and will only increase over time *even* with AI and robots that will replace *other* niches in VFX.

- **Procedural animators/particle effects artists**

Now, if there is ever a singular-niche type of VFX role that will survive the impending upheaval of the industry (ok, perhaps more like a slow boil; the change wouldn't be as violent as the word 'upheaval' suggests), it's the people who specialize in procedural animations and particle effects. These roles include hair FX, fur animation, environmental FX, et cetera – anything that really constitutes something that is almost *impossible* or too difficult to replicate in real-life due to the physics involved. Basically, anything involving simulations is going to stay for a while until technology advances to allow actual real-world physics modifications (which is unlikely, but hey, let's imagine the possibility for a second). I mean, really, name me a production that was able to *realistically* replicate a *real* lion's fur *acting* the way it's supposed to in a shot, on-camera – impossible, and you'd have to manipulate that using VFX procedurals and particle FX, for sure (which also defeats the purpose of bringing a real lion on set). Now, if you somehow learned how to *force* a lion to control its hairs to act for the camera the way you want it to, defying physics, do share that with me (or exploit it for yourself to become the next billionaire). For now, I am assuming that there presently is no way to control a lion (or any animal) to do that consciously on its own accord, hence, particle FX artists and procedural animators (you know, the ones who are Houdini whizzes, who are probably rejoicing in the background) will continue to remain as the precious commodities that they are today. Yes, even today, Houdini artists, particle FX, and procedural VFX artists are *highly* sought after and will most likely also be *highly* paid. Personally, I wouldn't know as I have not yet utilized my Houdini skills in a professional setting, but of the few Houdini artists I do know coming out of SCAD who are out there working in the trenches, let me assure you that they do get paid *a lot* (even entry-level Houdini artists are paid significantly higher than your entry-level compositor or texture artist). Make of that what you will, but I will say that whatever still remains impossible to replicate in reality (even in the future) would continue to have a market in VFX.

- **Tool developers/programmers**

If I haven't hinted at the patterns enough in my last sub-chapter, the trend is this: developers and programmers are here to stay and there will only be *more* opportunities for these people in VFX in the future. I mean, technologies are cool and all that, but tool developers and programmers are most likely always going to be needed in order to manipulate, track, and systematize the boatloads of data the VFX process generally produces. Even if AI gets so advanced in the future that it can intelligently assess and simplify the VFX data coming in, tool developers and programmers will most likely still be employed by various studios in order to customize their systems or software in order to give said studios the competitive advantage over other VFX studios. I don't really have much more to add other than developers and programmers certainly exist in the VFX industry today and that we will certainly be needing *more* (not less) of that as newer technologies and tools avail themselves to our industry. It is likely that there will be a heavier emphasis in the industry on people who can code or who can modify code of software and tools; there really is no better time to be a programmer than today, even if in anticipation of brighter tomorrows.

VFX supervisors, producers, shot creators, layout/previs/postvis artists, coordinators, and the like, are but a few of the roles that will most likely be long-term stays, in my opinion. Basically, if you happen to be in any of these positions right now, don't want to upgrade yourself, and *like* staying put where you are at, at your present company, then you can consider yourself safe from when the industry shifts and jobs get thrown out the window out of futility and a lack of utility in the future. While some roles are highly dependent on how future roles pan out, others like the VFX coordinator position may actually be good stepping stones to becoming a VFX producer or a studio general manager. Heck, certain VFX studios may even combine the coordinator position with general studio management roles like a studio manager. The important thing to note is that a lot of this depends on how technology continues to develop in the future and how the VFX market responds to said developments. Of course, this isn't *just* about VFX. Hollywood as a whole will also have to respond to these technological developments and, sometimes, they just might have a stronger (louder) voice than the VFX industry on its own. We'll just have to wait and see, really.

311

## The future of talent in the world of film and entertainment

Speaking of Hollywood, it is time we scale back into the broader market of the film world. Firstly, it is no mistake that the future of talent will also change in filmmaking just as it changes in VFX. The pattern is still the same regardless: generalize, generalize, generalize. Certainly, contractors and employees in the film industry themselves have long been forced into being or becoming generalists due to the nature of the film industry (especially when one is just starting out). However, I do believe that the tendency for more master generalists is only going to become stronger as time goes on and the competition from pools of specialists increases to a saturated oblivion. I mean, really, what is going to make John the gaffer different from Suzy or Tommy the gaffer? Other than experience, track record, and reputation in the film industry, soon we will eventually come to a point where John, Suzy, and Tommy are all look-alikes in résumé, reputation, and records that it will all boil down to pricing and rapport (though, it is almost certainly going to be a price war in most cases). Hence, with all this saturation and competition (filled with equally capable talent or equally deceptive walking cesspools), it is only a matter of time before the master generalist storm catches up to Hollywood as an important and valuable differentiator of *true* talent. Indeed, one can be excellent in one thing – just like the billions of other people in society – or one can be excellent in *many* things (which is even rarer and makes you stand out even more).

Of course, with the change of tides in talent in the future, expect competition to make an initial drop *and then* increase intensely in the film industry as more and more people slowly catch up to the differentiated means of assessing talent, and more and more people get exposed to lifelong or continuous learning and development in one's lifetime. Whilst the competition won't be as intense as before when everyone and their mom could get into film by specializing only in one area, the competition would be, well, interesting to say the least – and this would be for the betterment of the film industry and Hollywood as a whole.

As for the future of talent in the broader context of the entertainment industry, depending on the industry, certain roles will continue to be "safe" as specialists. Perhaps positions that involve a lot more risks, financial investments, or finesse will fall into that category. Overall, I would imagine that unless the position involves a lot of technical know-how or years of specialized, concentrated experience (as in programmers and developers), most positions will generally evolve into more generalist-type roles. Whether you are in themed entertainment, game development, or the music industry, generalists will be the new mainstream as multitalented artists and multihyphenates prove to be more useful and worthier of a studio or company's investment dollars than singular-niche specialists. In fact, it is highly likely that companies in the future will then be buying into the personal brand of their hired talents rather than just hiring them for their individual talents alone. And on that note, personal branding and the cult of personality will also become a major selling and differentiating point in the selection of future talent in entertainment. No longer will talent simply be pawns to be used by companies to fulfill their agendas; future talent will soon become deliberately calculated investments and hires for profiles that fit each company's brand (basically, the hire *could* feel more like a collaboration than a pure employer-employee relationship).

From hiring an independent record producer with one million followers to help "boost" a record label's own presence and notoriety to recruiting someone on the basis of how they portray themselves (and their values) online, the entertainment industry as a whole is definitely heading in the direction of leveraging more from their talent hires (and not just in areas of talent and skill alone).

This is especially true in the film industry and in Hollywood: if you think that your online persona and personal brand plays a big role in you being hired today – just wait till years down the road. The future of talent as well as the future of how talent is being hired and selected will change – for better or worse – and will become more complex than it has been or presently is today. Dear reader, here is where I advise extreme caution and anticipation: anticipate that you *may* have to pick up a few new skills in order to be more useful (and employable), *especially* when it comes to working in the film industry (again, this is slightly different than in VFX). You should also be cautious about how you are perceived online (if you have a searchable or public presence online). On that note, if you happen to have a ton of followers or a strong base of support from fans of your niche, the future is certainly going to be a lot brighter for you as those numbers eventually become your employment leverage when it comes to working in certain entertainment sectors (again, the value of this depends on the industry and on the position in question).

In the end, the future of talent will change as other factors *in and out* of the industry come into play. From the emphasis on personal brand leverage to the seeking of multifaceted brilliance, the future of talent in the world of film and entertainment is bright as it is dark, depending on which side of the fence you are on. ... And here's your list for the ones who are perpetually lazy and didn't read the above:

- Becoming a unique and differentiated generalist will be key to thriving in the future of film.
- Certain roles within certain sectors of the entertainment sphere will most likely always be safe due to the importance placed on specialists in those types of fields and work.
- Companies and studios will leverage the personal brand of their hires to help fulfill and execute their agendas.
- Public personas and fan bases of certain hires will start to matter to companies as a means of getting the best "bang for their buck" in their hires.
- Employment on the basis of personal branding and public persona may start to feel more collaborative, going beyond a strict employer-employee working relationship.

- The trend will be in investing in multitalented individuals with a strong, favorable public persona that fits their company profile.

Based on my understanding of human behavior, we as a people really do enjoy having variety in our lives – whether it's doing different tasks, different things, or turning different hobbies into businesses and lucrative skills to be utilized, et cetera. The people in creative industries such as filmmaking and other forms of entertainment, clearly, are no different. The larger trend as far as the future of talent goes in these fields is a preference towards individuals who are multitalented and multihyphenated. The world of film will experience a surge of people with a diverse skill set and almost little to no specialization, if this is not already occurring. To top that off, I would say, it certainly does appear that what were once considered periphery requirements for the job (a favorable personal brand or public persona) will soon take center stage in a future where personal names and brands start to matter more, *in addition* to being able to execute and deliver results. Welcome to the future.

## Where entertainment is potentially headed

As I already established at an earlier point in this book, certain markets and industries move in conjunction with one another. The entertainment industry as a whole is normally controlled by its sub-industries more so than the other way around; however, there may occasionally be scenarios where life imitates art and art imitates life. Obviously, the development of entertainment has always been closely tied with where society is headed – sometimes with entertainment even leading the development of society – so there are certainly many variables and factors involved in encapsulating the complex future of entertainment. I will attempt to simplify and summarize my predictions as to where entertainment is potentially headed as an industry as best I can (not just about the future of its talent, as we've covered in the previous sub-chapter).

You see, entertainment is a powerful tool and voice – that fact is not going to change. In fact, entertainment is only going to become more pervasive (perhaps even to the point of subconscious intrusion and attention-diversion) and interactive with its audiences – engaging and utilizing multiple mediums more than ever to get at its target audience. Of course, we already see this happening today with tracking cookies and just, well, trackers of your activity where companies and advertisers are able to read, analyze, and profile just what you like, don't like, what you do, when you do it, and how you prefer to do whatever it is that you do. Expect this to be doubled down tenfold in the future as entertainment heads in the direction of persistent engagement; basically, entertainment will be coming *to* you rather than the other way around, whether you like it or have the time for it or not. What this also means is that there will most likely be a select few who will eventually dominate this revised form of pervasive and persistent entertainment whereas the rest of entertainment that fails to catch up will most likely be tossed into the trash heap; sure, there may be a few nuggets of gold floating around in there but for the most part, that content will be relegated to obscurity (hence, a kind of oblivion, like trash) compared to entertainment that will become annoyingly persistent for eyeballs (also known as your attention).

That being said, with the rise and continued developments and investments into interactive technologies, whilst entertainment will become more pervasive, it will also start to be more open to viewer control – especially in the sense of the story said viewer wishes to receive and/or dictate. Meaning, another attempt at interactive storytelling will most likely happen again. Yes, yes, having viewers and audiences control the direction of a story or film narrative has been harped about (and hyped about) for years now, and having worked at and with a few VR startups and filmmakers deliberately looking to attempt that with VR, I can only say that this idea has been *very* popular with filmmakers and people in entertainment alike. The thing is, their attempts have always backfired or performed terribly with viewers finding the process of controlling the narrative cumbersome, annoyingly taxing, or just plain dumb. Unfortunately for entertainment, this is a fad that refuses to die and stay dead – and perhaps for good reason. It is likely that entertainment is potentially attempting another variant of interactive storytelling and this time, I am not just talking about the pathetic flop of interactive VR content or film either. Remember real-time VFX and 3D VR content on the horizons of VFX's future? That's one hint I'll give for now. And yes, there are certainly those startups out there that try to make virtual reality more like its namesake – a literal "virtual reality" – but my only comment to that is, "Mm, ok."

Back to being realistic, it certainly takes a while for these things to develop, but trust that societal movements will most likely be developing alongside motion picture content and technology. If the need for interactive storytelling is warranted then in the future, then, dear reader, the market will be tolerant and more accepting of its hundredth re-attempt. Until then, I can only affirm that pervasiveness, persistence, and *attempted* viewer/user directives and control will be trends we could see in the future, where entertainment is potentially headed.

As for entertainment, in terms of content style and type, I would say that you can expect content to become more cerebral, intellectual, rational, and poignantly scientific – while at the same time willing to defy the "norms." Let me enlighten you with what we have today. Today, what we *really* have in terms of content, is this: emotionally charged, politicized, polarized, dramatic, politically laden content that attempts to justify or only show one side of the story or situation that supports the director or screenwriter's view of the world. Basically, very biased, very one-sided, and very emotional. Ironically, where I am seeing entertainment heading in the future will be in stark contrast with popular opinion. Instead of entertainment becoming even *more* polarizing and stupidly emotional, I sense and predict that entertainment will surprise us (for the most part) by doing a complete 180 on its viewers, being enlightened and more intellectual and rational in thought. Of course, there is always going to be the same – if not, even worse – emotional, highly dramatic, and biased content out there in the future of entertainment, but you'd be surprised by how logical people can truly be as well as how much bias one person can eventually tolerate. Pile this up with the public consensus on the blatant bias portrayed by the mainstream media in America, as well as people's lowered threshold for polarizing idiocy, I do believe entertainment will anticipate the weariness of audiences and attempt to "flip" on them in order to capitalize on their cumulative fatigue from previously biased content. As I've said, entertainment, in general, is all about entertaining and engaging people; regardless of where you stand on the political spectrum, expect entertainment to pick up on these subtle cues and be open to being the panacea by having less polarizing, more rational content.

Ultimately, be prepared to be surprised (and not-so-surprised) by where entertainment as an industry is headed and how it plans to get there. In short:

- Entertainment as a whole will become more pervasive, persistent, and powerful than it currently is today.
- There will be a select few individuals or entities who will control and dominate the success of pervasive and persistent entertainment, potentially dictating the market's future direction.
- Interactive storytelling through updated and advanced interactive technologies will be making another comeback in a different way.

- Users and viewers will be granted even more control in how they wish to receive their content, in the sense of even controlling the outcome of said content to their desires.

- Entertainment, once polarizing and emotional, may make a surprising U-turn in becoming more intellectual and rational in order to tap into the viewers' increasing public disdain for biased content.

While these predictions aren't exactly crazy exciting or totally out-there, I do believe that the entertainment industry is beginning to bring about some changes. In the end, it is important to emphasize that the human psychology involved in the process is most likely going to be the sole constant throughout these developments in entertainment. That is, we as humans love and *want* to be entertained, educated, or enlightened through our entertainment, regardless of who executes and delivers upon those needs, and how it is done. Does pervasive entertainment sound exciting? Heck, no. But it sure does make consuming entertainment more convenient to the masses. It is all about predicting the development of the everchanging taste buds of our future viewers and audiences – and you can bet the farm that attempting to appease viewers as well as giving them some semblance of controlling the narrative are going to be key directives in entertainment's future direction. Soon, there may even be an addiction to the convenience and power derived from this type of malleable, pervasive content. Don't say I didn't warn you, dear reader; the writing is already on the wall, you've only got to take a closer look to see what it spells out.

# 11

# THE TRUTH ABOUT
# BEING A VFX ARTIST

Finally, the moment you have all been waiting for. Or, if you're impatient, you will have just skipped right to this chapter because that's what you do. I wouldn't want you to miss out on all the other juicy tips and insights but hey, to each their own. If you haven't yet caught on, most of the truth was sprinkled all over this book thus far, but every book needs to have its summative or headlining chapter, and this is it. Before delving into each truth, however, I'd like to premise that all these insights are simply data gathered from my many years working with and at many VFX studios in the capacity of a VFX practitioner. Sure, you could argue that I could be biased in my data interpretation but sometimes, it's easier to hear the cold hard truth from someone who technically enjoys

VFX and for whom VFX is a passion (and is still able to maintain a degree of objectivity and discernment). We all know we need more frankness these days – it will save you a ton of time if you're just wired differently. With that, here goes.

## You are never going to be your own boss (even if you own a VFX studio)

The VFX industry predominantly depends on Hollywood, and to a lesser extent, other avenues such as games, commercials, and maybe ancillary industries like medical and architectural visualization. The truth is, even if you start your own VFX studio, unless you are well-funded enough to produce your *own* productions through that studio (if that was your aim), you are always going to have to rely on incoming projects from the paying storytellers (also known as clients) of Hollywood. Sure, you may be the boss of your own company, but you are not *really* the boss, no. You are still beholden to the paying client, who can, at any moment, decide to pull out their production and go with a different competing studio that offers them better bang for their buck. And you will have no control over that – assuming you have done everything you could to keep and retain that client. In fact, this happened to one studio I had worked at: one of their largest (and possibly the only largest) clients, Disney, decided to stop outsourcing their graphics work and turned everything in-house. That move alone basically led that VFX studio to downsize drastically from over twenty artists in an entirely leased office building (with their logo and plaque plastered everywhere) to the bare bones of three artists, jammed into a tiny, plain rented room in some random corporate block.

Having owned my own company in 2016, we were in a similar situation considering and anticipating that when we would exhaust our runway (look up this start-up term on Google if you don't know what it means), we would have no other immediate or viable option but to take up productions and projects from well-off clients (whether they're independent filmmakers or corporations). This would then, of course, detract you from doing the thing that you formed your company to do to begin with. It is the reality of such a predicament. So, unless you yourself are well-off or have the means to attain that – which deserves a whole other book, that I will only care to elaborate in the distant future – you will *always* be beholden to your company's main source of funding: the client(s) or the investor(s).

As disclosed, VFX *is* an ancillary industry. They function and exist primarily to serve a larger industry or market – whether it be Hollywood, advertising media, or themed entertainment. If you get into VFX by starting a VFX studio or business, you are going to be in the business-to-business (B2B) category and rarely ever in the direct-to-consumers (D2C) category. And while being a B2B business sounds fancy, it probably also means that whatever product or service you are providing is going to first be filtered through the marketing lens of your business client. What do I mean by that? Well, easy. If you are executing VFX for a film produced by Studio123, which would be the studio that actually organizes and finalizes the production, then whatever work you have delivered will most likely be branded *under* Studio123's branding and logo. This also explains why you don't and will most likely never see the logos of VFX studios and houses in the opening credits. This, of course, makes total sense since your work was meant to be hidden and you *are* in the B2B business as a VFX studio. So, unless the consumer is an avid VFX fanatic, most consumers will most likely only know the businesses that served them the final product – those would be your Warner Bros., Paramount Studios, Happy Madisons, and Jerry Bruckheimers of the world. You know, *your* boss(es).

As such, even if you do end up running your own VFX studio, you will still be at the beck and call of your clientele and of the production studio(s) that hired your VFX studio – and in extension, hiring you.

## Say goodbye to making your *own* movies

Another truth about being a VFX artist in Hollywood is that you can basically kiss your movie-making dreams goodbye. I don't mean to be cruel, but you are *never* going to make your *own* movies (as a legitimate career) if you work as a full-time (or even part-time) VFX artist. It all comes down to the logistics, timing, and honestly, monetary returns of being in the position of a VFX practitioner. Sure, I have seen a few (and by few, I mean one or two out of the thousands of artists I encounter and work with at various places) who managed to transcend from being a VFX artist to being a director of a *major* blockbuster movie or *major* technology project, but the vast majority of VFX artists who share scripts or stories with me of their aspirations of becoming a director of their own pet projects, well, let's just say they remain just that – stories and aspirations lost to time and the lack of financial resources. Heck, even if these VFX artists were very resourceful, the schedule of a VFX person simply does not allow you to go around pitching your script or story. Let's not forget that I did talk about how you most likely won't get filthy, stinkin' rich doing VFX until you are really in your old age and that's the norm for this industry. And, for the sake of an argument, let's say you do reach that point of being rich from many decades spent in VFX: you will most likely only have the spare funds to fund one or, at max, two films of your own – then what? I hope you see where I am going with this.

This is why – harkening back to my previous point on asking yourself why you would like to get into VFX – I kind of snicker a bit when people say they get into VFX to make movies. Well, sure, you get to *help* make movies, but they are never going to be *your* movies, nor will you be credited as the mastermind of the ideas and stories channeled by the movies you *helped* create. You don't and will *never* own them (ever). So, let's just say that VFX is not for the ravenously ambitious – those who want to have their cake and eat it too (multiple times, perhaps multiple cakes). If we're running with the cake analogy here, VFX is the part where you get to have the cake, but unfortunately, that's as far as it goes. You won't get to taste that delicious, yummy cake and you certainly won't get to experience how it feels and tastes as it melts in your mouth. That's VFX in a nutshell. Again, yes, you get to *help* create other people's movies, but you won't ever get to create *your* movies – unless you have access to huge piles of throwaway cash that you don't need to use to pay off your acquired loans or other random debts. Now, to be honest, I can't really relate to bad debt or loans (as I've had neither bad debt nor loans in my life), but I can most certainly guarantee that you, dear reader, most probably don't have that extra throwaway cash to invest into creating your own films.

Well, VFX ain't going to help create that extra throwaway cash for you to invest into creating your own films, not unless you want to be at the age of eighty when you get to make your very first well-funded, self-funded movie.

The point is, if you really want to make a career out of making your *own* movies – don't be a VFX artist. Remember, the VFX industry is an ancillary industry; it is one that serves a larger industry as a whole and does not actually create any marketable end product of its own that reaches the end consumer (your typical movie-going audience). Don't get into VFX thinking you can somehow magically flip your career into bringing your own scripts to life. It doesn't work that way and the industry is certainly not designed to allow that transition to be easy. As a VFX artist, you will be working long and hard hours – with plenty of overtime days – in front of a computer screen (or running around on and off set, if your VFX position allows for that) where your sole purpose is to execute and deliver on *somebody else's* vision. And no, unless your VFX position involves a direct channel of communication and exchange with the director, your creative ways and ideas of how to design that shot will not be heeded – because, again, it's not *your* movie. Sorry, it's just the truth and you shouldn't be offended by it. Think about it: if you were a well-funded director or filmmaker of your own project (with over two thousand crew members from pre-production to post), would you accept creative ideas from all two thousand crew members because they wanted to feel like it was their own project too? Probably not. It's called having a singular vision – again, it's just the truth; it's how the industry works to keep itself thriving.

## Forever an unsung hero

Now, I did touch on this a little earlier in the book but I'm sticking this point here in this chapter because it is the truth about being a VFX artist. Unless you are a VFX supervisor of an *entire* production (not just a Head of 2D or Technical Director at a random VFX studio), any other position in VFX most likely does not get nearly enough credit or recognition. Even then, as a VFX supervisor, you also do not get nearly as much credit as the guys at the top – or above-the-line crew – of any production. Sure, you will get a pretty on-screen title card as a VFX supervisor, but to what extent does that matter to your viewing audiences? It doesn't. Again, unless the audience members are raving VFX fanatics who will even remember the names of Georges Méliès' films, it is unlikely that they will even care who the VFX supervisor on the project is, and you shouldn't blame them because objectively VFX supervisors are not *meant* to be the remembered heroes of any film production outside of the VFX world (and to a certain extent, Hollywood).

Yes, this all sounds rather pessimistic, but what did I say about the truth? Sometimes, it ain't going to be pretty or what you want to hear but it's not about what you want to hear at all. In fact, it is about what you *need* to hear. Of course, anything and everything comes down to how you *choose* to perceive and see things, but I'd like to believe that if you ever had greater aspirations in life than just being a cog in the machine, then you ought to be able to hear and swallow the objective truth.

Know this: if you like being publicly revered and credited for your work, being a VFX artist is not the way to go. Sure, you get your name in the credits, on IMDb, or both; but again, apart from the Hollywood crowd and VFX insider circles, no one in the audience will even know your name nor care about who you are – at least not compared to the directors, writers, and actors of a film. Heck, even producers don't get as much recognition, unless they are the J.J. Abrams or Brian Grazers of producing. Of course, don't let me dissuade you from becoming (or remaining) a VFX artist if that's what you *really* want. Hey, if this really is your passion, you won't be convinced otherwise. So, if you're fine being in and playing VFX for the long haul, go ahead. Just don't expect to be remembered in history outside of your niche and relevant circles. I mean this seriously too: you have no idea how many people (outside of the industry) are not even aware of what visual effects is, let alone the kinds of roles available. When ordinary people think of jobs in graphics, their first line of thought goes to Photoshop and poster design, advertising, or animation (as in cartoons or full-3D films). The fact that VFX is just not that well-known as a field outside of, well, the film, VFX, and animation world, already shows where you stand in the public consciousness and awareness of important or memorable lines of work. I'm not saying that what we do isn't important – it just isn't something your average Joe or a random neighbor down the block would know about, let alone be intent on learning more of (and that's okay).

All I am saying is this: be aware of your goals and go into this with both eyes open. Your position is most likely *always* going to be that of an unsung hero (which is absolutely okay if that's what you want or what you can live with).

## Your other talents will be wasted and unrecognized

As someone who enjoys exploring and honing my many other talents, this one really hits it home for me. And of course, as the VFX industry shifts and evolves over time, things may change and multi-talented individuals (however rare and limited they may be) may become the norm. For now, however, it is important to acknowledge that if you have any other skill or talent you wished to explore and develop further, you're best doing that in your own free time. The VFX industry is really keen on selecting and keeping highly-specialized skilled workers concentrated in one area of VFX – be it compositing, animation, rigging, texturing, lighting, et cetera – so, while an expression of possessing multiple talents isn't a negative, it isn't something most VFX studios will want to pay (especially if you are looking at extra pay) to hire you for. As described in an earlier chapter, just because you have other VFX skills doesn't mean that they will all be utilized at your applicable job.

In essence, being a VFX artist (especially in a specialist type of position) is not for the versatile or multi-talented, or really anybody with a diverse spectrum of skills; and I am not just referring to skills related to design and graphics, oh no. This applies to any *other* skills you may have, such as public speaking, accounting, computer programming, linguistics, et cetera. Once more, this all boils down to the fact that, as a working VFX professional, you are hired to essentially execute your job according to the studio's needs and demands. A studio, being a business, does not really like having routines and protocols thrown into the air for the sake of it, and with each introduction of an employee or freelancer, the studio has to spend the time and money in getting that employee or freelancer acquainted with its established protocols and systems. If you have someone coming in who wants to inject a whole load of other unexpected talent into the team, well, let's just say that it would be harder to re-establish all that protocol once the dust settles. Unless you are working at a startup or on an independent film production, it is *highly unlikely* that you will be able to utilize *any other talent* outside of your VFX niche (let alone, even talents *within* VFX that are not directly related to your job or specialization). Pigeonholing is the norm in our industry since that's traditionally how an artist will be able to ascend the career ladder (though you'll basically be stuck doing that one thing forever).

If you really want to use *all* the talents and skills at your disposal, try being an entrepreneur instead (not a VFX artist). And no, starting a VFX studio – that in essence, does the same thing as what you were doing independently anyway – is not really being an entrepreneur in *my* book (to me, starting a stereotypical VFX business is akin to franchising a business model that has already been tried-and-proven; basically, you're cloning a business and becoming a business owner/manager rather than an entrepreneur, if nothing else significant about your business model changes). If you're not convinced, see the first truth in this chapter about owning a VFX studio. You are free to debate me on my opinion if you'd like – just remember to take everything in its proper context.

In short: being a VFX artist is not ideal for the multi-talented vertically (any other skill involving VFX) and laterally (relating to skills *outside* of VFX) as there is a *high chance* that you'll be pigeonholed the moment you start to establish yourself in any one niche in the VFX world.

## Let's be real – it's still a desk job, but with pixels

Finally, and most importantly, behind all the smoke and mirrors (and the perception of the glamour of Hollywood life), let's be real: ... VFX is *still* a desk job. You still report to work at a set time, sit in front of a desk (if you work a post-production role), and work for a set number of hours pushing pixels. Alright, so I stand corrected: it's a desk job, but with pixels. Sure, you could argue that the output you are creating involves much more finesse, grace, and design work than the stereotypical desk jobs you see in movies (those jobs that literally require pencil-to-paper work), but remove that variation and you *still* have the fundamentals that create a desk or office job. Make of that what you will. Tying this truth in with the fact that you will most likely gain weight whilst working as a VFX artist, not have much of a life outside the VFX studio, and will lose your most prized currency (youth and vitality) as you age over the years (all factors that frankly apply to almost all office jobs across all industries), I personally fail to see how being a VFX artist is any different from a job working as an office clerk at a law firm or even as an accountant hired by a Fortune 500 company. Yes, anything and everything is what you make of it but to put this bluntly – and if we just view this profession objectively for a moment – you are *still* waking up at a set time to report to an office or location, perform a task you are paid to perform (nothing more, nothing less), and then rinse and repeat. Would you willingly show up to work if you *weren't* getting paid to do so? Be honest with yourself – most of us wouldn't do it for free even if VFX were our life, blood, and passion (it just isn't realistic to expect passionate talent to be exploited for free labor – because that said talent would then starve to death and perish all in the name of passion).

With that, let's take a moment to pause, think and combine all the truths revealed in this chapter. Why do I want to do VFX? Do I *really* want to do VFX? Look, there is no pressure. You don't have to make a decision now (or ever, even) to commit to VFX for the rest of your life – you could even just try it out for a day, a week, a month, or a year and uncover your own truths relevant to your own scenario and your own life – just be sure to keep everything I have said in mind if you ever reach an impasse about whether VFX is the right path for you to achieve your greater life goals. Remember: behind the facade of glamour and pseudo-fame, VFX is just like any other industry out there that requires you to report to work, meet deadlines, and most importantly, help somebody else achieve *their* filmmaking dreams and goals by telling *their* stories. As a VFX artist, you are but a hired hand, an executor of graphics behind-the-scenes; you won't be publicly recognized to the notoriety of the project's producers, and you will be paid from a pre-determined budget with *zero* opportunity to reap benefits and rewards from how the production does in the box office, as well as on other distribution platforms and channels. And while you won't get dinged if the production you worked on happens to perform poorly at launch, you also won't be rewarded either; your position as a hired hand shields you from both risk and reward and in most cases, when there is no risk, there is also little to no reward. It is what it is.

The bottom line is that *most* VFX work involves sitting in front of a computer screen at a desk – as such, it is a desk job through and through. You wake up, show up, work some overtime, get paid, go home – rinse and repeat, rinse and repeat. That is the cold, hard truth and reality of being a VFX artist.

# 12

# WHY I DO VFX

And that dreaded question returns. You know, the one that I ranted on about earlier. The question that sometimes gets asked by co-workers at studios. The question that you should ultimately ask yourself before getting into VFX (or any field, for that matter). Why do you do VFX? Why do I do VFX? Why do we do VFX? With my fatigued hands strained from all this typing thus far, I must say it has been incredibly cathartic to express all these insights, observations, and analyses onto paper, sharing it all with you, dear reader. You must reckon by now that the VFX industry is by no means an industry for the foolish, the power-hungry, or the immensely adventurous. It is an industry that is stable yet uncertain, technical yet endlessly creative, and fleeting yet all-consuming in its ability to consume your presence and mental efforts. So, you *must* ask yourself the very important question:

why *do* you do VFX? Is it for fun? Were you inspired by some movie (I hope not; see the earlier chapter on stupid reasons to get into VFX)? Does VFX run in your family? Or are you simply using VFX as an outlet to get your fill of creative problem-solving? Coming close to a decade (almost; just shy of a year as of the writing of this treatise), I have come to understand clearly why I do VFX, why I continued to do VFX, and most importantly, how VFX has come to fit or no longer fit my personal agenda and macro goals in life.

## For self-expression

Earlier I expressed my sentiments on using VFX as an outlet for self-expression, remembering the times when I was younger with that camcorder. What really lured me into VFX was ultimately video-editing, which allowed me, a child without a voice – having that voice squashed by traditional Asian cultural beliefs of children being seen but not heard and being obedient and non-defiant – to craft a strong, powerful voice. VFX was and is that megaphone and amplifier to the once shy and reserved girl in class. If you have the right skills, know how to push the right buttons in a sequence, and know how to solve the right problems, VFX can be that magic wand that allows you to do whatever you want to your reality. You want to go to Egypt? Create that with Autodesk Maya, After Effects, or Photoshop and you're there. Want to be a leader of a zombie apocalypse? Use Houdini to create your hordes of zombies and Nuke to composite all that jazz in. Anything and everything is possible if you know how to do it.

This is all me though. I am sure you have your own reasons for pursuing VFX. I would ask you to share that with me if we were on an interactive platform – of course, you can always email me and I'll be happy to entertain any conversation in that regard – but I would imagine if you have the proper motivation to get entrenched in the industry (or get this far ahead in the book, thank you, reader), you are intrinsically motivated by some kind of gratification that could only come from within. And whilst I always like to believe I am unique and one-of-a-kind in many ways, I am sure there are others out there who, at the very least, can relate to using VFX as a means of self-expression.

All in all, VFX *can* be very rewarding and empowering in that regard. With the right tools and innate knowledge, you could mold the world to your liking and become a God of that universe – as fictional as it is in actuality. VFX *can* be that great escape and pathway to unleashing and expressing your deepest of desires and innermost thoughts – provided that you also control the narrative and are in charge of that production, that is.

## The thrill of the hunt

Now, as a self-described person-who-gets-bored-with-the-mundane-fairly-easily, VFX to me gives the gift of excitement and thrills of problem-solving. The more difficult or challenging the shot, the more pleasure and excitement I derive from completing the task. It is all about problem-solving. Man, do I *love* problem-solving. It is just as stimulating as what your average Joe would find stimulating online, if you know what I mean. Being engaged in such a mental endeavor definitely assures your mind never takes a day off – provided that you are not in one of those mind-numbing entry-level roles.

Regardless of what your actual specialty is in VFX, I know there was never a dull moment when it came to my work. Whether I was compositing, creating 3D models of buildings, or flooding said 3D models of buildings with particles – every day was a field trip when it came to VFX. Heck, as a VFX supervisor on indie projects, I even got to visit the usually inaccessible working lots of Universal Studios and CBS in California; again, all in the name of returning props or shooting scenes for VFX in post.

Having been involved with VFX from the production and post-production side of things, I guarantee that the thrill of the hunt is present during all phases of production when it comes to VFX. On set, you will simply be solving problems – and troubleshooting miscellaneous unexpected issues – with prepared solutions that you will have already discussed with the relevant departments (though it is always tantalizing to see your ideas executed on set, in front of your very eyes); whereas during post-production, you will get a variety of problems to solve from the set, usually with a very tight deadline. No matter how you slice it, you get the stimulation of a thrill, regardless – or at least I do anyway.

## Variety of stimulation (problems)

Speaking of stimulation, I also do VFX for its *variety* in stimulation. In other words, it won't just be a repetitive, mindless task – if you are in the right position. As a VFX compositor, I always find myself excited at the prospect of solving a huge variety of problems; and if you're looking for a faster pace of work, try doing VFX for pilots and television series. Man, those were the days. Intense, exciting, thrilling; it definitely would have stimulated the balls off of me if I actually had any physical ... well, you know. In fact, to illustrate just how broad and varied your problems will entail in VFX (at least, in my position), here are just some of the things I've done or been asked to complete, as a VFX compositor:

- Remove earrings off a baby's ears: yes, that did happen. Why didn't they just remove the earrings on set? Beats me.
- Driving comps: compositing of car shots
- Crowd duplication
- Blood and muzzle flash additions
- Removing boom poles from shots
- Removing camera equipment from shots
- Removing crew members visible in shots
- Cleaning up reflections of crew members, equipment, et cetera: you get the picture.
- Replacing graffiti or copyrighted art
- Removing logos or replacing them with fake company logos
- Enhancing or adding artificial lighting in a shot
- Removing scars, marks, blemishes, or tattoos from actors
- Slimming down actors
- Screen and monitor replacements and design
- Insect composites
- Shot destruction: in other words, creating an apocalypse
- Entire shot generation: using nothing but a green screen shot

- Portal creations: including entering and exiting effects
- Creating 2D animations with compositing
- Compositing particle effects: including fake rain
- Compositing 3D rendered elements
- Multi-pass composites
- Rotoscoping and compositing elements from various shots
- Face replacements and tracking
- Set extension and re-design
- Cleaning up a shot and designing it with various software at record speed

Again, I could list them all, but that's not the point of my list. The point is that you do in fact get to tackle a *lot* of different kinds of problems. You are most certainly not going to get the same problem – in the sense of it being the exact same shot, same setup, same shot design – twice. Sure, you will most certainly encounter certain types of shot problems multiple times; for example, I can definitely assure you that I have done at least one shot involving the removal of a crew member reflection, camera equipment, or boom pole at almost every relevant working studio I have been at. It's perfectly normal for production hiccups to occur, and having crew members or equipment clearly visible in your shot is one of them. It's a costly mistake but it does happen – and it does happen *often.*

If you are not keen on any post-production VFX, well, fret not, as VFX production also offers up its fair share of problems in the stimulating variety. Here are just some of the varied problems I have had to solve on set, as a VFX supervisor:

- Shot design of VFX apocalypse destruction
- Planning of the execution of teleportation effects and in-camera works
- Post-production cooperation and counsel, which offers a host of its own variety of problems to solve
- Green screen shoot planning and lighting checks: which changes depending on the shot and camera work involved
- Shooting of extra plates to ensure necessary materials are captured for use in post-production
- Planning of props, set decoration, and wardrobe that may be involved in VFX
- Timing of camera shots to perform in-camera VFX

Et cetera, et cetera, et cetera. How could I ever possibly get bored with all this variety? Thus, VFX to me is like waking up every day not knowing what to expect for your meals because it's always going to be something different in one way or the other – and that's part of the joy of doing VFX.

## The fallacy of sticking to one field for the rest of your life

And yet, with all that being said, here is where the excitement and thrill of VFX *fail* to meet my current wants in life. Thus far, VFX has always met my needs for self-expression and self-stimulation. It is like a form of ecstasy to me. I get a shot I have to complete as fast and as accurately as I can, my eyes glued to the computer screen and sometimes hours will go by and I'll look up and see that it's lunchtime. No problem there. However, having experienced a vast number of compositing situations and experiences (in my opinion) and anticipated what my career could continue to be like should I invest another five or so years into VFX, I have come to the conclusion that VFX will not satisfy the larger and greater goals in my life. I told someone about this, and his immediate response was, "Well, so now you just did that VFX degree for nothing then?" To add some context, this person is a traditional-minded, old-fashioned, and old (literally classified as elderly now) Asian man living in Singapore, which pretty much explains his stupid question and reaction. This fallacy that just because you studied and obtained a degree in a field does not mean you are bound to that field for the rest of your "miserable" existence. In addition, just because you are well-known for it, or even profit immensely from it (to the extent that I have), does not mean you should force yourself to stick to it if you are no longer viscerally and innately satisfied by what you are doing. Heck, I was good at a lot of things when I was younger (and probably still am) – I was fantastic at chemistry and biology (science), a whiz at computer programming (coding), pretty good at drawing and the literary arts (traditional and written arts) and was an awesome public speaker by school standards (without having enrolled in any kind of "professional public speaking" courses). I was also good at voice acting to a certain extent, having done it casually almost every night for about eight years. Just because you are *good* at something (or make good money from doing something), doesn't mean you should make it your life's calling if you have *zero* interest in turning those talents into career paths.

I could have become a computer programmer but honestly, that was not where my heart was at – even though you can make tons more as a programmer than as a VFX artist, honestly. So don't let anyone tell you that you can't change your mind midway into the game. You may have studied it, you may have made tons of money off of it, you may even have been well-known for it, but if something no longer meets your wants in life (or gives you the bliss you used to experience), then don't be afraid to pursue something else. Yes, you most likely will have to start from scratch, but at least it is something that brings you the pleasure you've lost over the years doing the thing you once loved. It is all about perspective here. Who knows, maybe you will make an even *bigger* killing, obtain even *more* notoriety, or ascend to even *greater* spiritual heights with this shift or transition, but you will never know if you don't at least try. So, think of all that potential upside and try. Don't let your family's outdated (ought to be extinct, dead, and buried in the ground) beliefs hold you back, ever. I strongly believe it to be a fallacy to stick to one field for the rest of your life just because you studied it, are well-known for it, or profit from it. I will say this: if it no longer floats your boat, cut the rope (you heard it here first).

## When self-expression no longer cuts it

That serves as a nice segue into the part where I acknowledge how VFX as an avenue for my self-expression no longer cuts it for me. Sure, in VFX, I get to do anything and everything I can't in reality. You can literally kill someone in VFX and get away with it – all in the name of storytelling and selling the narrative. However, being the sole person walking this earth who knows myself best, I have long known that I have a growing appetite for bigger and better things. And I don't mean material goods or objects when I say that, I mean *bigger* and *better* goals and milestones. So, while I do have a blast with VFX, working as a VFX artist (more specifically a compositor and occasional supervisor) and meeting mostly talented and fantastic people along the way, VFX no longer provides me with enough stimulation to fuel my days. Somewhat ironic, isn't it?

Yes, self-expression is a process, and a developing one at that. It changes and morphs just as you and I do, over time. Personally, I just find that VFX no longer fuels this process enough to feed my ambition. You see, I don't just aspire to be an awesome VFX compositor and that's it (because let's be honest, that's really the highest pinnacle for most ordinary people in that position). I have far *greater* ambitions in my life and VFX is simply an insufficient conduit to reach and achieve the grand designs I have set out for myself. There is only so much you can do as a time-strained, time-starved VFX professional – whether you are an entry-level artist, mid-level supervisor, or veteran-level business owner – and sometimes, you've got to realize when to step away from a field in order to pursue avenues that will bring you closer to your ideal reality. To be honest, I also have zero interest in becoming an obese chick in the future – and as you've read in an earlier part of this book, VFX *really* is just another desk job (and most desk jobs fatten you up rather quickly, needless to say).

## Heed your *Ambition*

The real question is: whatever happened to raw *ambition?* I contemplated this concept one night, foreseeing and anticipating how my career path in VFX would pan out. At best, you are still subject to whoever the paying client or studio is. At worst, you stick to what you are still doing right now – that is freelancing at multiple studios and working on amazing projects. Sure, the latter isn't as bad as it sounds but that is just not where I want to stay for the rest of my life. Even with the limited upward mobility in VFX, you are *still* subject to obeying somebody else's schedule, somebody else's demands, and somebody else's creative decisions. Also, to be realistic and to reiterate, not many manage to successfully transition laterally into a different type of position. I know of many creatives who want to jump into a more administrative role (yes, that does happen), and only one out of seven actually do. Likewise, vice versa – though that ratio is probably one out of ten. It just doesn't happen often in VFX and frankly, studios *do* want to keep you in one basket or keep you pigeonholed as it only serves in their benefit to do so.

As a ruthlessly and aggressively ambitious person, I must say that those odds simply won't do it for me. And yes, while there will always be that one person who egotistically thinks that they will be that one exception to the rule, that one guy who will beat the odds, unless the industry takes on a titanic shift as a whole, I'd personally rather place my bets on guaranteed wins (even though nothing in life is guaranteed, but we will debate that some other time) than play against the odds, foolishly *hoping* that I'll prove to myself to be that exception. The only point you will prove is that you have watched way too many movies about startups (more specifically, that tiny minority of less-than-one percent of startups that go on to make billions). In the name of *bigger*, *better*, and *greater* things, your ambition appetite should still tie into your greater goal in life and if the two no longer co-exist harmoniously, it's time to analyze your current situation and pivot. Do not make the mistake of thinking that I have lost the love or passion for VFX though – you can still love it and not want to be with it *for now*. It's like dating and relationships: you can love multiple people or objects and not want to continue being with that or even bother getting closer to them. It's weird, but it's only human, and we humans are much more complex than we give ourselves credit for. We are also much more complex than the movies make us out to be.

All in all, you should be asking yourself this very important question: are you satisfied knowing that when you die, you will *only* have done XYZ and you will *only* have been known for XYZ? If the answer is no, then you should heed your ambition and feed your ambition. Give in to it and dare to follow it intuitively. Pay attention to your ambition appetite and do what is necessary to fuel it.

To get a bit extreme and morbid as well: when you die, no one will know who you are if you are *just* a VFX artist. Sure, if you manage to win a few awards and become quite revered in the industry, the niche of VFX may mourn your loss. ... Then they'll forget about it after two to three days and move on. If you're lucky and *that* important, you may get an annual anniversary article or two about your accomplishments and contributions in VFX, but then these too will pass (until the next anniversary of your death).

If your desire is to go down in history and to be remembered far more than just on the anniversary of your death ... then VFX is certainly the *least* favorable route to go.

Heed your *Ambition*, feed your *Ambition*. It all comes full circle now.

# 13

# NEXT

When I was younger, I had no friends. I was the quiet and shy person no one bothered to look at, the one that you'd forget if you ever saw her in the classroom. And when I was good at something, anything, I was told that I should just be a scientist, a programmer, an "insert-whatever-subject-role-you-happened-to-be-good-at," that I am "uncreative" simply because I was extremely organized, and that "I should work at a large corporation and not a startup." I'm sorry (no, not really), but I don't love the sciences or programming *that* much to make them my career, and frankly I *hate* (alright, maybe hate is a strong word, let's just say *dislike*) working for others. Yes, while I do take joy in VFX as a means of self-expression, I find that my capacity to go *all the way out* for *any* studio or *any* entity outside myself to be limited to the amount of ownership and autonomy (and in some way, monetary

351

compensation) I have as a creative. VFX is a creative endeavor only in its execution, not in its ideas. So, if you are a truly creative individual with ideas of your own, you are better off taking the risk of being a director or producer of sorts than working as a VFX artist. If you enjoy executing others' ideas and only focusing on the creative processes of the execution, then sure, VFX could be for you, at least for now.

Ultimately, I am not here to lift you up nor sugarcoat the true life of a VFX artist, but rather to remind you that just like almost *any* artistic or technical career under *somebody else's* studio roof, it is – and most likely always will be – a 9-to-5 office job (if you don't include the overtime); a contribution towards a project you will *never* own nor be *justly* and *fully* credited for bringing into existence (and rightfully so, it's just how the industry works). If you are seeking a *true* expression of your creative ideas, don't get into VFX or animation thinking that you will eventually get to take over the studio and have them execute your projects. You still are and will be beholden to your shareholders and high-paying clients, who will become your new bosses even if you are technically the "boss" at that VFX studio.

I got into VFX out of the urge to use this platform, this channel, as a form of self-expression. If you are fine creating work to achieve someone else's vision of self-expression, by all means, jump right into VFX. For me, however, I need something *much* bigger than that to satisfy my ambition appetite. So, dear reader, this is why I do VFX, and this is why I did VFX. I may return, I may not, or I may just stay after getting it all out in this book;

whatever it is, I'd like to keep those plans solely to myself. So, if you would really like to know, you know how to reach me. I look forward to hearing your personal story and journey into/currently in/out of (you know what to do, strikethrough the ones that do not apply, ha) the crazy world of VFX.

# ACKNOWLEDGMENTS

I am not one for writing long, mushy acknowledgments (that most people won't actually read) so I shall go against the publishing industry standard and use this page as a list of credits instead (kind of like those you see in the movies). Makes sense, right?

Thank you to:

- Leif Einarsson — for the foreword
- 100 Covers — for the book cover design
- Colum Hill — for copy editing
- Madison Bishop — for the audiobook production

See? Simple and straightforward.

# ABOUT THE AUTHOR

Vicki Lau is a visual effects (VFX) artist/generalist, virtual reality (VR) developer, TEDx speaker, entrepreneur, and educator from Singapore who broke into Hollywood as a foreigner and outsider, landing her first break working on AMC's *"The Walking Dead"* (Season 4).

She has worked on more than 30 projects with over 20 studios and filmmakers on independent and major productions. Some of her work can be seen in *"Guardians of the Galaxy," "Aquaman,"*

*"War for the Planet of the Apes,"* and *"Grey's Anatomy."* In addition to Hollywood, Vicki has also worked with tech startups in Silicon Valley and Los Angeles.

With her unique background in visual effects, computer programming, applied psychology, and business, Vicki teaches VFX and filmmaking to over 80,000 students from more than 182 countries.

She is a nominated finalist of the WinTrade Award for Women in Tech (an international business award) and the WeAreTheCity Rising Stars Global Award for Achievement.

Vicki is also a bodybuilder, making her one of the first female VFX artist-bodybuilders to exist.

**Connect with Vicki at:**

Website: lauvicki.com

IMDb: imdb.com/name/nm5130924 (**"Vicki Lau"**)

Instagram: instagram.com/vickicup (@**vickicup**)

# ALSO BY VICKI LAU

This is my first book, so I don't have any other titles to share for now. However, if you'd like to elevate your learning/VFX experience to the next level, you may explore the other avenues below (beyond the medium of this book).

I encourage anyone interested in reaching out to me to do so at my official website.

If you enjoyed this book, please let us know by *leaving a fantastic book review* on wherever you found this book.

**Mentoring**

bit.ly/VFXmentor

If this book hasn't convinced you enough of the pitfalls of VFX - and you still want to get into VFX - I offer one-on-one mentoring on MentorCruise.

For more information, head on over to that link attached.

**Online Courses**

bit.ly/VFXsupe

If you want to learn VFX and filmmaking directly from me, I have a ton of courses on various educational platforms out there. Here is one for those keen on becoming VFX supervisors - link attached.

### 3D Models

sketchfab.com/vickicup

If you simply want to download a bunch of ready-made 3D models for 3D printing, personal projects, or self-learning, here is one of the 3D stores I own online. There are both paid/discounted and free models for your modeling pleasure - link attached.

* * *

Printed by Amazon Italia Logistica S.r.l.
Torrazza Piemonte (TO), Italy

28946665R00217